T0396609

Queer Chinese Cultures and Mobilities

Queer Asia

The Queer Asia series opens a space for monographs and anthologies in all disciplines focusing on non-normative sexuality and gender cultures, identities, and practices across all regions of Asia. Queer Studies, Queer Theory, and Transgender Studies originated in, and remain dominated by, North American and European academic circles. Yet, the separation between sexual orientation and gender identity, while relevant in the West, does not neatly apply to all Asian contexts, which are themselves complex and diverse. Growing numbers of scholars inside and beyond Asia are producing exciting and challenging work that studies Asian histories and cultures of trans and queer phenomena. The Queer Asia series—the first of its kind in publishing—provides a valuable opportunity for developing and sustaining these initiatives.

Selected titles in the series:

As Normal as Possible: Negotiating Sexuality and Gender in Mainland China and Hong Kong
Edited by Yau Ching

Boys' Love, Cosplay, and Androgynous Idols: Queer Fan Cultures in Mainland China, Hong Kong, and Taiwan
Edited by Maud Lavin, Ling Yang, and Jing Jamie Zhao

Conditional Spaces: Hong Kong Lesbian Desires and Everyday Life
Denise Tse-Shang Tang

Contact Moments: The Politics of Intercultural Desire in Japanese Male-Queer Cultures
Katsuhiko Suganuma

Falling into the Lesbi World: Desire and Difference in Indonesia
Evelyn Blackwood

First Queer Voices from Thailand: Uncle Go's Advice Columns for Gays, Lesbians and Kathoeys
Peter A. Jackson

Gender on the Edge: Transgender, Gay, and Other Pacific Islanders
Edited by Niko Besnier and Kalissa Alexeyeff

Obsession: Male Same-Sex Relations in China, 1900–1950
Wenqing Kang

Queer Bangkok: 21st Century Markets, Media, and Rights
Edited by Peter A. Jackson

Queer Politics and Sexual Modernity in Taiwan
Hans Tao-Ming Huang

Queer Singapore: Illiberal Citizenship and Mediated Cultures
Edited by Audrey Yue and Jun Zubillaga-Pow

Shanghai Lalas: Female Tongzhi Communities and Politics in Urban China
Lucetta Yip Lo Kam

Undercurrents: Queer Culture and Postcolonial Hong Kong
Helen Hok-Sze Leung

Oral Histories of Older Gay Men in Hong Kong: Unspoken but Unforgotten
Travis S. K. Kong

Queer Chinese Cultures and Mobilities

Kinship, Migration, and Middle Classes

John Wei

Hong Kong University Press
The University of Hong Kong
Pokfulam Road
Hong Kong
https://hkupress.hku.hk

ISBN 978-988-8528-27-1 (*Hardback*)

British Library Cataloguing-in-Publication Data
A catalogue record for this book is available from the British Library.

Cover image: Rainbow Road Rhön, photo by RobertMeyer1205.
Source: Wikimedia Commons, https://commons.wikimedia.org/wiki/File:Rainbow_Road_Rh%C3%B6n.jpg. Licensing: Creative Commons Attribution-Share Alike 4.0 International.

10 9 8 7 6 5 4 3 2 1

Printed and bound by Paramount Printing Co., Ltd. in Hong Kong, China

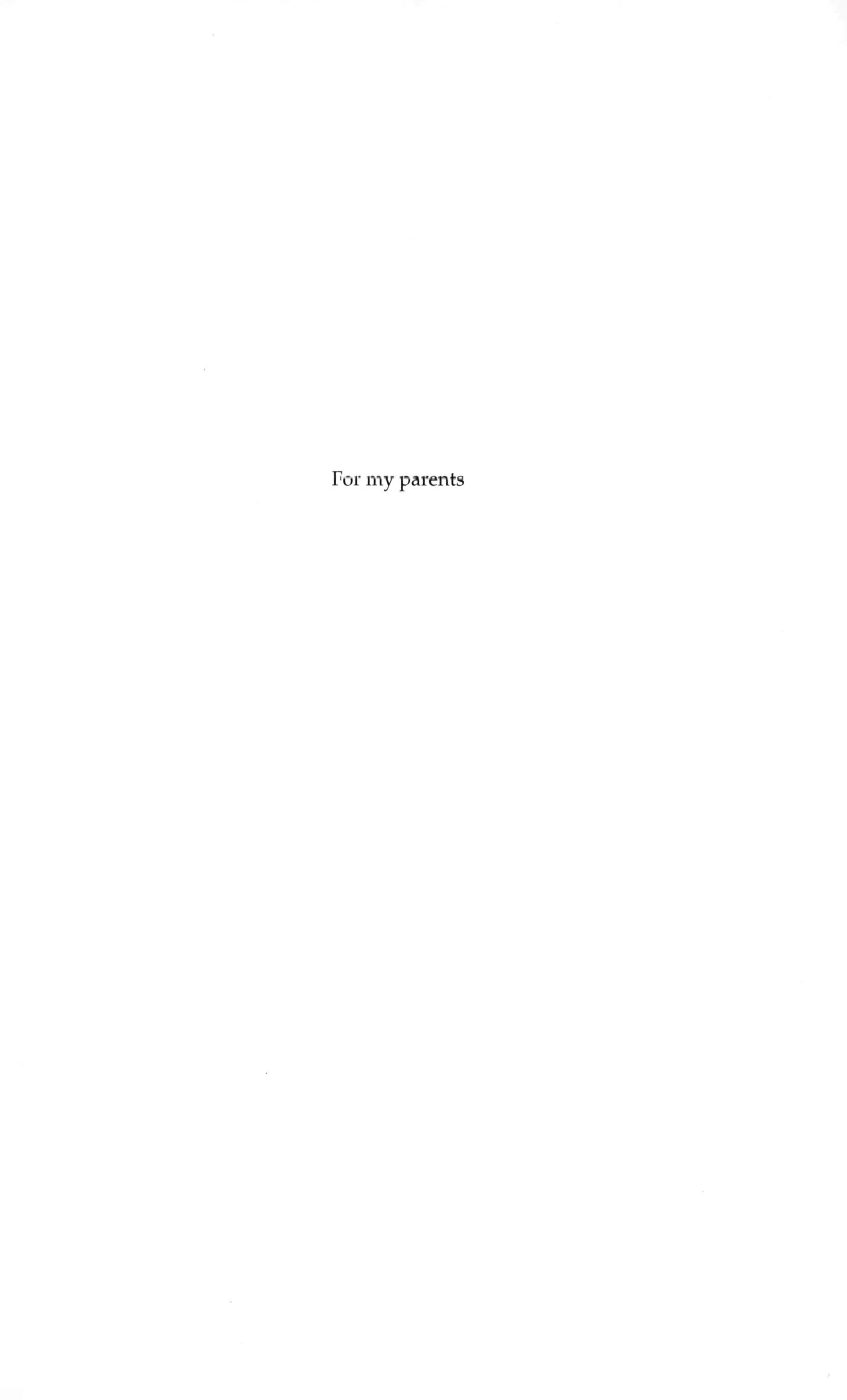

For my parents

Contents

Figures

Acknowledgments

Every intellectual voyage needs guidance and assistance to navigate through the unknown water and reach the promising new land. This book crystallized from my previous research on Chinese-language queer films, and my gratitude goes to Katherine Sender, who helped nurture this project from inception to near completion. Audrey Yue and Fran Martin have been the lighthouse in my journey, whose inspiration has been a tremendous instrument that I keep close to my heart.

I am also grateful for Song Hwee Lim, whose generous and thoughtful feedback was invaluable for the publication of this book. My thanks extend to Kenneth Chan for his feedback and encouragement. Segments of this research have been presented in early forms at numerous conferences; I wish to especially acknowledge the excellent support and feedback that I received from my colleagues at the 2018 Association for Asian Studies Annual Conference: Travis Kong, Louisa Schein, Shawn Mendez, Nicole Constable, Wei Wei, Wenqing Kang, Petrus Liu, and Gail Hershatter.

Editors of the *Queer Asia* series—Chris Berry, John Erni, Peter Jackson, and Helen Leung—have been very supportive for the publication of this book. I met most of them in 2014, at the Frontiers of TransQueer Studies Conference at the University of Sydney, and must thank them for their interest in my work when it was still at an early stage. Eric Mok and his colleagues at Hong Kong University Press have provided wonderful editorial guidance. I also thank the anonymous reviewers whose comments have helped improve this book.

Part of Chapter 3 first appeared as "Queer Sinophonicities in (South) East Asia: The Short Films of Desmond Bing-Yen Ti" in *Intersections: Gender, History and Culture in the Asian Context*, no. 38. I thank Carolyn Brewer for her permission to include it here with revisions.

Finally, I offer the warmest regards to my informants and interviewees, as well as many other people behind this book, without whom this research would be impossible. This book is written for them and for the brave queer people who have been working relentlessly to create a better tomorrow and a bright future.

Notes on Chinese Romanization

In most cases, I have used Hanyu Pinyin to romanize Chinese characters, save for habitual terms (e.g., Kuomintang) and for people outside mainland China (e.g., Ti Bing-yen and Lai Jeng-jer). Chinese names are presented as surnames followed by given names, unless the persons concerned are already well-known otherwise (e.g., Ang Lee and Stanley Kwan).

Introduction

On a bright summer night in 2013, I found myself in a small apartment with twenty people or so, sitting in front of a digital projection screen. It was a film-screening session hosted by a local gay and lesbian organization in Beijing. *Literature, Auteur, and Same-Sex Love: A Film Perspective* was the theme, and the film clips shown were edited and remixed from over a dozen English-language queer movies. Led by a guest speaker, we viewed these audiovisual materials and discussed the issue of love and romance in same-sex intimacy. After the screening, a few people gathered for dinner in a small restaurant nearby. They all looked quite young, save for the guest speaker, and some of them were apparently college students. We discussed film, literature, musical, opera, and other relevant topics over the meal. With their passion for film and art, these well-educated young men came to network with like-minded "queer comrades" and enjoy a night of quality entertainment.

This scene struck me as a completely different form of queer cultural practice in today's China. The exquisite taste in art-house cinema and the cinephilic euphoria lingering throughout the night served as a strong contrast to what I initially had in mind before putting myself in the field: cruising gay men lurking in public parks and toilets in search of sexual encounters, as depicted in the film *East Palace, West Palace* (*Donggong Xigong*, Zhang Yuan, 1996) and in early gay ethnographies conducted in China (e.g., Li and Wang 1993). The film club also felt strikingly different from the urban gay bars recorded in Elisabeth Engebretsen's (2014), Loretta Ho's (2010), and Lisa Rofel's (2007) fieldwork conducted in Beijing's queer communities. This urban queer film scene, together with other traditional and emerging forms of queer social and cultural practices, inspired me to embark on this journey to explore various types of queer cultures and mobilities in China and other Chinese societies in the early twenty-first century.

Chinese Societies in Transition

The rise of Asia (especially China) on the global stage has caught wide international attention and intellectual interest in its rapid and ongoing social transformations. The last three decades have witnessed several major legislative changes in various Chinese societies regarding sexual conduct between the same sex. In 1991, Hong Kong became the first Chinese society to decriminalize private sexual intercourse between two consenting male adults, although it was not until 2006 that the minimum age for consensual sex was equalized between homosexuals and heterosexuals.[1] Mainland China decriminalized inter-male sex in 1997 and depathologized homosexuality from the *Chinese Classification of Mental Disorders* in 2001.[2] Taiwan, in contrast, has never explicitly criminalized sodomy and homosexuality (Martin 2003, 12–14). It has also become the first Chinese society that bans discrimination based on sexual orientation in education and at work,[3] which set the tone for its endeavor to legalize same-sex marriage in 2017, after several unsuccessful attempts since 2003. Echoing the LGBT (lesbian, gay, bisexual, and transgender) social activism thriving in the West, such transformations in legislation and medical science in the Chinese world have arguably raised the social visibility of sexual minorities, contributed to the development of local queer communities, and underscored the increasingly diverse queer cultures at the turn of the twenty-first century.

Almost two decades into its membership of the World Trade Organization (WTO), China has surpassed Japan to become the second-largest economy and overtaken the United States in key benchmarks to become the world's new economic leader.[4] As the new regional and global economic engine with a vast and fast-growing domestic market, mainland China has seen an influx of capital and talent from both the West and other Chinese societies, such as Hong Kong and Taiwan. Moreover, the return of Hong Kong's sovereignty to China (1997) and the Economic Cooperation Framework Agreement (ECFA) between mainland China and Taiwan (2010) have further tightened the connections among these Chinese societies. These changes have reshaped the production and circulation of queer cultures across traditional geographical and geopolitical boundaries. Along with the economic development and the further opening up of its domestic market, China has also put its cultural policies in transition.

In 2008, China's then-State Administration of Radio, Film, and Television (SARFT) banned cinematic portrayal of *tongxinglian* (homosexuality) in an official announcement but later abolished this announcement in 2010.[5] However, SARFT did not specify whether they had lifted the ban. On 17 May 2013, the International Day against Homophobia, Biphobia, and Transphobia, independent Chinese queer filmmaker Fan Popo applied for "Disclosure of Information" at the film bureau concerning the regulative policies for queer visual content (see CQIF 2013).[6] This rather political move called wide domestic and international attention to China's film regulation and LGBT issues. The bureau replied that, after abolishing the policy specifically banning homosexuality on-screen, the clause in effect reverted to the previous one from the last century that banned all kinds of "obscene" visual content.[7] What counts as "obscene," however, is subject to the bureau's own interpretation without any clear definition.

But this ambiguity does leave a space, however limited, for the cinematic portrayal of queer characters in China's mainstream cinema. *Let the Bullets Fly* (*Rang Zidan Fei*, Jiang Wen, 2010), a box-office hit in the local film market, has a supporting male character self-mockingly expressing his attraction to the same sex. Albeit not the first gay character on China's commercial film screen, he is perhaps the first one without effeminate stereotyping, compared to previous portrayals of gay men in popular films such as *If You Are the One* (*Fei Cheng Wu Rao*, Feng Xiaogang, 2008). In a minor storyline of *Finding Mr. Right* (*Beijing Yushang Xiyatu*, Xue Xiaolu, 2013), a critically acclaimed commercial film, a Chinese woman in labor is accompanied by her lesbian partner and her American sperm donor. This might be Chinese audiences' first experience of cinematic lesbianism in China's commercial movie theatre. However, this very short sequence only shows a gentle kiss on the forehead between the lesbian couple after the childbirth, with the voiceover "let's bless them"; some viewers may not fully realize the lesbian undertone at all. *Sweet Eighteen* (*Tianmi Shibasui*, He Wenchao, 2012), a low-budget production released in China, also implicitly hides female same-sex intimacy in one of its multiple plotlines.

These transitions, albeit on one level minor and trivial, have opened up a space for the negotiation of queer cultural practices in the new millennium. The rapid development of technology and the rise of cyberculture and social media have also profoundly reshaped queer cultural production, circulation, and consumption. In addition to digital video production and grassroots queer filmmaking, the emergence of the camera-embedded smartphones has made phototaking and videoshooting even more accessible and affordable for average people without specialized knowledge and skills. Social networking services have also become integral to many people's life via the increasingly ubiquitous 3G/4G cellular networks and domestic and public Wi-Fi hotspots. These changes have begun to shift queer cultural productions and consumptions to digital screens—online queer social media, mobile dating apps, and digital queer films and video series, to name a few—which further underline the changing queer cultural landscape in the ongoing socio-technological transformations.

However, these social transformations do not suggest the realization of equal gay rights, nor do they imply a fundamental shift of the social ethos concerning transgressive sexualities in Chinese societies. The legislation of same-sex marriage or civil union, for example, has only seen progress in Taiwan—notwithstanding a strong local backlash and a failed referendum on 24 November 2018 to legalize same-sex marriage under the current Civil Code. Concealing one's sexual orientation and marrying the opposite sex is still a common choice among same-sex attracted people, while quasi-marriage (*xingshi hunyin*, or a set of fake heterosexual marriages between a lesbian couple and a gay couple) is not uncommon as well, especially in mainland China. Centered in the Confucianist kinship values, filial piety has long been the dominant social discourse that sees hetero-reproductive relationships as both a familial responsibility and a sociocultural ideal. Sexual minorities are still often stigmatized and marginalized in Chinese cultures, while queer film festivals and LGBT NGOs (non-government organizations) still face the authority's crackdown in mainland China.

The sociocultural transitions concerning queer sexualities in Chinese societies and the resilience of existing heteronormative sociopolitical structures have conjointly reshaped queer social and cultural practices in the twenty-first century. In the case of China, on the macro level, these transitions lead to the increased visibility of sexual minorities in cultural materials, cyberspaces, as well as the society at large, while the struggle of queer people against the dominant heteronormativity remains a prevalent theme in queer cultural productions and social practices. On the micro level, LGBT organizations and businesses are emerging both in China's urban queer communities and on digital platforms, while these organizations and businesses are still closely monitored by the authority and often struggling to secure a venue and a social space for their communal and commercial activities. Today, in short, while the changing social attitude towards queer people provides a somewhat positive environment for sexual minorities and queer cultures, the unchanged sex-related social norms and values remain strong and robust.

(Homo)capitalism without Democracy

Gender and sexual diversity is not necessarily contingent on a Western capitalist modernity. From Petrus Liu's thesis of "Queer Marxism" (2015) to Rahul Rao's critique of "Global Homocapitalism" (2015) and "Queer International Relations" (2018), recent scholarship on non-Western/non-white genders and sexualities tends to further disentangle the assumed correlations between queer cultures and global capitalist modernities and democracies. This body of literature, despite its various disciplinary origins and intellectual genealogies, elicits the arguments that (1) the mobilization of gender and sexuality is not necessarily a function of liberal-democratic and linear-progressive policies and politics; (2) similarly, it is not bound up with the "gay rights as equal rights" agenda that often comes through transnational capitalist expansion and liberal pluralism; (3) the development of global queer cultures does not always follow, nor does it necessarily benefit from, global capitalist production and its neoliberal reconfiguration of market and desire; and (4) contextual changes in LGBT-inclusive policies and legislation may further highlight the dependence of queer politics on state actors, but the role of the state in regulating/reproducing queer desires should be further contextualized and problematized, be it through the lens of homonationalism or queer Marxism.

Capitalism is integral to the formations of both homophobia and homonormativity. Critics from the Left see capitalism as the root of modern homophobia, in the sense that it has created a need and a necessity to pass on private wealth to offspring and hence precludes non-reproductive desires between the same sex (Wolf 2004). John D'Emilio argues that it is the capitalist development that has made possible an independent gay identity and the emergence of "chosen family" out of the register of consanguineous kinship, when expanded wage labor and socialized production have undermined the material foundation of traditional family life and released sexuality from imperative procreation (1983). To that end, the capitalist free market has also enabled self-expression and placebo gay emancipation through consumption, even though such emancipation is not achieved through progression in state legislation or activist social reform (Puar 2006, 77). The folding of queer desire and sexuality in capitalist production has reproduced a homonormativity signaled by individual participation in the market and a consumerist sexual citizenship hailed by capitalism, in which queer people are recognized as good citizens not through their deviant genders and sexualities but through their contribution to the market and to capitalist production and consumption.

In the new millennium, the neoliberal reconfiguration of capital and labor has continued to underline international development bureaucracies, while the leading institutions of global capitalism such as the World Bank and the International Monetary Fund (IMF) have extended their developmental agenda from gender equality to equal LGBT rights. These shifts are expected to create workplaces and economies that are more inclusive to improve the efficiency in the allocation of labor resource and human capital, when gender/sexuality-based exclusions are believed to be financially costly for capitalist production (Rao 2015, 38–39). The neoliberal states, whose function lies in creating and securing a free market, are hence incentivized to pass legislation to protect gay rights in employment, education, military, and other social institutions. Globally, as poor countries are believed to be more homophobic with less gender equality, economic incentives (e.g., the injection of capital) have been offered by their more developed neighbors in the West if they take up the inclusive gay rights agenda underpinned by neoliberal capitalist expansion, while economic punishment (e.g., the withdrawal of capital) may follow if they fail to comply (see Rao 2015 for case studies). The issue of gender and sexual equality has been reworked into global capital and labor resource allocation in the name of financial aid and international collaboration, reminiscent of a colonial "civilizing" mission in its promise of growth through a singular model of development (Rao 2018, 142).

China, a willing recipient of and an active contributor to global capitalist expansion with its particular trajectory of growth, has benefited greatly from the neoliberal blueprint of development while simultaneously remaining more or less immune to some of capitalism's assumed imperatives. As a beneficiary of globalization, China has been actively participating in the international market led by the West (e.g., through the WTO) while at the same time undermining its rules and principles set by Western countries. Controversial as it is, China has proved its capability in growing its economy and society without resorting to a liberal-democratic political and social system commonly found in the West that is often assumed necessary for continued (capitalist) economic development. After more than four decades of strong growth, China has started to assert its economic power and geopolitical ambition to become a new regional and global leader—a privilege previously grasped tightly by the more developed superpowers in the West. For those who remain skeptical, China has shown its determination through its previous and ongoing successes in pursuing its power and growth on its own track.

This is conjoined by a narrowing civil society when China's political leaders have further tightened their control on media, academia, NGOs, and many other aspects of public and social life. The middle classes who have benefited from the country's economic miracle lack the motivation and incentive for change and reform, as any social upheavals may put their hard-earned and newly acquired wealth at risk, while the pervasive nationalist yearning for China's revival engineered by the state has been increasingly satisfied by the country's rise to power on the regional and global stage. The Western world has also become more dependent on China since the turn of the twenty-first century, thanks to the opportunities China has offered in trade, business, and investment through its continued supply of skilled labor and international students and tourists, as well as its newly emerged urban middle classes with a large and growing appetite for global consumption. The relation with China has become crucial for many countries in their post-global financial crisis (GFC) recovery amid a series of social, economic, and political crises facing today's Western Europe and North America. The West has become somewhat reluctant to offend China for fear of the latter's economic retaliation, although the ongoing clashes in trade, cybersecurity, and intellectual property have further complicated the geopolitical tensions between China and the West.

That is to say, while China opened its doors and participated in the global capitalist development, the liberal-democratic progression and the human rights agenda that usually accompany Western capitalist expansions have been stopped by the authoritarian regime at its doorstep. The West has lost its bet on China—the long-anticipated political reform is unlikely to come—and the once-motivated local queer activists have been disappointed that the political conditions do not allow a reformist agenda based on a gay-rights/equal-rights model.

This may change in the future, but the past and recent evidence does not suggest an optimistic way moving forward. The current political status has largely throttled queer activists' dream that China will follow a Western (predominately US) paradigm that enables gay emancipation nested in a liberal, progressive model that China will eventually follow. This dream has long been nurtured by various LGBT activists and organizations supported by their Western counterparts since the turn of the twenty-first century, through which they have been saliently and laudably encouraging queer people's self-acceptance, leading and facilitating community building, and raising the public awareness of gender and sexual diversity. Their reformist agenda, in contrast, has been less fruitful and may have politicized queer issues in the eyes of the authority because of their equal-rights approach and their connections with Western NGOs, which are both deemed potentially subversive and regularly cracked down on by the party-state.

The problems here are not only political but first and foremost cultural and social. At the cultural level, Chinese people have long been obsessed with a Confucianist familism centered on (1) reproduction and the continuation of the family line and (2) filial piety and the obedience to parental authority. These have jointly maintained and reproduced a hierarchical Confucianist family and social order that has been a cornerstone of Chinese culture and society throughout its long history. Non-reproductive queer sexualities are apparently at odds with this long-lasting cultural ideal, while an independent gay identity and lifestyle enabled by a capitalist market economy outside the nexus of the family appear incompatible with the fundamental Confucianist social order and hierarchy. This incompatibility between the modern constructions and practices of homosexuality and the Confucianist family and kinship structure has deeply troubled queer people in Chinese societies. At the societal level, thanks to various social upheavals throughout its modern history, China's premodern inclusiveness of sexual diversity has also been replaced by an intolerance of gender and sexual deviance based on an obsolete Western sexology that is still strong and robust. The identity-based modern LGBT politics from the West may have raised the social visibility of queer people in China but also reinforced existing social stigma and intolerance of same-sex attracted people based on an essentialist belief of sexuality. Despite various developments in legislation and public health policy at the turn of the twenty-first century, recent census data still indicate a prevalent lack of social acceptance of homosexuality in today's China (see Hu 2016; Xie and Peng 2018).

This is why the noble cause of "equal rights" in Western LGBT activism seldom attracts a large support in China's queer communities and wider society: it is inherently a different mode that neither resonates with Confucian culture nor appears compatible or indeed relevant to China's social condition and convention. Its curtailed ability in addressing the sociocultural underpinnings of the difficulties and challenges facing queer people has frustrated the most willing followers of its agenda. To put it another way, the lack of progression of LGBT rights in China owes not only to the political constraints and a highly concentrated and increasingly consolidated single-party leadership, but more fundamentally to the lack of collective sociocultural groundings of the liberalist gay rights claim. Even if we recur to the neoliberal model of labor-resource reconfiguration and its underlying imperative of capitalist growth, the potential gain in productivity through a more LGBT-inclusive economy still fails to present a strong incentive to overtake the predominant cultural ideal of the Confucianist familism that has been sustaining Chinese society for two thousand years. This deeply rooted and widely held family and social order appears particularly strong and robust that rejects the folding of gender and sexual diversity merely into the capitalist process and liberal social progression in the name of modernity and development. Rather, at both the state and the societal level, the tsunami of global capitalist expansion seems to have further provoked a resurgence of and a stronger holding onto traditional Chinese cultures and values against Western influences, offering a striking contrast to the neoliberalization of China's urban cultures that is often attributed to China's participation in global capitalist production.

While it is erroneous to locate China's queer cultures and social practices completely in its economic development and modernization, attributing China's queer issues as "merely cultural" is equally negligent and oblivious to the capitalist reconfiguration of gender and sexual diversity. Indeed, queer issues are most saliently hailed in China through the process of capitalist development and consumption, exemplified by the popularity of the venture-capital-driven mobile gay dating apps and social networking services in China's emerging "pink" (queer) economy. When China's social, cultural, and political conditions offer a rather limited space for transgressive genders and sexualities, the economic realm seems to be the most promising place where queer issues are visibly tolerated by the state and financially incentivized by the country's private sector.[8] This appears redolent of Lisa Duggan's critique of "a privatized, depoliticized gay culture anchored in domesticity and consumption," which is essentially a homonormativity that fails to contest the dominant heteronormativity and its social, cultural, and political institutions (2003, 50).

More important, although China's development does not dissolve its sociocultural preclusion of non-reproductive queer sexualities, the capitalist reconfiguration of the labor force and human capital has fundamentally changed queer cultures and social practices, making queer issues inseparable from the process of neoliberal capitalist expansion and its many imperatives and contingencies. First, migrations within and beyond China have become increasingly common among today's young people for better education and employment. These development-induced migrations have shifted the focus of queer issues from within the family to a long-distance kinship structure between queer people and their families of origin, underpinned by their increased geographical mobilities and desire for social mobilities. Second, the mobilized migrating bodies and desires have also contributed to the increasingly frequent and fluid queer cultural flows across traditional boundaries, where China's expansive growth and capital power has made it a focal point in regional and global queer Sinophone/Chinese-language cultural mobilities. On top of that, driven by a development-induced desire for a better life through upward social class migration, the pervasive and zealous pursuits of social mobilities in today's China have further continued and sustained existing social inclusion and exclusion along the lines of not only gender and sexuality but also who has the power for capital accumulation and who has access to capital.

In other words, gender and sexual injustice may find its roots in the lack of equality in both economic distribution and sociocultural recognition; the former precludes those with less access to capital and material wealth from exercising their voices, while the latter precludes their voices from being heard and recognized on an equal footing. Along with China's rapid rise and growth, queer people's lack of social recognition has been increasingly conjoined with the issue of development and distribution. If the low sociocultural acceptance depicts a hopeless future for queer people, then the development-induced mobilities in pursuing educational, cultural, social, and economic capital may offer a slim hope through which a privatized, depoliticized queer future may be possible in a country like China. That said, development itself does not solve the issue of sociocultural misrecognitions of gender and sexual diversity, nor does it address the problem of the widening inequality in capital and wealth distribution. Overall, the emerging and established forms of queer mobilities (and, in any case, immobilities) have started to challenge our previous understandings of queer issues in China and other Chinese societies and communities. We urgently need new lenses and frameworks in social analysis and cultural critique to make sense of today's ongoing social transformations concerning queer people as well as the changing queer cultural landscapes, when China is marching into internal economic reform and ambitious international expansion for its great dream of revival in the twenty-first century.

Queer Cultures and Queer Mobilities

It is against this backdrop that I situate this book in post-2008 queer Chinese cultures and social practices. The year 2008 arguably marked several historical moments in China that conjointly opened a new era. In addition to the Summer Olympic Games held successfully in Beijing, 2008 marked the thirtieth anniversary of China's reform and opening up (*gaige kaifang*) that led to the country's strong development in three consecutive decades as the world's fastest-growing economy. The year 2008 also marked the beginning of the second decade of Hong Kong's rule under China, and the tightened connections between mainland China and Taiwan, when the Kuomintang (the Chinese Nationalist Party) regained leadership and began to ameliorate its cross-strait relation.[9] In a broader context, 2008 witnessed the peak of the GFC that led to a worldwide economic downturn, although China managed to avoid a recession despite a slowdown in its growth. Escaping the GFC relatively unscathed when many advanced economies in the West contracted, China has become increasingly confident in its global power assertion and geopolitical ambition over the ensuing decade vis-à-vis the sluggish recovery of the West. Since the GFC, local and global investors and businesses have also been eagerly searching for new opportunities in emerging economies and markets (such as China's gay market), while transnational collaborations on cultural productions have helped boost capital injection and redistribute potential financial risks. It was also in 2008 that Google android devices first appeared on the market and began to bring affordable smartphones to consumers, after the debut of Apple's more expensive iPhone in 2007, and foresaw the popularity of mobile social networking and locative dating apps. Within merely a few years, the smartphone had become integral to many people's day-to-day life as well as the new frontier in queer sociocultural practices and mobilities. In short, 2008 was a turning point that triggered a series of ongoing social, political, economic, and technological transformations that have been shaping and reshaping queer social and cultural practices in China and other Chinese societies in the early twenty-first century.

The emergence of a disparate and diverse range of queer cultural and social practices both online and on the ground since 2008 has provided a wide array of cultural materials and sociological data for critical analysis and investigation. Germinated from my interest and background in film and media studies, this project identifies and locates post-2008 queer Chinese cultures and mobilities across three interrelated and expansive cultural domains and social spaces: queer video/filmmaking and autobiographical queer cinemas; urban queer communities and queer film clubs (i.e., regular communal film screenings and discussions); and mobile queer social networking platforms and large-scale online queer communities.[10] I treat these socioculturally contextualized and contested spaces and practices of non-conforming genders and sexualities as rich and deep social and cultural reservoirs that offer a certain breadth and depth through which we can gain a substantive insight into the lived experiences and expressions of queer people.

At any rate, I was less concerned with the aesthetics, forms, and styles of queer cultural materials than with the underlying social issues behind them.[11] In other words, I look both at and through these materials and practices as vehicles to scrutinize the wider social changes and cultural shifts concerning queer communities and mobilities. Along this line, I have identified *kinship*, *migration*, and *middle classes* as the three key points in post-2008 queer Chinese cultures, as these themes have most frequently surfaced and resurfaced across all the queer cultural realms and social spaces that I have investigated in this research and empirically experienced in the past fifteen years or so in China's queer communities both online and on the ground. Indeed, these three factors all play essential roles in today's queer Chinese sociocultural practices. First, kinship has always been the top concern among queer Chinese people when their sexualities are at odds with the fundamental Confucianist family and social order. Second, queer kinship has been further complicated by the growing internal and international migrations as a result of China's ongoing economic development since the turn of the twenty-first century. Third, one's social position and class affiliation have a significant impact on the process of migration and kinship negotiation, to the extent that mobility is often a privilege and kinship negotiation may heavily depend on one's socioeconomic status.

These three elements conjointly constitute what might be termed *queer mobilities*—the motions (geographical relocations) and emotions (psychological readjustments) of queer people and their families across the queer/non-queer and local/non-local boundaries in the intersections of geographical, cultural, and social class migrations. In the first instance, the increasingly frequent internal and international migrations have separated queer people from their families of origin and inevitably changed today's queer kinship structure in China and other Chinese societies (the result of *geographical mobilities*). Second, the flows of queer cultures along the migration routes have become increasingly diverse and fluid across national and geographical boundaries (the manifestations of *cultural mobilities*). Third, it is the pursuit of upward social mobility and social class migration that drives people to leave home and embark on migration journeys (the underlying driving force of *social mobilities* and the stratifying force of inter- and intra-class segregations). On top of that, "queer" itself delineates gender and sexual mobilizations beyond traditional boundaries; it is hence impossible to talk about queer cultures without considering and evoking the issue of mobility. Speaking of queer kinship, migration, and social class, we are essentially talking about *how today's queer cultures are shaping and shaped by post-2008 queer mobilities in China and other Chinese societies and communities*.

Although the term "queer mobility" is hardly a neologism, my project reconsiders and requalifies this concept through a triple lens: (1) the horizontal, geographical relocation of people, (2) the multidimensional cultural flows and counterflows, and (3) the vertical upward social class migration. This reconsideration of gender and sexual mobilities owes to two parallel sets of scholarship: mobility studies and queer geographies. First, since the "mobile turn" and the "global turn" of social sciences in the late 1980s, we have actively recast mobility from a sideline "epiphenomenon of more basic material, social or cultural formations" (D'Andera, Ciolfi, and Gray 2011, 150) to "an evocative keyword for the twenty-first century and a powerful discourse that creates its own effects and contexts" (Hannam, Sheller, and Urry 2006, 1). Mobilities have become less an option than an obligation as a fundamental sculpting and ordering force in contemporary life, ranging from micro-level daily commuting to macro-level transnational flows of capital and culture (Gössling and Stavrinidi 2016).[12] This mobile shift has enabled us to reframe the issue of gender and sexual diversity through the lens of mobilities. Queer theory, in its anti-fixity propagation for more fluid and flexible gender and sexual expressions and experiences, thus finds an intellectual alliance with mobility studies in their anti-sedentism common ground.[13]

Second, both a "sexual turn" and an "emotional turn" have become evident and prevalent in the interrogations of mobility experiences that consider sexuality and affection as two critical, if not decisive, forces in the imagination and enactment of migration (Mai and King 2009, 296). This dual lens effectively highlights the lived experiences and affective labor of mobility and migrancy that encompass feelings, desires, and memories in spatiotemporal movements. The emotion thus finds its material bearing and grounding in the motion and mobilization of the body, the forefront carrier of feelings and desires in the pursuit of love and comfort through migration, which has been a major focus in queer geographies and geographies of sexualities (Gorman-Murray 2009, 441–47).[14] These developments in mobility studies and humanistic geographies have laid a solid foundation for the interrogations in this book of the conditions and consequences of queer cultures and mobilities in twenty-first-century China and other Chinese societies and communities.

Politics of Sexual Identities

The ongoing social transformations have paralleled the development and diversification of sexual identities and identity-based politics in Chinese societies across everyday vernaculars and academic research. Terminologically, various identity labels have been adopted to describe sexual minorities: *memba* in Hong Kong (Kong 2011a), *piaopiao* in Chengdu (Wei 2006, 2007a, 2007b), and *gaizu* in Taiwan (Lim 2008a)—although these regional slang terms are less known in the Chinese world as a whole.[15] Other terms such as "same-sex," androphilia/gynephilia, and men who have sex with men (MSM) and women who have sex with women (WSW) are mainly used by researchers in social sciences and in public health and HIV/AIDS intervention. However, there exist numerous widely adopted and highly contested identity labels including homosexual or *tongxinglian*, gay and lesbian, LGBT(Q), *tongzhi*, *jiyou*, and queer or *ku'er*. These identity labels have presented more complicated issues in the negotiations and reproductions of sexual identity politics in Chinese societies under the influence of the intermingled localizing and globalizing forces since the turn of the twenty-first century.

The birth of homosexual/*tongxinglian* as a sexual category was an interesting case in China. In the West, it was not until 1869 that journalist Károly Mária Kertbeny published his coinage of the terms *heterosexual* and *homosexual*, a dualism soon picked up by sexologists and psychoanalysts to categorize human sexualities (Bonnet 1997). Since then, social understandings of sexuality were increasingly folded into a dichotomous medical and pathological discourse (see Foucault 1978). In China, intimate same-sex bonding was visible throughout its ancient history and often described with poetic metaphors in lieu of pathologized sexual classifications (see Xiaomingxiong [1984] 1997; Hinsch 1990; Vitiello 2011; Wu 2004).[16] Same-sex desires and heterosexual reproductions were not considered mutually exclusive, and those involved in same-sex relationships were often able to maintain a heterosexual and reproductive marriage. This attested to "the prevalence of bisexuality over exclusive homosexuality" in premodern China (Hinsch, 11)—or, more accurately, a fluid way to balance one's familial/patrilineal responsibility with the object-choice of one's sexual desire before the modern categorizations of homosexuality and bisexuality came into being.

However, the nuanced and fluid same-sex tradition was reduced to silence when the imperial period came to an end and China underwent dramatic social upheavals from the mid-nineteenth century through to the first half of the twentieth century. Humiliated at the hands of Western colonists, China went through a series of social transformations aiming to reform and strengthen the country. Especially during the Self-Strengthening Movement (*Yangwu Yundong*, 1861–1895), whose slogan was "learning the Western strengths to strengthen ourselves," and the New Culture Movement (*Xin Wenhua Yundong*, 1915–1921) that valued science and democracy as China's salvation, Chinese people began to frantically cast away traditional cultural values for a new society established on a Western paradigm. Roughly at the same time, sexologists in the West began to construct new medical knowledge on homosexuality, which was imported by then-Chinese intellectuals who were borrowing modern science from the West to modernize China, often through Japanese translations of Anglo-European texts when Japan was also undergoing social reforms and modernization driven by Western colonialism and internal social upheavals.

Thus, the categorization and the knowledge of homosexuality were imported from the West when China and Japan eagerly looked at Western modernity and scientific knowledge as a model for their own survival. The Chinese word *tongxinglian* originated from the term *tongxing'ai*, literally "same-sex love," a direct adoption of the Japanese word *doseiai* that was in turn a transliteration of the English word "homosexuality."[17] That is to say, China's more nuanced premodern understanding of same-sex intimacy was reshaped and reproduced by the imported modern, Western classification and pathology of homosexuality (Chou 2000, 249; Hinsch 1990, 139–66; Kang 2009, 2010; Wu 2004, 3–5).[18] Since then, the conduct-based sexual practice was to some extent replaced by the modern scientific discourse that criminalized and pathologized non-normative sexualities.[19] When the native same-sex cultures were cast away together with other traditional values, the Chinese Civil War (1927–1950) led to the establishment of the Marxist-socialist regime in mainland China and the retreat of the Kuomintang to Taiwan. During the Cold War, socialist China was mostly cut off from the West—the origin of the imported sexology where knowledge of sexuality continued to develop.

More important, the umbilical Chinese traditions including premodern same-sex cultures were further cut off in China in the nationwide pursuit of Maoism and the rejection of "obsolete" premodern values during various social upheavals, including the massively destructive Cultural Revolution (1966–1976). What remained from early sexual cultures was further denied and despised, although same-sex intimacy was still practiced (and punished once discovered) through these turbulent times (Kang 2018). When China once again opened up to the world, the obsolete sexual norms imported from the West at the turn of the twentieth century were taken for granted by Chinese people and had become so shockingly strong and robust that even today's more advanced sexology from their source of origin (the West) cannot overthrow them (Hinsch 1990, 165–71).[20] This is why, in today's Chinese parlance, the term *tongxinglian* still conveys the image of pathologized sexual deviants who need medical diagnosis and treatment. In some school textbooks in mainland China, for example, *tongxinglian* is still described as a disease and homosexuals as patients (*huanzhe*).[21] Partially due to this derogatory connotation, "homosexual" and "*tongxinglian*" have gradually lost their appeal among same-sex attracted people, in Western countries and Chinese societies alike, and have often been replaced by other sexual identity categories such as gay and lesbian, or *tongzhi* and *jiyou*.

The power of the term "gay" probably lies in its simplicity with only three letters and one syllable, constituting the most concise articulation of sexuality that proclaims a certain identitarian empowerment. This English term probably spread to China in the 1990s. In Li Yinhe and Wang Xiaobo's pioneer research of same-sex attracted man in Beijing (1993), none of their informants self-identified as "gay" in the late 1980s. But in the revised edition that includes follow-up research (Li 1998), many interviewees directly used the English word "gay" as self-identification while describing heterosexuals as "straight." In this case, the influence of Western gay emancipation contributed to the emergence of a self-conscious gay identity and a minoritarian and identitarian awareness among queer Chinese people, underpinned by China's continued participation in the global capitalist development through which the consequences of globalization had become more prominent in gender and sexual mobilization. The gay-straight dichotomy essentially follows the same pattern as the homosexual-heterosexual binary but has largely moved away from pathology and sexology. That is to say, this identity label has empowered the once criminalized and pathologized homosexuals "to be cheerful and gay" (pun intended).[22]

Such identification has also granted people a sense of connection with their Anglo-American counterparts in the transnational and global flows of gay cultures. However, this "global gayness" (Altman 1996, 1997, 2001) derived from Western, urban, white, male, middle-class gay cultures may appear inadequate in addressing the cultural and historical specificities of local same-sex desires and traditions in China (Rofel 2007, 85–110). In a broader context, it also underlines the emergence of an imagined global gay community of "horizontal comradeship" that potentially flattens the differences among various cultural locales, although this critique risks a "cultural particularism" that claims what it represents is unproblematically authentic and genuinely different (Chiang 2014a, 27–36). At any rate, it is equally problematic to conflate Western and Chinese gay cultures or to argue for a unique Chinese gayness that circumvents global flows of gay texts and images and completely marks itself off from the global gay community.[23]

However, "gay" is probably one of the most problematic identity labels, and those self-identified as "gay" in Chinese societies are not often fully aware of its connotations. The term "gay" was first and foremost a synonym of "cheerful" before it became an alternative and less pathological descriptor of homosexuals.[24] In today's vernacular, the word "gay" has often become associated with a certain level of pride and self-consciousness about one's sexuality and an expressive desire to declare and proclaim one's sexual self. More important, in today's English parlance, "gay" often alludes to a pejorative stereotype associated with a flamboyant quality, a metrosexual glamour and flair, and perhaps a "drama queen" personality that is inseparable from the homocapitalism and the late-modern consumerism discussed above. Then what about those who do not identify with such culturally marked and self-reflexive body images and gay habitus? What about those who do not share the gay-style pride and self-awareness? What about those who dislike the unapologetic, identitarian, and minoritarian conception of gay individuality and sexuality?[25] Has the label "gay" confined them, as much as it has freed others? Are they gay (cheerful) to be gay?

On top of that, to quote Kai Wright's writing of queer youth of color in the US out of context, gay people are understood as "white people . . . with a proud, self-proclaimed sexual identity" (2008, viii). At any rate, the intertwined *gayness* and *whiteness* have little to do with the lived experiences of sexual minorities in China. Their experiences and understandings of themselves may not resonate with, or appear relevant to, the "whiteness of gayness" (107) and the "gay euphemism" (77) in the West. If we simply label same-sex attracted people in China as "gay," we risk assigning them an identity category that some of them can come out with but never fully belong to. Even though many of them self-identify as "gay," they are not often aware of the connotations attached to this label, while the "gayness" that they have experienced in China and other Chinese societies may be very different from that of their Anglo-American counterparts.[26]

To further complicate the case of sexual identities, while "gay" sometimes serves as a gender-neutral term for both men and women in English-speaking countries, this word is unmistakably linked to male-male bonding in Chinese societies. Gender-distinctive terms such as "lesbian" and the Chinese term *lala* are instead often adopted for inter-female intimacy. "Lesbian" is a word sometimes attributed to ancient Greek poetess Sappho, who resided on the Greek island of Lesbos and whose poetry proclaimed her love of female (Bonnet 1997, 147–48). The history of its usage in designating same-sex desires and intimacies is probably longer than that of "gay."[27] The emergence of Chinese lesbians was also contingent on the reconstructed local understanding of women and homosexuality based on imported Western physiology, sexology, and social theory (Sang 2003, 15). In Chinese societies, the label *lala* has become popular as the nickname variant of "lesbian," given that the Chinese word *la* puns on *les*, which derives from the character *La-zi* in the renowned Taiwanese lesbian novel *The Crocodile's Journal* (*Eyu Shouji;* see Martin 2003, 224–36).

"Gay" and "lesbian" have in turn formed part of the shorthand LGBT(Q), which is also well known and widely adopted in China's queer communities. Here, grouping various sexual preferences and practices in a single alphabet mixture may potentially obscure the differences among and within each and every category, insomuch as the needs, demands, and interests often vary across and within different sexual minority groups. More important, how many identity labels will be enough? When the term "queer" was first borrowed by social activists from queer theory to append LGBT, they were already hoping that the newly added "Q" could become an umbrella term to cover different gender and sexual categories. However, once an analytical weapon in our theoretical arsenal has been reduced to the simple capital letter Q in social activism, it becomes yet another somewhat essentialist category that queer theory tried to criticize in the first place, as well as another label that not everyone is comfortable to identify and come out with. Since then, we have continued to add more labels to create an alphabet soup of LGBTQQIAAP.[28] More recently, this has become the more concise but equally tasteless LGBTQ+. Appending a plus sign ("+") to LGBTQ marks the latest attempt to include potentially indefinite gender and sexual categories as we continue to create more labels along with our diverse sociocultural practices. One day we may realize that not every difference needs a prescribed label and not everyone is willing to be reduced to and represented by a symbol, be it a capital letter or a mathematical sign.

While these Western creations never fully fit in Chinese cultures, the label of *tongzhi* has flourished in Chinese societies since the early 1990s. *Tong* literally means "same," while *zhi* can be understood as *zhixiang* (goal, aspiration, ambition, or intention). *Tongzhi*, a fixed iamb meaning "the same goal," was first used in *The Discourses of the States* (*Guoyu*), an ancient collection of historical records dated to the fifth to the fourth centuries BCE (Tang and Qu 2008, 270). The modern meaning of *tongzhi*—people who share the same political ideology or who belong to the same political party—was borrowed from the West at the turn of the twentieth century through the Japanese translation of the English word "comrade." Its popular use is frequently attributed by historians to the dying wish of Sun Yat-sen, founding father of Republican China: "revolution is not yet accomplished and *tongzhi* must endeavor to carry it on." After the establishment of the socialist PRC (People's Republic of China), *tongzhi* also became widely adopted as a friendly, politically correct, potentially equalizing, and gender-ambiguous term for people to address and greet each other in everyday life.[29]

The appropriation of *tongzhi* for homosexuals was first introduced in 1989 by the organizer of the inaugural Hong Kong Lesbian and Gay Film Festival and disseminated to Taiwan's Golden Horse Film Festival in 1992 and then to mainland China in the mid- to late 1990s (Chou 2000, 2; Lim 2008a, 237; Tang and Qu 2008, 271). Chou Wah-shan argues that the term *tongzhi* implies a "sameness" between the pathologically divided homosexuals and heterosexuals and potentially transforms the former from sexual perverts to equal citizens who share the same feeling of love and intimacy (2000).[30] The emergence and popularity of *tongzhi* as a native same-sex identity label and sociopolitical discourse further diversifies and problematizes local sexual identity politics in various Chinese societies. However, for those who grew up in mainland China in and before the 1990s, it is still rather uncanny to apply this term to sexual minorities, as it used to be the daily vernacular they adopted to address each other. This local term may also cause confusion in international liaison between Chinese and overseas LGBT organizations. Beijing *Tongzhi* Center, a prestigious NGO well known in the local queer communities, has chosen "Beijing LGBT Center" as its English name despite the completely different implications and genealogies of the two terms. Due to its strong political and historical underpinnings, the term *tongzhi* has gradually lost its charm among the younger generation in mainland China to new identity labels such as *jiyou*.

As a slang term, *jiyou* literally means "gay friend" or "gay buddy." This neologism changes the Cantonese transliteration of gay ("*gei*") to its Mandarin pronunciation ("*ji*") and bridges it with the Mandarin character *you* ("friend," literally). In Cantonese-language areas, "gay men" are often called "*gei-lo*" in which "*lo*" denotes "male" but also connotes "men from the lower social classes" and is hence classist and sexist (neglecting same-sex attracted women) at the same time (Chou 2000, 79). The new portmanteau *jiyou*, however, wipes off the classism and most of the derogatory meaning of *gei-lo*. Its designation of "gay friend" relocates homosexuality into the register of "friendship" and frees it from pathology and sexology, as I have discussed elsewhere (Wei 2012), as well as from Western-style gay euphemism and local *tongzhi* politics. *Jiyou* soon became a popular term designating all kinds of intimate bonding in both online and offline vernaculars, often in the form *hao jiyou* ("good gay friend"). There has also emerged a gender-distinctive feminine label *hao li you*—literally "good beautiful friend."

This set of terms has been adopted by the young generation to describe and make sense of same-sex intimacies, albeit in a rather jocular way. Having emerged recently at the dawn of the 2010s, *jiyou* is better understood as an outcome of the intermingled local sex-related values and traditions, the influence of Western gayness, the vibrant cybercultures and youth cultures in China, and the (con) fusion among English, Cantonese, and Mandarin. In this sense, the term itself has become a site to negotiate sex-related desires in a globalizing world when the social visibility of queer people is gradually increasing in China. In his study of the use of *jiyou* among college students, Wei Wei (2017) sees the term as both a demonstration of homosociality and an identity management strategy to renegotiate the public display of heteromasculinity. When this term is generalized beyond the scope of homosexuality, *jiyou* becomes less an identity label than a way to understand same-sex social bonding by young Chinese people. Because of its jocular nature and ambiguous and expansive connotations, *jiyou* remains a problematic term despite its popularity among the youth.

This is why we need the term "queer"—as an analytical tool and conceptual framework, not an umbrella identity category. "Queer" as in queer theory has been a highly contested term adopted by scholars and artists in both the East and the West. Marching into its fourth decade and having generated a vast intellectual and artistic repertoire, queer theory offers invaluable insights into the social construction of sexual identity categories and the problem of identity politics. However, those of us working under the "queer" banner do not necessarily agree with each other on the use of "queer" in different contexts; after its initial emergence as an analytical and critical tool, queer theory itself has become a polyphony chirping in different branches of cultural and social theories.[31] I understand queer theory as a view that draws attention to the social construction of our understandings of gender and sexuality, challenges the fixity of sex-related categories and identity-based politics, and questions the dualist, naturalist, and essentialist view of gender and sexuality. I also embrace queer theory as an empowerment to highlight the cultural and conceptual diversity and complexity of marginalized and non-conforming bodies and desires under the dominant heteronormativity.

However, transplanting and implementing queer theory in Asian/Chinese societies is often controversial. Queer theory arguably "remains rooted in Western, primarily Anglo-American discourse" (Welker and Kam 2006, 5), and researchers still hold divergent views about "the salience and appropriateness of 'queer' as a descriptive term and analytical category" in Asian contexts (Blackwood and Johnson 2012, 442). As Ara Wilson beautifully summarizes,

> the term queer appears to represent a loose domain of disparate non-normative genders and sexualities, although it does not solve any problems of English-language hegemony or ethnocentric categorizations of sexuality. It is not a gloss for Asian vernaculars, nor is it necessarily a term of choice for Asian actors. (2006, 2)

At any rate, the problematic use of queer theory in Asia "may not resonate with local meaning systems regarding sexuality and gender" (Sinnott 2010, 20). A noticeable suspicion of queer theory's value in the study of Chinese gender and sexual diversity is also evident in Hong Kong, Taiwan, and mainland China, although connecting China with queer theory is potentially revolutionary, as it links two distant locales of the Orient and the West and makes them once again intimate (Liu 2010, 296). This both disrupts the East-West binary and reminds us of "the constructedness of Chineseness" in decolonizing the US-based queer theory and further connecting it with the underlying Marxist intellectual and cultural traditions in Chinese societies (Liu 2010, 300–307; Liu 2015; Liu and Rofel 2010, 283–88).

In other words, the power of queer critique in Chinese contexts first and foremost lies in its revelation of how gender and sexual classifications are socially and discursively constructed, dichotomized, and colonized. That said, I do not mean that "queer" can be used as an overarching term to blur the material-bodily and psychosexual differences among individual people, but that it offers enough intellectual flexibility to address the diversity and embrace the non-conformity of genders, sexualities, bodies, feelings, desires, attractions, and texts and images (Sinnott 2010). In this project, I follow Ara Wilson and Megan Sinnott to use the term "queer" as academic shorthand but *not* as a label of identification. I have titled this book *Queer Chinese Cultures and Mobilities* but would like my readers to keep in mind that "queer" is neither the common vernacular among Chinese sexual minorities nor an identity label widely adopted and recognized by Chinese people.

As much as terminology is concerned, "queer" and its Chinese transliteration *ku'er* are mostly used by artists and intellectuals in a way that often has little appeal to the masses. In this book, my use of "queer" as academic shorthand owes to its epistemological liberating power—an intellectual emancipation beyond gender and sexual emancipation—to highlight the diversity and heterogeneity among and within communities, societies, cultures, and mobilities. I agree with Evelyn Blackwood and Mark Johnson that we use "queer" in Asian contexts as it "effectively highlights the possibilities and constraints of different systems of gender/sexuality" and makes explicit our concern with the "relative instabilities inherent in and productive of both normative and transgressive bodies and practices" (2012, 442). In this case, "queer" and other terms discussed here are by no means monolithic; in fact, these terms themselves have long been the sites of negotiations and resistance in the global flows of sex-related cultures and discourses.

Finally, I hope this section has been able to shed further light on the complexity of sexual identities as well as on the power and the limits of "naming" and "labeling." None of these identity labels can single-handedly capture the complexity of sexualities and the lived experiences of people; in sex-related Chinese cultures and social discourses, homosexual or *tongxinglian*, gay and lesbian, LGBT(Q), *tongzhi*, *jiyou*, and whatever comes up next all have their roles to play and cannot be used simply interchangeably. Here, I am fully aware of my deep skepticism of identity-based politics, my discontent with stereotyping and sexual dualism, and my preference for fluidity over rigidity in the understanding of sexualities. These have further underlined my choice of "queer" as a more flexible analytical tool and conceptual framework as well as my intellectual, epistemological, and critical shorthand instead of a categorical identity label. This section, I hope, has further cleared up the terminological ground for the rest of the discussions in *Queer Chinese Cultures and Mobilities*.

Doing Queer Ethnography in China

This project is not completely ethnographic; rather, it is highly interdisciplinary in its scope and methods that include (1) focused ethnographic fieldwork and community research; (2) textual and contextual analyses of queer cultural materials, mainly autobiographical queer films and online video series; and (3) digital anthropological studies of large online queer communities and mobile queer social networks. As far as fieldwork is concerned, I would like to make two notes regarding the research methods. First, "focused ethnography" refers to a method of carrying out short, intense ethnographic research in one's own culture to study its certain aspects, when an ethnographer is already (more or less) familiar with the research field but has difficulty securing long-term research stays (Knoblauch 2005; Kühn 2013; Wall 2015). Derived from my previous experiences in China's queer communities online and on the ground, my focused ethnography from 2013 to 2014 consisted of three fieldtrips to China, each lasting for over a month. I participated in a large number of communal events organized by various LGBT organizations, including more than twenty screening sessions combined in five queer film clubs—three in Beijing, one in Shanghai, and one in Guangzhou—although I was unable to include all of them in this book. I devoted my fieldwork to participatory observations as well as semi-structured, in-depth interviews with community leaders and stakeholders in these queer social enclaves.

Second, my fieldwork was conjoined by a digital anthropological study (Horst and Miller 2012) that originated in 2011, when I joined a major online queer community, and then expanded to numerous China-based online and mobile queer social networking platforms between 2013 and 2016. This multi-year digital fieldwork, or "networked anthropology" (Collins and Durington 2015) or "virtual ethnography" (Hine 2008, 2015), has enabled me to not only participate in and observe online queer social interactions but also closely scrutinize the development of specific virtual queer communities contextualized by the ongoing social transformations concerning queer people. In other words, I "lived" with these people online for several years to study virtual queer communities as social and cultural sites that constantly generate their own voices and stories, instead of simply treating digital platforms as representations of real-life communities (cf. Underberg and Zorn 2013, 10) or merely connecting with interlocutors through digital networks (cf. Collins and Durington 2015, 4–6). This method is of particular importance in China, where queer people have limited public space and many of them can only come out anonymously online while hiding in the closet in everyday life. This also holds true for people from less-developed areas, where queer social groups and events are scarce. The cyberspace has been a central stage for queer social life and cultural production in China, through which we can gain a deeper anthropological understanding of queer cultures and mobilities in the early twenty-first century.

Despite my decade-long experience in China's queer communities before embarking on this research, I came across a few obstacles in the ethnographic field. These include: (1) the timing and the method in approaching the gatekeepers and initiating field rapport, (2) the balance between participation and observation in the ethnographic sites, and (3) the negotiation of the researcher's own identity in the field and how this identity defines and confines the ethnographer's access to the sites. These three factors presented various problems at different stages of my fieldwork, especially given that my previous experiences were not gained through the NGOs or LGBT groups that were organizing and supporting the queer communal events that I set up to research. Also, before the onset of this project, I only had limited experiences in Beijing, my main ethnographic site where several queer film clubs and many other queer social groups and organizations were in active operation.

When I started my ethnographic fieldwork, how to reveal my researcher's identity and initiate field rapport became my first concern. Loretta Ho's (2010) experience in Beijing as an ethnographer was still alarming: she was directly taken by an informant to meet with other gay activists in the city, who openly showed their distrust in this newcomer foreign to the local queer community. More important, for queer social activities organized by or in association with local NGOs, the gatekeepers often have already seen academics coming to these places for research purposes. Before I had the chance to disclose my identity in a film club, for example, the club organizer mentioned that there were researchers coming to the club to "study them," as distinguished from real participants coming for films and for dating/networking. Although he said immediately that the club welcomed researchers as well, I felt an invisible line suddenly emerged in the thin air between me (as an observer and outsider) and other club members (as participants and insiders).

I had to wait for the right time to "come out" in this particular club. First, I participated in the discussion about the short films we saw and shared my stories with other members. Then the next day I met a new friend in another social group who wanted to explore the local queer film scenes, so I brought him with me to the next screening session in this film club. When I disclosed my researcher's identity in that second session, the organizer was grateful that I brought a friend to the club. What I did had unintentionally demonstrated my willingness to contribute to the development of the club by introducing new members; in so doing, I had convinced the gatekeeper that I indeed cared about the film club instead of treating people as mere research objects. My practice in the research field, merely out of my love for film and my enthusiasm to introduce people to queer cultural spaces in the city, unexpectedly turned into an effective ethnographic strategy to strengthen my rapport with the key informants.

To put it another way, actions always speak louder than words when it comes to building field rapport, while taking initial steps to observe how things work in particular ethnographic sites may turn out to be fruitful. In my case, furthermore, participating in film club sessions not only demonstrated a certain level of devotion and commitment to these queer cultural spaces but afforded me the chance to share my stories and feelings in post-screening discussions. Therefore, by the time I revealed my identity as a researcher, the gatekeepers and other participants already saw me as a person with stories and emotions, instead of a total stranger coming to "study them."[32] However, this role between an insider and an outsider was at times awkward. Even after the disclosure of my identity, I often felt that I was lingering on the borders of these urban film spaces that I was studying, neither fully committed as a member nor totally detached as an observer. On an optimistic note, this minimized the risk of "over-rapport" in my fieldwork and allowed me to participate in and withdraw from the ethnographic sites with less emotional and personal attachment. But I was also uncertain about how to balance participation and observation in the research field.

When I first set foot in queer film clubs in urban China, I was always quite wary about how I should participate in the post-screening discussions. For one thing, it was not clear to me the degree to which an ethnographer should partake in the cultural scenes he was observing. For another, I was caught in the cultural difference regarding speaking and listening. Having received graduate education in the West, I was accustomed to speaking out during group discussions. However, Chinese culture is largely listening-centered ("*tinghua*"), as the entitlement to speak is often a privilege of the senior and the leader (Chia 2003; Gao and Ting-Toomey 1998). As a newcomer to the local queer communities, I was concerned that my potential talkativeness would appear aggressive to other more established members in the film clubs. Listening to what they had to say would better fit my role as an observer and show my due respect for their seniority as long-term members of the clubs.

However, I gradually realized that my involvement in the discussions offered a better chance for me to gain further access to the field. Once the club organizers and participants became aware that I had a background in film studies and queer studies, for example, they would become very curious about what I had to say on relevant issues. Some participants indeed showed a strong interest in cinematic art and relevant theories, and sometimes I clearly felt the pressure that I had to deliver some critical analyses of queer films and social issues in order to win their trust. Showing a good knowledge and understanding of queer cultures and queer studies thus became an effective ethnographic strategy to approach the field and strengthen the rapport. Later, when I theorized and wrote about *gated communities* in this book, I started to realize that I actually offered some cultural capital for exchange in the field that earned me membership in these queer communities gated and walled by knowledge, education, and cultural tastes and interests.

This discussion reveals another issue in my ethnography—the negotiation of my own identity in the field. I was fully aware of my image as young, urban, and educated overseas in these queer cultural spaces. This image may well have influenced, if not determined, which queer groups and individuals were willing to befriend me and which groups and individuals I was able to establish a strong rapport with. Before my first fieldtrip to Beijing, I had earned a master's degree in film studies in an English-speaking country. In the field with my informants, we engaged in many discussions about queer cinematic art, kinship negotiation, and "coming out as coming home" (see Chapter 1). My knowledge of English-language scholarship on queer Chinese cultures often became a point of interest that they were keen about. Together we also visited art-house movie theatres, art galleries, concert halls, and opera houses in the city. It was not until that point that I realized that my key contacts in the field were exclusively young gay men who had completed or were en route in geographical and social class migrations. All of them migrated to Beijing from other parts of China, and most of them had college degrees or were studying at elite universities, who had demonstrated distinctive middle- to high-brow cultural tastes. Although not all of them came from what we can describe today as urban middle-class families, they were overwhelmingly successful in their educational or employment-orientated migrations underlined by the overall increase in Chinese people's development-induced mobilities.

Thinking retrospectively, the roots and routes of my own migrations have largely shaped my identity and image in the research field. My experience of migrating from an underdeveloped small town to Beijing and then to the West itself presented a successful story of geographical, cultural, and social mobilities.

My decision to study China's urban queer film clubs was also led by my own cultural interest in cinematic art and my academic training in film and media theories. My very identity as a researcher returning to China from the West indicated advantaged cultural capital and certain social privilege that both defined and confined my ability in approaching the ethnographic field. I was able to earn entry to urban film clubs because my own cultural profile fitted in these social groups, while many others might have been precluded from such urban queer cultural venues. Along with the progression of this project, class-related social distinctions became increasingly clear as a strong and prevalent indicator underpinning the queer sociocultural phenomena that I was examining. Although I never intentionally selected my informants and interviewees based on their class status, this project largely materialized as a study of China's queer middle classes, insofar as the cultural products and the social spaces in question were noticeably produced and dominated by those with middle-class capital and those desiring and willing to work for such social privilege.

In this case, despite their different geographical origins across a large span of China's territory, my informants were in fact demographically limited in a group of young, all-male, well-educated, and successfully migrated queer people. At any rate, those left behind in geographical, cultural, and social class migrations seldom have access to the vibrant queer cultural spaces and social organizations in China's major metropolises that I was able to approach and research. The elderly, the rural, the undereducated, those with disabilities, and other transgressive (e.g., transgender) sexual minorities who are underrepresented in these places are precluded from this project, in spite of my earnest intention to cover a wide range of queer social practices and cultural spaces in China.[33] Every research has its limits and pitfalls; that said, I do believe that the findings of this project can shed further light on wider social issues concerning queer cultures and mobilities that potentially benefit a more diverse range of social groups beyond this relatively narrow demography.

Kinship, Migration, and Middle Classes

In retrospect, a complex interplay of historical, sociocultural, economic, political, legislative, and technological forces has contributed to the formulations and interventions of the lived experiences, social practices, and cultural expressions of today's sexual minorities. The issue of queer cultures and mobilities is deeply intertwined with (1) the locations and dislocations of Chineseness and the globalized Western gayness and (2) the negotiations and contradictions between the sex-related social norms and the emerging queer cultures that have assumed more social visibility and economic values. The issues addressed in this book are not simply a growing number of queer social practices and cultural products that have been struggling to secure their social legitimacy against the ongoing familism and the ongoing process of neoliberal development, nor are they mere lineages of ancient Chinese sexual cultures or simple imitations of modern, Western gay emancipation. Rather, *Queer Chinese Cultures and Mobilities* examines the germination and movements of queer cultures and social practices across geographical locations, cultural conventions, and social stratifications, when the configurations of gender and sexuality and the understandings of gendered and sexual cultures have become less stable/sedentary and increasingly mobilized beyond traditional and conventional frameworks, categories, and boundaries.

Following this introduction, Chapter 1 and Chapter 2 continue to discuss the issue of compulsory familism and hetero-reproduction facing queer Chinese people, as well as their coming-out and kinship negotiation strategies and the processes of queer homecoming and homemaking through migration. These chapters draw insights from both my ethnographic fieldwork and my analyses of post-2008 autobiographical queer films and digital video series to examine the changing queer kinship structure (the result of *geographical queer mobilities*). As kinship negotiation with the family of origin has been the predominant concern among queer Chinese people under the strong and ongoing familism, I put these chapters up front to address this overwhelmingly common and primary question in queer Chinese communities. I argue that the so-called "coming out as coming home" strategy no longer works in today's Chinese societies, and "home" has often become an impossible location for people to return to; queer kinships are often physically and emotionally distanced when people leave their original families to pursue education and employment through internal or international migration. I have therefore developed a new paradigm of *stretched kinship* to consider a wide range of family/kinship arrangements and various practices in queer homecoming and homemaking, so as to better understand and make sense of the changing queer kinship structures that are shaping and shaped by today's queer Chinese cultures and mobilities.

Chapter 3 furthers the discussion of migration by engaging both mobility scholarship on geographies of sexualities and Sinophone scholarship on settlement and localization to analyze border-crossing queer migrations and cultural flows between mainland China and Sinophone societies such as Hong Kong, Taiwan, and the Chinese community in Malaysia (the manifestations of *queer cultural mobilities*). I examine various forms of queer cultural flows to question and "queer" (i.e., destabilize) the concept of Sinophone and to reconsider mobilities through the concept of queer Sinophonicities. By developing and problematizing the idea of *Sinophone mobilities*, I look at the ways in which we can shift our focus from post-migration settlements to a broader range of mobilized migrating experiences beyond roots/routes and origin/destination. My analysis extends to the flows and counterflows of queer cultures and migrants between mainland China and the Sinophone sphere, in which China itself has become a site for Sinophone cultural productions. Through these discussions, I question the many problematic imperatives and assumptions in the conceptualization of the Sinophone cultural sphere to examine the intentions and enactments of migrations as well as their conditions and consequences in Sinophone theories and ontologies.

Chapter 4 and Chapter 5 deal with social inclusion and exclusion, cultural capital and social distinction, and social class migration in China's queer communities (the underlying driving and stratifying force of *queer social mobilities*). Drawing upon sociological analyses of various forms of human capital, as well as academic inquiries into the issue of *suzhi* ("quality") and into the rising and aspirational middle classes in today's China, these chapters analyze the ongoing social stratifications both inside China's queer communities and in the society at large. Through an investigation of China-based online queer communities, mobile social networking platforms, and urban queer film clubs, I argue in these chapters that the state-engineered discourse of *suzhi* has to some extent expired, but the lingering myth of *suzhi*/quality continues to underline queer social distinctions. The politics of proximity on locative mobile media also evoke the issue of social position and class affiliation, while online and urban queer communities are often segregated by class-related cultural tastes and capital as well as the affiliated social status and privilege as *gated communities*. The pursuit of upward social mobilization and class migration led by China's development and expansion has reproduced larger social stratifications and segregations in today's queer communities, when the rising and aspirational urban middle classes have assumed more social visibility and economic significance in today's China.

Synthesized under the theme of queer cultures and mobilities, these threads come together in the final chapter to highlight and further interrogate some of my key analyses and arguments through the lines of kinship, migration, and middle classes. With a focus on the dual pressure of compulsory familism and compulsory development facing queer people, this final chapter considers the values and pitfalls of the development-induced mobilities and post-development syndromes. The discussions extend to the claims of China's neoliberal cultures and desires, the conception of China's middle classes and intra-class stratification, the emergence of an economy of loneliness, as well as how stretched kinship functions as a resilient strategy amid the ongoing social changes that will continue to shape the understandings, expressions, and practices of nonconforming sexualities and transgressive desires. Through a critique of China's neoliberal capitalist process and its role in queer cultural productions and social practices, this chapter concludes with a consideration of the extent to which this book may have presented a queer Sinophone Marxist analysis and critique, and further envisages a possible future for queer people in twenty-first-century China and Sinophone Asia.

1
Stretched Kinship

Queer sexualities are often at odds with the family's expectation for the continuation of the family line through heterosexual reproduction. A widely scrutinized issue in queer Chinese studies, *kinship* is the cornerstone of Confucian culture and a predominant concern both in queer people's daily lives and in various queer social and cultural practices that have emerged at the turn of the twenty-first century. The ongoing social transformations in China have continued to shape and reshape the kinship structures between queer people and their families of origin, where "home" has become a problematic ontological and symbolic entity in its inevitable entanglements with sexualities. The issues of coming out, leaving home, building a family, and returning to the family of origin have constituted a complex nexus of kinship connections and negotiations between one's family and one's sexual self. Emerging from such negotiations is a changing kinship structure between queer people and their families across physical distance and psychological detachment, centered in which is essentially the locations and dislocations of home and family concerning gender and sexuality.

Impossible Home

Since the anthropological works of Claude Lévi-Strauss ([1949] 1969) and David Schneider ([1968] 1980, 1984), the view of kinship as a symbolic sociocultural system rather than purely biological blood ties has dominated kinship scholarship (Menget 2008). This turn from consanguinity to symbolic social connections has shifted the focus of research from procreative to non-procreative kinships (Shapiro 2010), through which studies on queer kinship have emerged in the West since the late twentieth century to make sense of what kinship means for queer people whose sexualities barely serve as reproductive vehicles. According to historian Heather Murray (2012), gay people in North America were able to live in discretion in the 1950s as a means to protect their sexual preference without offending their families. But, during the gay liberation in the 1960s and the 1970s, more queer people started to distance and detach themselves from their families of origin for increased individual sexual independence enabled by the continued development of a capitalist economy.

At that time, queer people were "decidedly excluded from the normative structures of family and kinship" (Eng 2010a, 3) to enjoy an emancipated urban gay life free from the constraint of the family, when the free-market capitalist economy successfully reproduced independent single breadwinners outside the traditional structure of kinship (D'Emilio 1983). "Moving out" from the family hence often becomes "coming out" to the larger world from the original kinship circle, while the childhood home has often been seen in today's queer mobility scholarship as an antithesis to queer desires that has to be abandoned and left behind (Fortier 2003, 115–16). In this moving-out/coming-out process, leaving home and building a new family have become equally important for queer people, where "home" is both the origin and the destination (116–17).[1] Home-leaving and homemaking thus become two focal points in queer kinship negotiation, centered in which is the all-important issue of motion (moving out) and emotion (detachment) vis-à-vis the family of origin.

In this sense, the negotiation of queer kinship first and foremost centers on a *queer mobility* that, often enabled by capitalist development, drives queer people to leave the family in search of sexual independence and build their own chosen families out of the original kinship structure. In her acclaimed *Families We Choose: Lesbians, Gays, Kinship* ([1991] 1997), Kath Weston observes that family-detached queer people often establish a strong rapport among themselves as their own "chosen family" out of the original kinship circuit. This kind of queer mobility functions as a process of "homing" or "homemaking" that creates family-like queer peer connections beyond blood relations as part of a spatial, temporal, and psychological journey of "uprooting and regrounding" (Ahmed et al. 2003; Brah 1996; Fortier 2000, 2001, 2003; Hannam, Sheller, and Urry 2006, 10; Mai and King 2009, 298). It is in this sense that queer kinship often becomes an issue of queer mobility that separates queer people from the original family and helps them build their own chosen home with their peers. In this case, any potential subsequent reconciliation with the family of origin is contingent on whether or not their family members accept their transgressive sexualities.

In the US, it was not until the AIDS epidemic in the 1980s that queer people once again became integrated to their families—HIV-infected gay men were allowed back into the sympathetic family to die at home (Murray 2012, 136–78). Formal national PFLAG (Parents, Families, and Friends of Lesbians and Gays) organizations and movements also took place in 1980s America (108–34), which marked a further reunion of transgressive queer desires and traditional families. Since then, non-normative sexualities have gradually re-entered the domain of family and kinship; towards the end of the twentieth century, coming out to the family became a ritual in the West for queer people to complete before moving out from the family (see Murray, 180). That is to say, the negotiation of queer kinship has often become a more complex attachment/detachment feedback loop in order for one's non-conforming sexuality to be reconciled within the traditional family structure. In addition, since the turn of the twenty-first century, same-sex marriage legislation in a growing number of Western countries further pinpoints queer relationships firmly in the domain of kinship that is largely based on a heterosexual model of family.

Paradoxically, coming *out* has therefore become an essential process for queer people to be accepted and integrated *in* their families. Queer kinship negotiation, in other words, increasingly entails an imbricated process of *home-leaving*, *homemaking*, and *homecoming* on the margins of traditional family and kinship production. This "coming-out/coming-in" dilemma is arguably more complicated in Chinese societies. Kinship often presents a troublesome issue for queer Chinese people facing the Confucianist obligation of filial piety. As the standard English translation of the Chinese term *xiao shun*, the notion of filial piety designates "a prominent Confucianist moral idiom generally associated with the obedience, respect and/or support [that] children *owe* to parents as a return for the 'gift of life,' so to speak" (dos Santos 2006, 288; my emphasis). Giving birth to and raising the children are traditionally understood in Chinese societies as a great bestowment of life and kindness, to which the children must *return* and *repay* through lifetime obedience and service to their parents, most notably by fulfilling their filial obligation through reproduction to extend the family line—and hence to continue the cycle of the bestowment of life to future generations.

This moral idiom of filial piety is the foundation of Chinese societies that underlines a strong and powerful familism and a cultural fascination with kinship (dos Santos, 277–81). In premodern China, same-sex relationships often coexisted with heterosexual and reproductive marriage, which did not endanger the continuity of the family line. Since the importation of the dichotomous Western sexologies at the turn of the twentieth century, homosexuality and heterosexuality have turned into mutually exclusive conceptual categories. While in practice people can still hide their preference for the same sex and choose a heterosexual and reproductive marriage, homosexuality has often been designated by an essentialist view of sexuality based on the obsolete Western sexologies/pathologies as a threat to the fundamental social order and the Confucianist cultural ideal. Consequently, queer people in today's Chinese and other Confucianist societies often face a strong dilemma between their filial piety for reproduction and their non-procreative queer sexualities.

As I have argued, this strong familism still rejects the folding of transgressive bodies and desires merely into the process of capitalist development and modernization. Rather, when China's older generation is still haunted by the country's deprived past and various social upheavals before the reform, the profound sense of economic and existential insecurities has continued to instill a pervasive preoccupation with material gain and financial security among Chinese people. Therefore, the family is not only an institution for the continuation of the patrilineal kinship and the cycle of the bestowment of life, but also an important socioeconomic unit to carry on family wealth and inheritance. Marriage is hence an economic transaction on top of love and affection to exchange wealth and establish material relationships between kin groups, through which the production of children further secures the transfer of inheritance within kin groups and ensures the survival and the longevity of the family.[2]

This is why procreative marriage is widely considered an indispensable social security mechanism in today's China, where compulsory heterosexuality prevails. Independent sexual identities and non-conforming queer relationships outside the register of kinship are precluded from the established, family-based networks of wealth exchange and inheritance in a country where people still lack equal access to social welfare. Private wealth thus functions as the building block of the material foundation of love and romance. Childless same-sex couples cannot be bestowed and entrusted with family heritage, if they have no one to pass on their inherited wealth to. In a broader context, the absence of offspring also means that same-sex couples will have no immediate family to look after them when they get old, which potentially drives them towards public elderly care and adds more pressure to the social welfare system that may already be drained by a large and upcoming aging population. While late capitalism in the West may no longer rely on the heteronormative family in its reconfiguration of gender and sexuality, today's China still relies upon the hetero-reproductive family (and, by extension, hetero-reproductive sexuality) as both a socioculturally steering institution and a socioeconomically stabilizing entity in its ongoing development and transformations.

The one-child policy enforced by the party-state in mainland China since 1979 has further complicated the situation by putting the filial obligation on the single child in the family to continue the family line and carry on the family inheritance to maintain and extend the family's stability and longevity. The child's singularity makes it especially difficult for same-sex attracted individuals to avoid compulsory heterosexual reproduction, as they often have no siblings to fulfill the filial responsibility if they keep a non-reproductive queer relationship. In 2016, the Chinese state loosened its control over reproduction, and more families were allowed to have two children as a means to deal with the downward pressure in population growth and cope with an aging society that started to loom closer. This change will have a profound impact over future queer kinship structures in China if more families are willing (and financially adept) to raise two children under the new policy, although such impact will not manifest at the societal level until the new generation born in the standard "two-child families" have come of age and come to terms with their sexualities.

The issue of queer kinship has also been further complicated by the confrontational and unapologetic coming-out strategy that has disseminated from the West to Chinese societies. In his widely influential *Tongzhi: Politics of Same-Sex Eroticism in Chinese Societies* (2000), Chou Wah-shan proposes the concept of "coming out as coming home" as a local, culturally sensitive, and non-confrontational strategy for queer people to mitigate the dilemma of coming out and coming into the family. The essence of this strategy is for a person to introduce a same-sex partner as a "good friend" to the family, and this "friend" will then frequently stop by and join in family activities from recreation to daily chores. Gradually, the family will accept this friend as a family member, whether or not the same-sex relationship is subsequently disclosed. This strategy precludes a confrontational declaration such as "Mom, Dad, I'm gay" and no longer entails the disclosure of one's attraction to the same sex. Rather, it aims to bring transgressive queer relationships back into the register of family and kinship. Although this strategy per se does not solve the problem of reproduction, it at least functions within the family structure and less deviates from the parental authority and familial hierarchy that are highly crucial in the Confucianist social order.

This strategy came from Chou's observation of and interviews with queer people in the 1980s and the 1990s, mainly in Hong Kong. According to Chou, this strategy often led to the family's *silent acceptance* of same-sex relationships when such relationships became obvious to the family. For Chou and many of his interviewees, this was an effective way to achieve familial harmony without scarifying one's sexual preference. The confrontational "coming out," on the other hand, was observed by Chou as often leading to direct conflicts within the family in Chinese societies. However, the ambiguity of one's sexuality centered in this "coming home" strategy may not always lead to positive outcomes. Liu and Ding's (2005) critique of Chou's theory, for instance, points out that "coming home" can be an endless journey that one may not be able to complete before family conflicts break out. Their discussion reveals that the "coming home" process lacks effectiveness and efficiency compared to the more straightforward "coming out" strategy and can be time-consuming and exhausting without any guaranteed outcomes.

This "coming home" approach presents further problems when the kinship structure in China is undergoing rapid and dramatic changes at the turn of the twenty-first century. Frequent redistributions of human resources, to begin with, have become de rigueur in today's neoliberal economic blueprint where the flows of the labor force play an important role. In the case of China, its rapid economic growth has resulted in significantly imbalanced regional developments across the large span of its territory. One of the most visible results has been a major increase in China's internal migrations from the agricultural countryside to the industrialized urban areas, from small towns to large cities and regional economic centers, and from the less-developed hinterland to the affluent coastal provinces. Since China's reform and opening up, hundreds of millions of internal migrants have constituted the largest migration in human history and an enormous and mobilized "floating population" in search of a better life.[3] The state-led higher education expansion (*kuozhao*) since 1998 has also contributed to a dramatic increase in education-oriented migration, while China's ongoing development continues to demand a large and well-educated labor force, and college degrees have become an entry ticket to urban middle-class employment (Goodman 2016, 7). More families that benefited from China's rapid economic growth during the recent decades can now afford to send their children to China's major cities or to foreign countries for education, further boosting China's internal and international migration in the early twenty-first century.

That is to say, it has become increasingly common for young people to embark on such development-induced migrations in search of better education and employment to build a better life. What has become the new norm in this process is a new kind of long-distance kinship: people who study and work in another city or another country often have very limited chances to go back home and visit their family. Public holidays are often the only option for family reunions, and many people can only go back to their families once a year, usually during the Chinese New Year. Long geographical distance combined with high living and traveling costs often makes today's young people reluctant to return home; the pressure they may experience from their parents (e.g., for heterosexual marriage) during family gatherings can also turn a family reunion into an ordeal (more on this below). In short, *homecoming* back to the family of origin has become increasingly difficult for today's Chinese people (especially young queer people) to fulfill.

Therefore, the close kinship tie with the original family has often been diluted and stretched to a long-distance connection that separates young people from their parents and only allows limited chances for reunion. This kind of distanced kinship is fundamentally different from the traditional Confucianist doctrine *"fumu zai, bu yuanyou"*—do not travel far if your parents are still around (and need your service). Today's parents in Chinese societies are more willing to spontaneously encourage their children to undertake educational and occupational migrations, be it internal or international, both to honor the family and to create a better life for themselves and for future generations. Underlined by China's rapid growth and expansion under global neoliberal capitalism, this new form of long-distance kinship often entails yearlong separations that cut people off from the Confucianist filial piety to accompany and look after their parents, and cut parents off from closely mentoring and monitoring their sons and daughters with their wisdom and parental authority.

In such long-distance separations, "home" often becomes an impossible location for queer people to complete the time-consuming "coming out as coming home" process. The partner-as-a-friend method reaches a dead end when the time required for the "friend" to become a family member no longer virtually exists. "Coming out as coming home" is largely contingent on the geo-proximity between queer people and their families; it works best only when a same-sex couple has the chance to frequently visit their families of origin to complete the "coming home" process. However, when people and their same-sex partners are half a country and half a world away from their original families, homecoming has become a mission hard to accomplish. For "coming out as coming home" to work in today's long-distance queer kinship structure, people have to complete this process before the home-leaving separation, or invite their parents to move to the area where they have built their own life, or return and settle down back in their hometown. Nevertheless, a positive outcome (i.e., the family's acceptance of the same-sex relationship) is still not guaranteed. This is why I argue for a new paradigm of *stretched kinship* to better scrutinize and understand today's changing queer kinship structure in Chinese societies and beyond.

Stretched Kinship

Stretched kinship emerges from various aspects and works on multiple imbricated levels of today's kinship structure. First, it relates to the physical separation and geographical distance that underline the struggles and negotiations between one's non-conforming sexuality and the family's hetero-reproductive expectation. In this sense, leaving home and staying away from the family becomes a practical way for queer people to better prepare themselves for potential disclosure of their sexualities or for other arrangements to fulfill their responsibilities under compulsory familism and heterosexual reproduction. Chinese or Western, confrontational or not, there does not exist a universal way to come to terms with one's sexuality in relation to the family; being physically detached from the family hence leaves a space for young people to explore their options. At the social level, those who have moved to populated metropolises also have better access to other queer people and peer support—from queer student groups at universities to LGBT NGOs and various support organizations. Thus, the flows towards the more developed and more diverse "queer cities" potentially offer young people a chance to acquire and secure a sense of belonging that they may not be able to enjoy at home.

That means queer migrants in larger cities also have better chances to learn from others' experiences for such issues as coming out, building a same-sex relationship, and kinship negotiation. Even for those who have little interest in queer social events or activism, populated urban centers are often a better place to stay invisible or to enjoy a generally more tolerant social environment. At the cultural level, migration enables people to observe and experience various queer lifestyles and vibrant urban queer cultures that are often more prominent and accessible in big cities compared to that in small towns and the countryside.[4] People who travel from one Chinese society to another, or from one country to a different culture, also have the opportunity to experience and learn local understandings of sexualities as well as local articulations and practices of queer cultures. Moreover, at the economic level, migration for education and employment will increase people's earning power, which offers them a better opportunity to become financially independent in case they are disowned by their parents and cut off from parental financial support if/when they come out. In this sense, migration is essentially a process to accumulate more social, cultural, and financial capital that potentially puts queer people in a better position in negotiating their sexualities with their families.

That is to say, in the first instance, stretched kinship refers to the separation and distance between queer people and their families that potentially allow them more time and space to acquire financial security and other resources to plan for subsequent strategies in kinship negotiations. The physical separation and geographical distance significantly reduce immediate family pressure for heteronormative behaviors, marriage, and reproduction, which gives queer people a chance to breathe and a space of their own to navigate their life at their own pace. For those who are uncertain about their sexualities, the more diverse metropolitan areas also provide better chances for them to further explore their sexual selves. In this scenario, however, the intimate kinship ties with the families of origin have been stretched thin, and the physical connections between family members have often been stretched to virtual connections through long-distance communications. The familial support and closeness are hence reachable only remotely. What has been stretched is not only the physical distance but also one's intimacy and openness with the family; a significant aspect of oneself, namely sexuality, has to be separated in another physical and mental space thousands of miles away from home. If concealing one's sexual preference from the family is already difficult, then the long-term physical separation only stretches the kinship ties and the affective connections even thinner.

This mental distance and emotional detachment constitute the second key factor in my theorization of stretched kinship, when the geographical separation stretches both people's physical connection and their emotional intimacy with their families. On the one hand, the stretched distance may intensify the underlying mutual longings between family members and potentially tightens their mental and emotional connections. On the other, this underlying emotional longing does not solve the conflict between one's sexuality and filial piety, nor does it compensate for the physical separation or make it easier for queer people to come out to their families. Moreover, when the kinship connections become increasingly stretched, it is not only the separation but also the reunion that can be a stretched experience, where physical closeness does not help with the mental and emotional distance between one's concealed sexuality and the family's heteronormative assumption. For some people, coming back to the family during the Chinese New Year can be a frustrating and exhausting experience when the physical reunion further intensifies the tensions derived from the mental and emotional rupture between them and their families of origin.

One may argue that Chinese parents relentlessly use their children as weapons for comparison, as a character remarks in *The Joy Luck Club*, a 1993 film by Wayne Wang adapted from Amy Tan's acclaimed novel. Chinese New Year often means an annual gathering of the extended family where the elder family members routinely compare young people's achievements, usually measured by career success, income level, and relationship or marital status. For young people, the major pressure and embarrassment during the family reunion are all the relatives actively probing into their relationships—known as the "annual interrogation" among the young generation in today's Chinese societies. The elder members in the family often enthusiastically match up young people with others in the larger collateral family and social circles for dating and relationship building. On such occasions, complete frankness about one's sexuality is often not possible, and queer people tend to make various excuses to explain their "singleness" and hide their sexual preference.

When such embarrassing interrogation and awkward explanations have become an essential part of people's reunion experiences, the physical closeness with the family does not solve the problem of the stretched emotional distance and the detached underlying queer mentality from the family's hetero-reproductive expectations. Before the Chinese New Year in 2014, gay social media company Feizan/ZANK released a video entitled "Nine Gay Men Teach You How to Go Home for the New Year" (*Jiuge Gay Jiaoni Guonian Huijia*). In this video "tutorial," the characters jocularly talk about strategies for gay people to more sophisticatedly deal with the family's annual interrogation about their relationship status. While the comedic *Nine Gay Men* video series is produced to market the mobile gay-dating app ZANK, this episode nonetheless demonstrates a deep sense of frustration among today's young queer people in China caused by the stretched distance—both physical and emotional—from their families of origin. Going home for family reunions becomes something that queer people in particular, and young people in general, have to carefully prepare for in order to cope with the stretched feelings from the family's expectations, even though the "annual interrogation" often comes with good intentions.

A video documentary depicting such stretched queer kinship negotiations and family reunions attracted over 100 million views online during the Chinese New Year in 2015 and caught international media attention to queer people's struggles over their sexualities and filial responsibilities in China.[5] Produced by China's national PFLAG organization, the documentary brings into question such "New

Year plight" facing queer people as well as young gay men's dilemma between fulfilling their filial piety and coming out to the family, when stretched kinship has become increasingly prevalent in this country since the turn of the twenty-first century. In the stretched queer kinship structure, that is to say, "home" often becomes a point of departure instead of a point of arrival, when the gap between the family's heteronormative assumptions and the undercurrent queer desires often appears hard to fill. In other words, the understandings and practices of "homecoming" in queer kinship negotiations have been fundamentally changed by the development-induced migrations and mobilities.

However, stretched kinship is not to be understood as a complete destruction of the traditional family and kinship structure; rather, it is a different form of family connection and kinship negotiation. Across the East and the West, people share the expression "blood is thicker than water" (*xue nong yu shui*) and stress one's responsibility for and connection to the parents and the family. The essence of stretched kinship is not to break up with the family but to keep the stretched connection *elastic* and *resilient*. That is to say, stretched kinship inherently entails and enables constant negotiations and renegotiations that connect queer people and their families across the physical and emotional distance. This is the third perspective from which I theorize stretched kinship: when neither "coming out" nor "coming home" can be achieved, stretched kinship always entails and implies a nuanced situation that is delicately balanced, constantly negotiated, and dynamically maintained between people and their families.

In other words, stretched kinship often takes the form of mutual dependence between people and their families across the physical distance to forge a stretched but nonetheless resilient and elastic connection. To maintain this connection, the families to some degree have to forgive their adult children for being "single," while queer people have to think about the next move when their families gradually lose patience and increasingly demand a hetero-reproductive marriage. From this point of view, the stretched kinship structure never remains in a stable state of being, nor is it merely confined in the fragmented and isolated moments of separation and reunion. Rather, it functions as *a dynamic process of becoming* that requires careful and constant negotiations between the two sides of the connection. Once the stretched balance is established, it will not remain static but constantly tighten or loosen its tension as people remotely or closely negotiate their non-conforming sexualities with their families in various ways. Previous understandings of queer kinship negotiations often appear somewhat static with expectable procedures and outcomes—from queer homemaking in Kath Weston's delineation of "chosen family" to Chou Wah-shan's argument for the "coming out as coming home" strategy. The notion of stretched kinship, by contrast, is more concerned with the complex and dynamic process of queer kinship negotiations as well as the resilience born within such tensions and contradictions—often with uncertain possibilities and outcomes considering the many imperatives and contingencies along the way.

However, when the family gradually loses patience, the situation may lead to an ultimatum: "bring back a boyfriend/girlfriend or do not come home for the New Year." This is when the kinship connection has been stretched for too long and too thin, so that people have to take action before it reaches the breaking point. When this happens, queer people will have a choice to make: faking it (bringing back a fake partner), breaking it (cutting themselves off from the family once and for all), or making their sexual preference known to the family. The first choice will continue and further stretch the already very intense balance, while faking it once may become faking it forever, which will add even more tension to the already tight kinship connection. At some point, such tension will become too heavy to bear and the stretched connection too tight to maintain; the fake relationship and the stretched kinship tie may eventually break and fall apart. The second option above is against the fundamental Confucianist dogmas and a choice that most people will not even consider. That means "breaking it" is not often a feasible solution to eliminate the tension by cutting off the kinship connection.

The third strategy seems wise but often involves many risks and uncertainties, which may end up in success, failure, and all kinds of possibilities in between. People who reveal their sexualities may be understood and accepted in the family with love and support, may be disowned and repelled, may be forced to seek medical or psycho-clinical treatment, and may evoke other reactions from the family that sometimes can be radical and violent—from passive-aggressive indifference to verbal and physical abuse and forced confinement at home. Here, on the one hand, revealing one's sexuality is already a challenge to the family's assumed heteronormativity and to the filial obligation for reproduction. On the other, if one's parents cannot accept non-conforming sexualities, then insisting on pursuing one's sexual preference will also challenge the parental authority and hence deviate from the fundamental filial obedience that underlines Chinese cultures and societies. Thus, the situation might be further stretched and become a prolonged battle between queer people and their families.

In stretched kinship, that is to say, what has been stretched is not only the kinship connection per se but also queer people themselves who are often frustrated and exhausted by the conflicts with their families and the rupture between their sexualities and filial responsibilities. Regardless of the outcome, the process of queer kinship negotiation itself can be a rather stretched and stressful experience with an enormous amount of pressure for those involved—a "stretched feeling," in short. This is a particular concern in mainland China, where three decades' enforcement of the one-child policy has put queer people in a tight spot to carry the very intense pressure alone as the only child in the family. This can be a double pressure, as I have discussed, in the sense that they have to deal with both heteronormativity and parental authority without any siblings to "cushion" the tensions with their parents.

This is the fourth aspect through which I develop the notion of stretched kinship, namely the prevalent "stretched" feelings and experiences that young people have to bear during both family reunions and distanced kinship negotiations when the tensions continue to increase and the kinship ties become further stretched. Stretched kinship, through this lens, is inherently *a kinship of unease* that causes both practical problems and significant mental and emotional stress in people's understandings and practices of family and sexuality. More important, the enactment of migration and the pursuit of social mobility through education and employment often increase the embedded tension in the stretched kinship structure, as this process is in itself highly time-consuming. When young people graduate from colleges and universities to start their career, they will soon reach the expected age of marriage and reproduction but still lack sufficient social, cultural, and economic capital to deal with the challenges and complexities in stretched kinship negotiations. They often find themselves running against time when their families start to keenly expect their marriage; the tension will continue to increase as the parents get old and become increasingly impatient for their adult children to get married. Time, in this case, is not queer people's friend.

That is to say, temporality is an indispensable and inexorable part of the stretched kinship structure, where *time* is the essence and *the lack of time* often contributes to the tension and the stretched feelings. Thus, in stretched kinship, how much time is allowed for further negotiations of one's sexuality is often a major pressure facing queer people. This dilemma often leads to a *filial panic* among young queer people under the increased time constraint and the growing tension in the stretched kinship negotiation. This filial panic parallels the aforementioned kinship of unease amid the conflicts and contradictions between the family's expectation and one's sexual orientation across time and space. In this sense, temporality is no less salient than is spatiality in the stretched long-distance kinship connection, thanks to the pervasive forces of the development-induced mobilities. The intermingled issue of time/space and temporality/spatiality thus marks the fifth constituent element of stretched kinship.

To push this *stretched* metaphor even further: just as different materials have different stretchiness and elasticity, queer kinship connections can also be stretched to different levels. Kinship negotiations often present a diverse and dispersed range of experiences depending on a wide array of social, familial, and individual factors. People's connections with the family can be stretched to various degrees, depending on the different levels of openness they have established with their parents, their current socioeconomic status, their knowledge of sex-related and family-related issues, and their own life stage and relationship status, to name but a few. When the kinship and family structure has become increasingly complicated in Chinese societies driven by various forms of mobilities, I highly doubt that there still exists a one-size-fits-all strategy such as "coming out as coming home" that works universally to resolve the issue of stretched kinship. Rather, in the present day, each negotiation strategy will entail and involve different risks and uncertainties that need to be carefully considered to ease the tension and keep the resilience of the stretched kinship connection.

For example, hitherto I have often cast the family as conservative, parochial, refusing, and repressing—i.e., an antithesis to the happiness of queer people. However, in some cases, the family can be tolerant, forgiving, understanding, and supportive even within the highly hierarchical Confucianist family order. In addition, the family is never a monolithic entity but a multiplicate formation of different values and beliefs from various members across the lineal and collateral family structure. One family member's attitude is not equal to the whole family's refusal or acceptance, although at some point the family (especially the parents) often has to reach an agreement regarding how they respond to non-conforming and often non-procreative sexualities. At any rate, queer kinship in today's China still functions within the larger Confucianist family system that prioritizes the virtue of family cohesion as the cornerstone of social stability, no matter how stretched such kinship connections appear to be.

However, even for an understanding and supportive family, stretched kinship also has its roles to play. Whether the tension in a stretched balance can be eased is still contingent on the degree to which the family has accepted the queer individual and whether the parents are willing to reveal their child's sexuality to the larger family. In the first instance, accepting a queer person in the family often takes time, while acceptance is not necessarily equal to pride and support. Moreover, for people who have come out to their parents, the situation facing them might become "*haizi chugui, fumu rugui*"—when the child comes out of the closet, the parents walk into the closet—which means Chinese parents are often reluctant to disclose that they have a queer child to their extended family and social circles. Thus, during family reunions, the "closeted parents" often have to make excuses for their children and to face interrogation from other and elder family members such as the grandparents.[6] The extended collateral kinship structure has therefore also been stretched, through which a new balance will be established with more tensions embedded. More important, while coming out may tighten or loosen the emotional tension between queer people and their families, the distanced and stretched physical separation across geographical areas remains the same as an ongoing result of migration. Such physical distance in stretched kinship will continue to deprive people of any immediate closeness to their families of origin, rendering any potential family support less accessible across the stretched time and space.

In addition to the process of homecoming, stretched kinship has another dimension in queer homemaking and family-building: *marriage*. For queer

Chinese people, marriage comes in many different forms, both fake and real. First, for people who choose to conceal their sexual preference for an incognito heterosexual marriage, the relationships between them and their heterosexual partners can be understood as a form of stretched kinship as well. This argument echoes a new Chinese term that has emerged in recent years, *tong qi*, which means "*tongzhi de qizi*" or "gay man's wife." It refers to a woman who finds out that her husband is attracted to the same sex only after their marriage. Such marriage involves little reciprocal sexual attraction, and the kinship connection established on this kind of "deception" is often stretched to a dangerous status that may break at any time. The most severe case occurred in China in 2012, when a woman committed suicide after she found out that her husband was attracted to men.[7] The issue of *tong qi* has since then attracted much public attention, and several *tong qi* peer support groups have emerged in China both online and on the ground (see Zhu 2018 for a detailed discussion from *tong qi*'s perspectives).

While concealing one's sexual preference for an incognito heterosexual marriage is not an entirely new phenomenon, the situation facing queer people has gradually changed in the recent decade. In a global context, growing numbers of countries have legalized same-sex marriage, which appears tremendously encouraging for queer people and activists in Chinese societies. Thanks to the development of local queer activism and to the increased self-consciousness and public awareness of gender and sexual diversity and mobility, queer people are making an increasingly visible social presence in Chinese societies. Under the circumstances, paradoxically, it is becoming increasingly difficult to hide one's sexual preference, especially when a person has married the opposite sex and established a stretched kinship tie with the partner and the entire family-in-law. People today are generally more sensitive to discovering such deceptive marriage; some gay men who have married the opposite sex and lived a double life for many years start to become worried about the recent development of global and local queer activism that has exposed and endangered their previous survival method, making it harder for them to continue hiding under the cover of heterosexual relationships.[8]

Another controversial practice of queer family formation in China that can be understood through the lens of stretched kinship is lesbian and gay contract marriage, also known as quasi-marriage, cooperative marriage, or pro forma marriage (*xingshi hunyin* or *mingyi hunyin* in Mandarin). This designates a set of fake marriages between a gay couple and a lesbian couple who pretend and get married as two straight couples (see Engebretsen 2014, 104–23; Ho 2010, 39; Kam 2012, 84–86). This appears to be a more "ethical" option, to the extent that the chain of fake marriages is arranged with the consent of all the parties involved. But it may also be a very risky choice in the sense that as many as four families will become involved in one single set of quasi-marriage. A chain of fake marriages like this stretches the kinship connection to an even more intense level;

if one part of the chain breaks down, then four interrelated families will suffer the consequences. In addition, issues such as reproduction still present major problems for people in these arranged contract marriages, and they still face the possibility that one day they may get tired of their fake heterosexual partners and/or lose interest in their real same-sex partners, at which point the kinship connections built on the fake marriages will be stretched too thin to maintain.

The most recent emergent form of stretched queer homemaking in Chinese societies is overseas same-sex marriage, often arranged through commercial agencies in the West. Although these marriages will not be legally recognized in their home states, for many people it is still an invaluable opportunity to get their same-sex relationship legally certified and have a wedding in a place where it is accepted. This emerging form of family formation entails a new kind of global queer mobility that mainly aims for marriage registration and wedding, often without fully immigrating to a different country. It also demonstrates a new type of queer homemaking and family-building that needs to be stretched to foreign soil for legal recognition. Gay adoption and surrogacy agencies have also come to people's attention in Chinese societies during recent years, but the actual process often occurs overseas, given that same-sex adoption and surrogacy are not legally recognized in any Chinese societies (although Taiwan's legislative progression offers some hope on this). Furthermore, all of these established and emerging forms of queer homemaking and family-building will inevitably raise the question of whether a same-sex marriage can be accepted by the family, or to what extent and for how long an incognito or arranged fake marriage can deceive other family members when these practices add more tensions to the already stretched kinship tie.

Overall, underlined by the general increase in Chinese people's mobilities, the kinship connections between people and their families of origin have often been stretched by (1) their prolonged physical separation; (2) the underlying mental and emotional detachment; (3) the elastic, resilient, and dynamic process of kinship negotiation; (4) the stressed feelings in the experiences and practices of the kinship of unease; and (5) the filial panic facing the time constraint on top of the spatial/physical separation. This stretched kinship structure and the stretched feelings of kinship may further extend from the parental family to the larger collateral family, as well as from the process of home-leaving and homecoming to people's homemaking efforts in building their own (real and fake) families. Today's young people often have to reconsider their practices of family and kinship facing the ongoing familism and the ongoing development amid China's changing social conditions, where the kinship structure has been fundamentally reshaped by the increasingly ubiquitous and imperative mobilities. The notion of stretched kinship, in this case, offers a promising lens and a new framework for our consideration and interrogation of queer cultures and mobilities in the twenty-first century.

Alternative Families

When queer kinship connections have often been stretched on many imbricated levels, and when homecoming and homemaking have become problematic and often impossible, various forms of alternative families have emerged in urban centers where young migrants abound and floating populations intersect. One such example is shared urban queer tenancies. The influx and conglomeration of internal and international migrants in China's major metropolises often boost local real-estate markets where housing prices escalate and living costs skyrocket. It has become increasingly unaffordable for young people to buy or to rent a property alone without parental financial aid. Co-tenancy hence becomes a popular solution for the young generation where shared households effectively turn into *alternative families*—which might be a better term than "chosen families" as many young people are driven into these shared living arrangements by circumstances, not by choice. An early form of gay co-tenancy in China was sharing housing information via online forums and looking for gay roommates, which to some extent remains popular today. However, in the context of increased queer social visibility and geographical mobilities, shared tenancies and alternative families have become increasingly diverse (and queer), which not only include co-habited gay tenants but sometimes take the form of gay-straight co-tenancy with mutual awareness and acceptance of each other's sexual preference.

Beijing-based queer social media company Feizan/ZANK picked up this theme of queer co-tenancy and alternative family in their digital video promotions. In addition to the aforementioned *Nine Gay Men* video series, Feizan/ZANK has sponsored and co-produced *Rainbow Family* (*Yi Wu Zan Ke*, 2014–2017), the first queer Chinese sitcom set in a shared urban household in central Beijing. After the release of the first episode online on 29 October 2014, *Rainbow Family* has become a multi-season video series subtitled in different languages and distributed through both YouTube and local Chinese video-sharing websites.[9] While this digital video series functions as a marketing and publicity tool for the mobile gay dating application ZANK, it also offers a timely foray into the experiences of queer migrations and co-tenanted alternative families. On many levels, this video series resonates with young people's lived experiences when development-induced mobilities have become increasingly pervasive and compulsory in today's China.

This sitcom is set in an apartment in a residential compound where the co-tenanted "rainbow family" consists of a young gay man, a straight woman who agrees to be his quasi-girlfriend, a gay tenant and his ex-boyfriend, and one temporary houseguest different in each season (Figure 1.1). The temporary houseguests include an athletic young model/actor who comes to Beijing for job search (season one) and a young man who returns from postgraduate education in the West (season two). In each season, both the gay protagonist and

Figure 1.1 *Rainbow Family* (season one promotional poster)

his quasi-girlfriend will have a crush on the houseguest, from where the drama of a triangular relationship unfolds that carries the main narrative weight. A "rainbow family" like this is inherently a queer family formed through domestic and transnational mobilities. Exilic young migrants, both gay and straight, reside in this shared, alternative place of abode outside their families of origin. They have formed an intimate bonding between each other and built a family of their own—an alternative form of kinship not connected by blood ties but by mutual understandings of each other's sexuality and the shared experience of migration. This kind of queer homemaking is above and beyond peer support groups that further connects gay and straight, local and non-local, and temporary and long-term tenants under the same roof in the nexus of mobilities.

This alternative queer family brings us back to one of the central questions in queer kinship negotiation: what is home and where is home for queer people? In my theorization of stretched kinship, homecoming often appears stressful and unsuccessful, while homemaking in the host cities, albeit often trouble-some, may afford young migrants a chance to build an ontological and symbolic alternative family, however precarious and transient. This sitcom arguably offers us a possible way to look further into alternative queer kinships as such. First, urban co-tenancy enables queer people to once again acquire and secure a sense of "kinship" to experience family-like intimacy and openness within a shared household. They are able to maintain an intimate connection with each other by sharing a living space and the living cost to build a life together in a host city.

Second, this alternative kinship system also potentially establishes camaraderie among its members who often face the same issues in their daily lives—the refusal and indifference of the host city and the increased hetero-reproductive expectations from their aging parents in the original families. Third, alternative queer families afford young queer migrants a safe enclave and provide a point of arrival on the margin of the localist/heteronormative productions of identity and sexuality. These alternative queer families are essentially heterotopic "third-places" or "non-places" in between the home of origin and the home of destination—a point to which I will return in the next chapter.

Here, to put it another way, an alternative family functions as a temporary sanctuary that provides a buffer between young queer migrants and the heteronormative family and society. Also, a quasi-heterosexual partner living under the same roof may offer a temporary solution for such situations as family reunions and annual interrogations, as we have seen in *Rainbow Family*. That is to say, this co-habited household offers its members protection and flexibility to cope with different situations and provides family-like support and mutual understanding—seemingly "a kinship at ease," so to speak. However, an alternative kinship like this does not solve the problem of queer people's stretched connections with their families of origin; rather, it may further stretch the original kinship ties, insomuch as it mentally and physically isolates young people from their families into a small queer heterotopia where sexual diversity is not only tolerated but celebrated. This heterotopic safe heaven still has to conceal its queerness from parental and public scrutiny as well as from the houseguests. An alternative family like this is inherently a stretched and fragile structure that shows a certain resilience but may eventually fall apart. At some point, its members have to come out of this alternative kinship circle and return to their original families in order to fulfill their filial responsibilities, as shown in the second season of this video series.

In addition, alternative kinship is not necessarily an antithesis to the original kinship connection but rather a different variation of the stretched kinship tie that both extends and deviates from the traditional family and kinship structure. The alternative queer family established through such co-tenancy is not only a means to share a living space and a temporary escape from the social and familial pressure for hetero-reproductive marriage. Rather, it potentially bridges the families of the tenants in a loosely connected network—if one tenant has an understanding and supportive parent, for example, then this experience can be shared with and extended to other tenants and potentially their parents. At a greater societal level, various PFLAG organizations in the West and in Chinese societies also play a similar role in connecting the families of queer people in a social network, which essentially functions as an extended family-like institution where the connections are established among the parents and friends of queer people.

In this sense, PFLAG organizations and other LGBT NGOs may also function as alternative families that offer queer people, especially young migrants, a family-like social support network where they can safely come out and come into. Along this line, urban queer film clubs operated by various LGBT organizations and social groups have also shown great potential to become alternative families and alternative kinship circles. As Seio Nakajima (2014) observes, a large number of film clubs have been operating in urban China in various styles: attached to cafés and bars, associated with university student groups, based on the internet, or supported by NGOs (55–56). Queer film clubs, which I define as regular gatherings of queer people for film screenings and discussions of relevant social and cultural issues, have recently emerged in China's major metropolises and regional economic centers with large numbers of young migrants from other parts of the country.

These film clubs often screen a wide range of queer and non-queer audiovisual materials of different country origins—from art-house and independent cinemas to mainstream commercial movies, digital videos, TV shows, and documentaries. They are often operated by or in association with local LGBT NGOs and university student societies, most of which are registered with local authorities under such categories as public health and HIV/AIDS intervention. In addition, each screening session will be publicly announced in advance on queer and mainstream social media, instead of being kept in secrecy as often seen in the underground operation of queer film festivals facing authorities' crackdown. In fact, these film clubs seldom entail a strict membership. Many participants are casual visitors who otherwise have little personal ties with the clubs or the LGBT organizations behind them. Only when a club continues for an extended period do some participants become regular members, from where a sense of community and a feeling of kinship emerge.

Here, the Concentric Circle film club presents a compelling case that demonstrates how an alternative family comes into being through a queer cultural space in a migrant city like Beijing. Concentric Circle organizes and hosts regular film screenings and discussions in Beijing LGBT Center (*Beijing Tongzhi Zhongxin*). As part of the larger Concentric Circle brand, a series of communal events initiated by a mental health counselor for queer people, this film club puts a great emphasis on encouraging the participants to open their heart and speak their mind about such issues as queer sexualities and kinships. They offer a space for queer people, mostly young migrants studying or working in Beijing, to talk about their genders and sexualities as well as other pertinent issues in everyday life that are not usually discussable in other social occasions and in their own families of origin. This club mostly screens short films and video clips in order to leave more time for post-screening discussions, and potentially all the participants will have the chance to share their stories and experiences that are related to the films and videos screened in the club.

Each session of the film club starts with the participants sitting in a circle and briefly introducing themselves, often in pseudonyms, which somewhat resembles a psychotherapy group or a mutual aid meeting. The organizers will then introduce the theme of the session, which is often based on the visual materials they are able to collect and group together between screenings. Then, two or three short films or video clips will be shown to the participants, followed by a brief freestyle discussion about the audiovisual content. The most special part of this film club is that, after the discussion, each participant will be handed a piece of paper to draw out his or her stories, memories, or fantasies that are most relevant to the theme of the films. Led by the organizers or a regular participant familiar with the procedure, the attendees will then take turns to tell their stories with the sketchings in their hands. The organizers will also ask the participants to sign their paintings in pseudonyms afterward and upload them to the public photo album of the Concentric Circle film club on the queer social media platform Feizan.

The three-step procedure of screening, sketching, and storytelling was carefully designed and developed by the organizers, with assistance from the founding mental health counselor who would like the club to focus less on film per se than on the participants' underlying emotional and psychological needs.[10] This three-step arrangement has become a signature of the club, each time offering the participants multiple opportunities to express themselves and share their stories and fantasies as a verbal narrative therapy through the visual mediation of film and sketching. This process is deemed crucial by the organizers and the founding counselor as an invaluable opportunity for the participants to share their thoughts and feelings in a safe and non-judgmental environment that otherwise may not be available to them in other places. They consider this safe environment a much-needed and much-valued space for queer people, upon which the club is able to maintain its popularity in the local queer community.

The organizers also believe that it is their responsibility to help people overcome their anxiety and the habit of concealing their personal feelings. They understand that people need time to get used to talking about their sexualities and relevant issues publicly, given that many of them grew up under the Confucianist parental authority and came of age in a society that strongly emphasizes social uniformity rather than diversity and individuality. Many people still need encouragement to participate in these communal events and open their heart to a group of strangers. In my interview with the founding mental health counselor of Concentric Circle, he attributed people's reluctance in opening up themselves to the strict Confucianist hierarchy and the traditional parenting style in Chinese societies, where the "great bestowment of life" puts people in a lifetime debt and unconditional obedience to their parents. As I have discussed earlier after Chia (2003) and Gao and Ting-Toomey (1998), Chinese culture is heavily centered on "listening/*tinghua*," as the entitlement to speak is a hierarchical privilege of the senior. Although the *fin-de-millénaire* has seen many developments in parenting styles in Chinese societies, such Confucianist doctrines and traditions of passive filial obligations have to a large extent survived, and many Chinese people grow up accustomed to listening to the parents and obeying their orders while keeping their own feelings to themselves.

The situation is worse in mainland China, where most people grew up without siblings due to the one-child policy enforced by the party-state—other than the parents whom they must obey and listen to, people hardly have anyone else in the immediate family to share their feelings and emotions with. In the PRC, people were also educated in the state-controlled educational system from a very young age under a socialist collectivism that every individual is a tiny small "cog" or "bolt and screw" (*luo si ding*), whose sole function is to ensure the operation of the overall society and the giant machine of socialism. Cogs and screws do not need feelings and individualities, and people only need to fit into the large social machine and serve for the society's functionality. In this context, it is even more difficult for queer people to talk about their transgressive sexualities that neither correspond with the hetero-reproductive Confucianist expectations nor fit in the standard socialist blueprint engineered by the state with little tolerance for "out-of-order" components.

This film club thus becomes an invaluable alternative family to accommodate the queer feelings, expressive or not, that often fall off the register of the traditional Confucianist family and the standardized production of good socialist citizens. People who do not feel at ease about their sexualities in the family and the larger society finally find an alternative home that offers an important outlet for the queer undercurrents on the margin of the social and familial hierarchy and heteronormativity. According to the organizers who had operated this film club for two and a half years when I interviewed them in late 2014, many participants were reluctant to participate in the discussions spontaneously; however, once encouraged and offered a chance to talk (e.g., through sketching), they often had a lot to share with others:

> F (one organizer): *If you just ask them [about their story], they may briefly say a thing or two . . . If you ask them about the sketching they did, they would share a lot. This is relevant to the theme of our club: self-expression. It is their own story, not the documentary films and videos that we have shown. Each time after the screening, we won't ask people to comment on the characters in the film, but instead ask them if they may have any relevant experiences, focusing on themselves.*
>
> D (another organizer): *We use film screening and sketching to induce personal thoughts and expressions. We are not commenting on films, as we are not a film review club for professional film studies and appreciation. Film and sketching are inducers—later we realized that it doesn't matter whether the participants are good painters or not, as long as the sketching can help them express themselves.*

It is also in this sense that a queer film club becomes a form of alternative kinship that enables and accommodates such queer articulations muted and silenced in people's original families as well as in the wider society. Film clubs like Concentric Circle both extend and differ from other queer social groups and "chosen families." In the first incidence, a film club organized as a counseling group offers an opportunity for mediated and intimate queer narratives and storytelling. As Ken Plummer reminds us in *Telling Sexual Stories*, the very act of storytelling replaces the voices of authorities with personal histories that create a sense of intimacy (1995, 151–60). The carefully induced process of storytelling through film screening and sketching enables a confession, or a condensed psycho-autobiography, that is irreplaceable in helping the queer storytellers define their individuality and sustain their subjectivity as gendered and sexual beings, to further borrow Jeremy Tambling's idea in *Confession: Sexuality, Sin, the Subject* (1990). The realized needs and impulses to narrate individual stories and confess personal histories have contributed to relieving queer people from the reproductions of the unconditionally obedient children in the Confucianist family and the uniformly standardized "cogs" in the socialist machine. In other words, the unsettled queer desires detached and stretched from the heteronormative family and society have found a home in the intimate queer storytelling via the visual and oral narrative therapy.

In addition to self-discovery through recounting personal histories and memories in a nostalgic past, queer storytelling in Concentric Circle has a parallel focus on an actively imagined queer future. The fantasy of a better queer life, often characterized by a long-term relationship with a committed partner and the family's blessing, has permeated the intimate storytelling and the participants' sketching in this film club. Writing on lala/lesbian activism in mainland China, cultural anthropologist Ana Huang (2017) notes that the commonplace nostalgia alone is not able to structure a sustained lesbian lifestyle and a long-term commitment in a same-sex relationship. As the founding leader of the China Queer Digital Storytelling Workshops in Beijing since 2010, Huang identifies a prevalent sense of precariousness among lesbians and gays whose romantic love lacks social recognition and the structural support of kinship, "resulting in a state of futurelessness" (233). Haunted by the painful experiences of breaking up with their partners who have to marry the opposite sex to fulfill their socio-familial responsibilities, lalas and gays often "float in a temporal limbo, longing for anchorage" (227). The prevalent lack of faith for a possible, proper queer future inevitably links the confession of the past (however painful to look back) with the fantasy of the future (however utopic and volatile to look forward) in the negotiation of kinship and sexuality in an alternative family like Concentric Circle.

Imagining a promising queer life, or what Ana Huang calls "daydreaming" after José Esteban Muñoz (2009, 144), frees the participants from the triad of the painful past, the insecure present, and the uncertain future, while still engaging "real longings" for same-sex love, family blessing, and social acceptance

(Huang 2017, 241). In one screening and sketching session in Concentric Circle, for example, the participants were asked to share an imagined life out of the closet and compare it to their experiences in the closet; in another session that I attended, we fantasized the moment when we propose to our same-sex partners even though same-sex marriage is unlikely to be legalized in China in the near future. At any rate, the value of fantasy for a queer utopia does not reside in "now and here" or "soon-to-be" when the social ethos and state regulation of sexualities have only shown slow progression (Huang, 234, 239). Rather, it is about the "then and there" of a queer futurity that breaks out of the liminal present and insists upon "a potentiality or concrete possibility for another world" (Muñoz 2009, 1) to engage and unleash a forward-dawning, anticipatory illumination of the future (28). If the videos and film clips shown in Concentric Circle help induce confessions of the past and reflections of the present, then the fantasized queer life in the sketching further mobilizes a conscious imagination of a queer future that has been brought forward, but in no way dictated, by past sufferings and present longings. The processes of confessing and daydreaming thus constitute the two pillars of intimate storytelling in an alternative family like this, allowing the participants to speak the otherwise unspoken and unspeakable.

More important, the sense of family-like intimacy generated through confessions and fantasies is particularly strong when the connections have been established at a deeper mental and emotional level among the film club members. These connections based on mutual support and understandings are "as strong as any family, maybe stronger because they are chosen rather than simply given" (Plummer 1995, 154). Alternative queer kinship connections like this are therefore even more resilient than are everyday social and familial relationships in which queer people often have to hide their feelings and desires. A film club like Concentric Circle goes above and beyond other queer cultural activities and social groups by providing the all-important mental and psychological support to forge deep connections among its members through therapeutic confessing and daydreaming. But it also differs from professional counseling services in offering a less serious and more relaxed environment through film screening, sketching, and collective storytelling. For queer people who feel uncomfortable seeking counseling services, often due to the social stigmas of mental health issues and of non-conforming sexualities, the club presents a less intimidating alternative for them to acquire better peer support in a comfortable and supportive environment. In this sense, queer film clubs like Concentric Circle have even greater potential in reaching and benefiting more queer people than do any LGBT organizations or counseling services alone.

The Concentric Circle film club also puts a strong emphasis on coming to terms with one's sexuality and coming out to the family. Although each session has a different topic, family and kinship has been a major thread running through this film club. A few months after its establishment in 2012, for example, the film club organized a session titled "Home without Closet" (*Wu Gui Zhi Jia*) to screen short coming-out stories and let the participants sketch real and imagined queer life inside and outside the closet. This session turned out to be quite popular, and since then the club has frequently chosen similar topics on family and kinship, including Father's Day, parental love, family reunion during the Chinese New Year, and *Modern Family* (American TV series), to name a few. In late 2014, one club session also screened the aforementioned queer sitcom video series *Rainbow Family*. During my field research in Concentric Circle in 2013 and 2014, kinship issues frequently emerged and surfaced in post-screening discussions. At any rate, intimate queer storytelling in an alternative family like this is every bit akin to the stories of the biological family for the participants to generate and share a feeling of kinship.

More important, the film club's focus on queer family and kinship temporarily relocates kinship negotiations from the register of the family per se to an alternative and family-like intimate social circle. Writing about printed queer publications, Ken Plummer contends that mediated queer storytelling creates a "sensed community" that is not based on any direct face-to-face contact but rather shared by the readers and the consumers of the story (1995, 44–45). In contrast, a queer family that comes together through a film club entails and enables ontological direct human interactions in the physical queer space and in the visual and verbal exchanges of stories and intimacies through confessions and daydreams. In this scenario, the narrator and the listener often alternate their roles in telling and receiving their respective stories and fantasies. This shared home can never replace the blood-tied family but nonetheless offers an all-important alternative—which is in itself a form of stretched kinship beyond consanguinity—that accommodates the homeless queer desires and expressions out of the original families in a migrant city like Beijing.

Furthermore, this psychotherapeutic film club is a highly mediated queer space that often connects passive film viewing with active sketching, through which people can both experience queer cultures on the projection screen and tell their own stories on the small "screen" (i.e., the blank paper) in their hands. The virtual album of Concentric Circle on Feizan also becomes a digital home that archives hundreds of sketches drawn by the participants in a few consecutive years. The combination of film viewing, sketching, and online picture sharing further strengthens the mutual connections in this alternative queer family through different forms of communication channels across the physical queer space and the virtual cyberspace. More important, for regular participants, coming to the film club resembles a very special *homecoming* experience, the destination of which is a family that they have built together and can regularly visit. It is also in this sense that queer space-making essentially becomes *homemaking* through which "home," albeit alternative and transient, once again becomes a possible ontological and symbolic place for the exilic queer migrants.

An alternative family, paradoxically, has become a place where real longings for acceptance and anchorage can be actively imagined and affirmatively enacted to engender a real sense of belonging.

In addition, the two organizers of the club believe that the mission of Concentric Circle is to encourage a life that people should live—be honest to oneself and to the family about one's sexuality:

> F: *The value [of the film club] lies in helping* tongzhi *with self-recognition . . . Only when people accept and correctly understand themselves can they develop a correct ethical value and avoid wandering into the wrong path. If they chose a wrong path [e.g., a deceptive heterosexual marriage or a contract marriage], then it means that they have seen themselves and the world through a wrong lens. Here [in Concentric Circle] a person can see that it is not only him who is like this [facing the pressure for heterosexual reproduction] and can understand that we are all the same. Then they can drop their concerns [and make the right choice].*
>
> . . .
>
> D: *We also want to influence people through our club. We communicate a healthy ethical value and encourage a life that* tongzhi *should live . . . this is a very good start for people's self-recognition and much more beneficial for them than going to a gay bathhouse or that kind of [cruising] spaces.*
>
> F: *This process is especially necessary for young people, such as college students.*

Therefore, coming out to the family is often discussed favorably in the club, while other strategies such as complete concealment and cooperative marriage are often questioned as deceptive and dishonest—and hence should be avoided at all costs. Through the years, the members of Concentric Circle have shared many coming-out stories that were successful, disastrous, or unsettled, as well as many troublesome situations of concealing one's sexuality for deceptive heterosexual marriages. The organizers believe that the participants are able to accumulate more "samples" when they hear more about other people's stories, based on which they can make an informed decision regarding their own strategies in stretched kinship negotiations and marriage arrangements.

This seemingly gentle nudge for queer people to "make the right choice" by watching and listening to other people's stories is rather underpinned by a "zealous pursuit for honesty" prevalent in today's LGBT organizations in China (Zhu 2018, 1085). Their agenda often includes promoting gays and lesbians as good (sexual) citizens who are honest about their sexuality and responsible for their choice of sexual and romantic partners. In this kind of one-size-fits-all agenda that treats coming out as a social responsibility, disclosure becomes increasingly compulsory when other choices have often been questioned as dishonest and unethical. This attempt to raise queer people's social visibility through disclosure coincides with the growing public awareness of and eagerness to know more "truth" about sexual minorities; such intermingled enforcement for truth and requirement for honesty are as oppressive as, if not more than, the soft violence of social and familial stigmas that keep queer people in the closet in the first place (Zhu, 1086). If "honesty" is the single right option, then other queer family formations such as heterosexual marriage and cooperative gay and lesbian marriage should all be condemned—gay should marry gay, and straight people should marry straight. Therefore, "homosexuality is tolerable only when it is unambiguously identified, wholeheartedly confessed, and most importantly, voluntarily quarantined from straight people's kinship systems" (1087). Behind such compulsory honesty, there still lies an essentialist view of innate gender and sexuality that, once identified and self-recognized, must be upheld and quarantined in their own right and for their own good.

This essentialization of homosexuality celebrates "coming out" as the ultimate strategy in proclaiming identitarian sexual emancipation and declaring a self-conscious minoritarian social visibility. During my field research in Concentric Circle and other NGOs in urban China, I noticed that these organizations often adopted media materials directly from the West as models and templates for local queer people to copy and follow in both coming-out and kinship negotiation. In an LGBT student group in Guangzhou, for example, we were instructed to "come out unapologetically" based on a slideshow made by a US gay activist group, even though anecdotal evidence and empirical research both indicate that this strategy does not conform with Chinese culture and may not lead to a positive outcome in Chinese societies. After all, "coming out" has long been a dominant (if not compulsory) narrative in the West across both theories and practices. When many LGBT organizations in China have strong ties with and receive funding from their Western counterparts, and when numerous Western countries are pioneering LGBT rights and same-sex marriage legislation, it is understandable that queer activists in China have turned their eyes to the West. However, intensively and blindly mimicking the West may obscure and marginalize other possibilities in queer activism and social strategies that are more sensitive to local cultures and traditions and to people's lived experiences of stretched kinship.

Echoing my argument, Huang observes that the common pragmatist and reformist politics in Chinese LGBT organizations based on a Western paradigm often misalign with local queer people's longing for anchorage and for the structural support of kinship (2017). In contrast, a "utopian queer politics of imagination" (e.g., through storytelling) offers a much more expansive method that addresses and responds to the lived experiences of precariousness and the affective needs of gays and lesbians. The conscious embrace of an imaginative future through collective storytelling instills a sense of hope and home-like grounding and belonging among queer people, which transcends the problematic pragmatist present and the unmaterialized reformist future. In this sense, the limited selection of mainly Western queer cultural materials in film clubs and other family-like social groups has often constrained people's active imagination and construction of queer futures, insomuch as the imagined queer fantasies often derive directly and sometimes exclusively from Western models of gay emancipation and reformist activism in a liberal-progressive paradigm. This has channeled people's visions of queer futurities and potentialities in a rather narrow and liminal scope.

This problem is further underlined by the fact that audiovisual materials such as short films and digital videos are often hard to find and collect between each film club session. When local queer visual contents are still relatively scarce, film clubs like Concentric Circle have been largely relying on foreign materials available online with Chinese subtitles. Their choices are hence limited. This is conjoined by other difficulties facing them. For instance, the two organizers of the Concentric Circle film club have full-time jobs and can only work for the club in their spare time. The film club does not generate any personal income, and they have not been able to find any other people for long-term commitment to organizing the screenings. The venue in Beijing LGBT Center may also become unavailable when the city is hosting major political conferences or other national or international events, during which authorities often temporarily shut down all the non-official organizations. Due to these issues, queer film clubs like Concentric Circle have often experienced interruptions from time to time.

The participants present another problem in these urban queer spaces and alternative kinship circles. During my field research, I noticed that frequent participants were often much more active and more at ease in the film club, whereas other people were prone to be nervous and cautious when they first joined in. This is a common problem facing social and communal events: frequent participants often unconsciously form a stronger bonding among them (a smaller circle within the circle) that is hard for outsiders (newcomers and occasional visitors) to penetrate. Once established, such a small circle of acquaintances and friends potentially excludes new attendees to join in the "family" and acquire a sense of belonging. Those who are new to the club, already nervous, are often left with insufficient time to share their stories and make themselves known to others, as the frequent participants become very active during the discussions. New members may soon drop out from participation when they are unable to acquire and secure the sense of family-like belonging that they are potentially searching for. In addition, as many participants utilize the film club as a dating space to meet other gay men, they may withdraw from participation once they have found a date and the film club no longer offers any value as a dating place. This has further highlighted the difficulties facing queer cultural spaces like Concentric Circle in maintaining an alternative family for queer migrants, when some members are themselves highly mobile and may not be consistent in their participation and devotion.

Overall, despite the many pitfalls of alternative queer families from shared urban tenancies to queer film clubs, today's young queer migrants are actively exploring and experimenting with new formulations and interventions of kinship connections outside the original, biological family. From "impossible home" to "stretched kinship" and "alternative families," this chapter has shown how the increasingly ubiquitous and imperative mobilities have reshaped people's understandings and practices of kinship. Since Chou Wah-shan's "coming out as coming home" thesis based on research data from the 1980s and the 1990s, our conceptual framework of queer kinship in Chinese and Confucianist societies has not been thoroughly reexamined and renewed for over two decades, despite the dramatic and ongoing social transformations in twenty-first-century China and capitalist Asia. These changes have to a large degree reshaped the ways in which kinship is structured and negotiated amid the increasingly diverse queer social and cultural practices in the age of mobilities. The issue of stretched kinship will be further interrogated in the context of queer homecoming and homemaking in border-crossing and transnational migrations, followed by considerations and examinations of queer cultural and social mobilities, in the rest of the book.

2
Home and Migration

Kinship and migration have long been the two focal points in queer cultural productions in various Chinese societies and communities. The early queer Chinese-language cinemas in the 1990s, for example, often portray the issue of love/affection and home/family through the imagination and enactment of mobilities. These include the Taiwanese queer immigrant's homemaking and family reconciliation in America in *The Wedding Banquet* (*Xi Yan*, Ang Lee, 1993); the gay couple's turbulent relationship and exilic love from pre-handover Hong Kong to Argentina in *Happy Together* (*Chun Guang Zha Xie*, Wong Kar-wai, 1997); as well as the young protagonist's actively imagined but unfulfilled migration from China to the US in *Lan Yu* (Stanley Kwan, 2001).[1] Cinematic homecoming and homemaking have since become a common theme in queer Chinese cultural productions, where filmmakers tend to rewrite queer issues in regard to local understandings of the family (Berry 2001), and same-sex relationships tend to "come back" into the kinship system rather than "coming out" of the family register. Also, same-sex intimacies in Chinese films often entangle with heterosexual relationships (Wei 2010), as compulsory familism/heterosexuality predominates and prevails over the characters' queer desires.

The focus on the issue of family and mobility in queer cultures has continued to more recent Chinese-language movies such as *Rice Rhapsody* (*Hai Nan Ji Fan*, Kenneth Bi, 2004), *Innocent* (*Zhi Ai Moshenren*, Simon Chung, 2005), and *Lilting* (*Qingqing Yaohuang*, Hong Khaou, 2014). Queer cinematic cultures have also proliferated and diversified as seen in the popularity of the queer youth genre and the emergence of lesbian film auteurs most noticeably in Taiwan and Hong Kong,[2] as well as in independent and underground digital queer films produced in mainland China.[3] Compared to their predecessors, recent queer filmmakers in Chinese societies tend to put a greater emphasis on ordinary queer life and the protagonists' own identity crises as urban queer youth, rather than on the metanarrative of radical social changes at significant historical turning points, as we have seen in early queer film masterpieces such as *Farewell My Concubine* (*Ba*

Wang Bie Ji, Chen Kaige, 1993). At any rate, the propagating and mushrooming queer cultures in Chinese societies have seen the milieu of high-profile international art and auteur cinema, where queer issues have been explored as an artistic theme, growing side by side with mainstream commercial cinema, where juvenile charm and youth corporeal delicacy have been exploited as a selling point for both gay men and straight women.[4]

In the recent decade, there has emerged another type of queer filmmaking and digital video production that is created *by* and *for* queer people in various Chinese societies, where a deep solicitude for queer people's struggles often emerges through an autobiographical lens and the filmmakers' real-life experiences. In this case, cinematic queer storytelling often becomes an intimate confession of the past and an active imagination of the future that make these films highly relevant to queer people's real longings and sufferings. Among the newly emerged, self-identified gay filmmakers, Kit Hung (Hung Wing-Kit) and entrepreneur-turned-director Scud (Danny Cheng Wan-Cheung) are two prominent examples. The former has directed his first feature film *Soundless Wind Chime* (*Wusheng Fengling*, 2009), winning multiple awards at international film festivals; the latter has funded and directed his ambitious queer film trilogy *City Without Baseball* (*Wu Ye Zhi Cheng*, 2008), *Permanent Residence* (*Yongjiu Juliu*, 2009), and *Amphetamine* (*An Fei Ta Ming*, 2010), followed by two experimental short-film compilations *Love Actually Sucks* (*Ai Hen Lan*, 2011) and *Voyage* (*You*, 2013) as well as feature-length productions *Utopians* (*Tongliu Hewu*, 2015) and *Thirty Years of Adonis* (*Sanshi Erli*, 2017).

Both these directors have explicitly, and so far exclusively, engaged queer issues in their repertoire to represent their own life experiences as transnational queer migrants and global queer filmmakers through large-scale multinational productions and direct portrayals of cosmopolitan queer life and global queer mobilities. The protagonists in their films, compared to those in early Chinese-language queer movies, are often much more self-conscious with and confident about their sexualities and body images, although the "sad lonely young men" (Berry 2000; Dyer 2002, 116–36) struggling to confront their identities and sexualities still have a stage in their work. In lieu of canonical queer film masterpieces or underground digital movies, this chapter focuses on the newly emerged (post-2008) queer cultures created by and for queer people and the underlying queer mobilities on and off film screens as vehicles to understand stretched kinship and the issue of home and migration through autobiographical and cinematic queer homecoming and homemaking.

Homecoming and Homemaking

While I developed the notion of stretched kinship mainly in the context of mainland China, here I turn to Kit Hung's and Scud's autobiographical representations of transnational homecoming and homemaking to further expand the conceptual and analytical scope of stretched kinship alongside global queer mobilities. Transnational and border-crossing queer migrations often play an important role in their films, especially in the protagonists' negotiations of kinship and coming to terms with their sexualities and identities. Moreover, transnationalism and multilingualism not only function as an underlying premise of their works but often serve as the leitmotif that closely parallels the filmmakers' real-life experiences of migration across different Chinese societies and between the East and the West. In this case, what has been uprooted and regrounded along the migrating routes are not only the queer migrants themselves on and off screens but their ontological and symbolic home and family. In other words, migration itself is often a homemaking and homecoming process in search of love and anchorage that accommodates feelings, desires, and intimacies.

Kit Hung's *Soundless Wind Chime* was shot across mainland China, Hong Kong, and Switzerland in German, English, Mandarin, and Cantonese, which echoes Hung's own international experience as a filmmaker and a gay migrant. Despite the transnational production of the film, *Soundless Wind Chime* demonstrates a strong underlying understanding of the issue of family and kinship in a Chinese/Confucianist context. Ricky, one of the leading characters in the movie, travels to Switzerland after his Swiss boyfriend, Pascal, dies in an accident in Hong Kong. Half of the movie focuses on how Ricky traces Pascal's past in Europe and contemplates on his own past with his now deceased partner. During this journey, Ricky meets and gets close to another Swiss man, Ueli, who has an uncanny resemblance to the deceased Pascal and seems to be the latter's brother (played by the same actor). But their connection is temporarily disrupted when Ricky returns from Europe to Hong Kong, and then to his hometown in mainland China to look after his mother who is dying of cancer.

One significant part of this story is Ricky's background: he is a young migrant from rural China to Hong Kong and works as a waiter and a delivery boy in a small restaurant. When he talks to his mother over the phone, he reassures her that he is working in the finance industry, taking clients to Hong Kong's stock market. He also suggests his mother see a doctor in the city for her illness, since "the hospital in the city is better." This scene is not uncommon in today's Chinese world, when young people migrate from rural to urban areas (and from one Chinese society to another) with the dream for a better job and a brighter future, only to find that they do not have enough training and education to take up a middle-class job with a decent salary in the host society. The worst part is that they are reluctant to disclose their situation to the family—partially to protect their already fragile dignity as disadvantaged migrants in the localist host city and partially to save their parents from getting worried and concerned about their struggles and ordeal. Therefore, as delicately captured in this film, the imagined urban middle-class life has often become a "white lie" adopted by the unprivileged young migrants to reassure their families.

In this scenario, the kinship tie is further stretched when young migrants live in the rupture between the host city's refusal and the family's expectation, and between their real and imagined lives blending the harsh reality with their dreams of settlement and middle-class employment. A stretched kinship like this is essentially a misplaced kinship, when the two sides of the family are physically separated across time and space and the remote connection is filled with deceptions, albeit well intended. The kinship connection is hence often misplaced in a mutually imagined and constructed picture of exilic and exotic urban middle-class life in the host society—a picture that the family may not often have the chance to see and in which the young migrants are in fact often marginalized and struggling to make a living. In *Soundless Wind Chime*, Ricky's connection with his family is stretched across rural China and Hong Kong and further intermingles with the life trajectory of his boyfriend, Pascal.

Pascal lives in Hong Kong as a pickpocket. He steals Ricky's wallet but only seems to find some loose change in it, for which his Caucasian partner is unsatisfied and enraged. Physically abused and raped, Pascal leaves his partner and once again runs into Ricky. He recognizes the latter and returns the wallet. The kindness then becomes mutual when Ricky shares his food with the homeless Pascal and takes him back to stay in his place. Their romantic relationship starts to unfold but soon ends when Pascal dies in a car accident. In later flashbacks, we learn that Pascal left his hometown at a very young age before eventually settling in Hong Kong. When Ricky travels to Switzerland after Pascal's death, what awaits him is an old, abandoned house that seemingly belongs to Pascal's family, a cemetery that seems to be the place where Pascal's parents rest in peace, and an antique shop operated by two unidentified characters who are presumably Pascal's brother and sister.

But the film does not disclose whether they are indeed Pascal's siblings, nor does it explicitly reveal if Ricky has confided Pascal's death and his relationship with Pascal to them. As the audience, we track Pascal's past in Switzerland through Ricky's eyes, but the traces of his early life are hard to find and identify. Ricky's journey to Switzerland is a trip returning to Pascal's estranged home place, a "homecoming" process that he wants to complete for his now deceased partner to make up for the latter's unfulfilled reunion with his family. However, this homecoming process is never visually or narratively achieved on-screen. In the movie, the symbolic image of "home" has been rendered as deserted (the abandoned house), deceased (the cemetery), and discontinued (one of the shop owners tries to sell the family antiques they inherited from their parents). Home, in this film, has always been an impossible physical and mental origin and destination that neither protagonist is able to fully return to.

Not unlike Ricky's family connection that has been stretched between rural China and Hong Kong, the kinship tie between Pascal and his family has been stretched far and thin as well. Pascal's connection with his family is now only traceable through remote and vague memories—short flashbacks on-screen in which young Pascal waves farewell to his mother on a gloomy winter day when everything around them is covered in heavy snow. In a later flashback towards the end of the film, we see Pascal's mother walking home alone after her son's departure, when two names appear on-screen with the dates of their respective life and death. This scene implies that Pascal's parents have passed away before they had the chance to see Pascal again. More important, this is also a tribute paid by the filmmaker Kit Hung to his boyfriend's parents. According to Hung, *Soundless Wind Chime* is adapted from his real-life story with his Swiss boyfriend, who came out under Hung's encouragement; his boyfriend's parents in Switzerland showed great support but passed away not long after the coming out.[5] This film is hence Hung's own lament for his deceased "parents-in-law," where mourning and grief are conveyed through Ricky's unfruitful journey looking for Pascal's family in the unreachable and impossible "home."

In a broader context of migrant and diaspora cinema and culture, "home" as well as "homecoming" has always been a recurring theme in the representations and understandings of exilic experiences. If the feelings of kinship are often negotiated through the idea of home, then homecoming necessarily "occupies a primary place in the minds of the exiles . . . for it is the dream of a glorious homecoming that structures exile" (Naficy 2001, 229). However, paradoxically, this predominant idea of home and homecoming is often represented through estrangement and alienation in queer migrant films: the reality of homelessness often appears persistent, whereas the glorious dream of homecoming often remains, merely, a dream. The happy place of home only resides in a remote, symbolic imagination as "a mythic place of desire" for exilic migrants—a place of no return even it is possible to temporarily return to the original geographical territory (Brah 1996, 192). The enactment of homecoming may only lead to the discovery of a shattered family that either no longer exists or is dying/struggling to keep its original shape, like Pascal's home in Switzerland and Ricky's home in rural China. The actual experience of homecoming barely aligns with the imagination of home in the exiles' minds.

This is also why queer migration is often structured and conditioned by the dual spatialities of "claustrophobia" and "agoraphobia." In queer migration, the experience of exile often intertwines with the trauma of coming out from ethnic enclaves and the homosexual closet into the localist and homophobic host societies; queer migration across the home/host boundaries and inside/outside the closet thus "entails and unleashes claustrophobic and agoraphobic spatialities" (Naficy, 310). Stretched between both sides of the closet and both ends of the migrating route, exilic identity and queer sexuality have to constantly shift their places and find their positions across the claustrophobic intolerance and the agoraphobic exposure. As such, the imagination of home and the enactment of homecoming can only be experienced through estrangement and alienation between the contradictory dual spatialities. There is no salvation and no purgatory: what is left behind and what awaits ahead are equally problematic (cf. Berghahn 2006, 148–55). Queer homecoming is, essentially, a stretched journey.

Soundless Wind Chime further reminds us about one significant dilemma in stretched queer kinship negotiation: when the young generation is making long-term plans to reveal or conceal their sexual selves, their parents are getting old and may not have enough time to wait for the final revelation or a quasi-heterosexual marriage. In Chinese cultures, one major Confucianist doctrine regarding filial piety is *"zi yu yang er qin bu dai"*—when children have the ability to serve their parents, the parents are getting too old to enjoy such services. Thus, how much time is allowed for further negotiation of one's sexuality in stretched kinship is a major pressure facing queer people, leading to the filial panic that I have described. The parents may pass away without knowing the true sexual preference of their children, if the disclosure takes too long, which can be a shame for some people who do not want to forever hide their sexualities from their families. In a different situation, the parents may not have enough time for a quasi-heterosexual marriage to be arranged and grandchildren to be born, which is against the fundamental Confucianist familism and can be a tremendous moral burden on young people. This kinship of unease, as shown through the story in *Soundless Wind Chime*, resides in the gap between one's sexuality and filial responsibility when the kinship connection has often been stretched long and thin across both time and space from the distanced aging parents.

Moreover, the process of uprooting and regrounding can be a long journey in pursuing geographical and social class migrations, which adds more tensions to the stretched kinship negotiations for queer migrants. The rise of the capitalist knowledge economy and the shift of the global job market to a knowledge-based and skill-intensive field ineluctably entail longer education and training in the production of work-ready employees. Combined with the traditional Chinese preference for education, these changes mean that today's young people are often expected to complete further and higher education to acquire advanced qualifications. This delays the time they become independent to sustain themselves and ready to build their own home and family, which further increases the pressure and the tension in stretched kinship negotiations facing the hetero-reproductive expectations from the aging parents. Here, it also means that the unskilled and undereducated migrants like Ricky and Pascal often have a hard time finding a decent job and have to spend more time at the bottom of the host society, which inevitably postpones—if not renders impossible—their "glorious" homecoming to their original families as well as their own homemaking in the host society.

When Pascal left his hometown in Switzerland, he might not have foreseen that he would end up as a pickpocket in Hong Kong; when Ricky came to this city from rural China, what awaited him was also not the middle-class job he imagined and later described to his mother. But, as young migrants, they have exercised their agency to navigate through the obstacles and negotiate a new life together in the gap between the left-behind hometowns and the hardship in the host city. After Pascal left his violent Caucasian partner and after Ricky moved out of his aunt's home where she worked as a prostitute, they were able to rent a small apartment together as a safe refuge for their exilic queer love (ditto to Hamid Naficy's *claustrophobic apartment* as a prevalent symbol in the chronotope of exilic cinema, 2001, 116–17). Pascal also found a job with Ricky's encouragement. As queer migrants in Hong Kong, they are able to build an ontological home secured by housing and employment as well as a symbolic home safeguarded by love and intimacy outside their left-behind original families (Figure 2.1). In this sense, their transnational homemaking as queer migrants is rather successful. They might have had a happy life thereafter in the home built by and for themselves, if Pascal had not died in an accident and Ricky had not returned to mainland China to look after his mother.

When stretched kinship meets transnational mobilities, the stretched spatialities and temporalities often conjointly condition and structure the process of queer homecoming and homemaking. Both characters in the film have eventually lost the chance to introduce each other to their respective family, as Pascal's parents have passed away in Switzerland and Ricky's mother is dying of cancer in rural China. Learning about her worsening illness, Ricky abandons his job in Hong Kong and returns to the Mainland. He labors in what seems to be a suburban area under rapid development to earn money for his mother's medical expenses. Toward the end of the movie, Ueli, the man who is supposedly Pascal's

Figure 2.1 Ricky (left) and Pascal in *Soundless Wind Chime*

brother, comes to China to look for Ricky. Ueli finds Ricky's mother but has not yet seen Ricky when the film concludes. We have no idea whether Ueli can be accepted into the family as Ricky's partner, or if Ricky comes out to his mother before she dies of cancer. For Ricky, "home" is also an impossible destination to fully return to. His intimacy with Pascal/Ueli never successfully enters the domain of the family.

Heterotopic Non-places

In addition to Hung's *Soundless Wind Chime*, Scud's queer films also put a strong emphasis on transnational homemaking and homecoming across and beyond Chinese societies, where the motif of home and migration is underlined by stretched kinship and queer mobilities. Scud's acclaimed autobiographical film *Permanent Residence* was shot in six countries across three continents, in which traveling and migrating across the East and the West constitute a major part of the protagonist's coming-of-age story and coming-to-terms with his sexuality. Ivan, the protagonist based on Scud's real-life archetype, was born in mainland China and raised by his grandmother. He moved to Hong Kong and worked in the booming local IT industry before immigrating to Australia, and then returned to Hong Kong to start independent queer film production, as self-reflexively portrayed towards the end of the movie. *Permanent Residence* contains two important homecoming stories that depict Ivan's journeys back to China to visit his grandmother, who was suffering from Alzheimer's disease and could hardly recognize her own family.

During his first visit, Ivan brought back a female colleague (who later comes out as a self-identified lesbian) as his fake girlfriend, in order to reassure his grandmother that he was in a relationship before it was too late for her to recognize his grandson. At the beginning of this homecoming scene, the camera waits inside the front yard of the grandmother's house and anticipates Ivan and his quasi-girlfriend. Ivan asks the latter to act well since "grandma is smart" and may discover the truth. The woman responds with "I'll try my best" before having an awkward tumble in front of the house, to which Ivan comments disappointedly that she is "worse than Mrs. Thatcher." His comment refers to the then-prime minister of the UK, Margaret Thatcher, who in 1982 tripped and tumbled down the steps of the Great Hall of the People in Beijing, where the leaders of the two countries negotiated the future of Hong Kong. In Chinese societies, Mrs. Thatcher's tumble is often seen as a symbol of China's diplomatic victory and Britain's "fall and fail" over the issue of Hong Kong. Here in the film, this anecdote offers a hint for the subsequent failure of Ivan's "fake-it" strategy in his own stretched kinship negotiation across Hong Kong and mainland China.

As soon as Ivan's grandmother learns that the young woman is Ivan's partner, she becomes thrilled and gives her a jade bracelet as a gift: "I have waited too long for this day!" In stretched kinship, the elders in the family often hold high expectations for the youngsters' marriage, but such anticipations are often stretched long and thin, if not left empty. In Ivan's case, his grandmother, who took the parents' role in his upbringing, becomes the person for whom he has to fulfill his filial responsibility. But the elder's wisdom is not to be underestimated. The smile soon disappears from the grandmother's face: "My grandson, you shouldn't have chosen this woman. She hasn't looked at you since you two came in. She doesn't really love you. You shouldn't marry her." Her observation is also evident in the cinematography, which puts Ivan and his grandmother in tight and intimate frames and leaves the woman alone in separate shots. Even when they are portrayed in the same frame, the fake girlfriend is often positioned on the margin of the composition, detached from the intimate family on another side of the screen (Figure 2.2). In other words, the quasi-girlfriend is never visually permitted and invited into the family. Apparently, Ivan would need to be better prepared if he wanted this "fake-it" strategy to work. But he does not have a second chance. His grandmother passes away when he is traveling with his boyfriend; his subsequent second homecoming only brings him back to her cold, motionless body and her wheelchair, empty under the pale moonlight.

While Ivan's homecoming only ends in death and sorrow, his homemaking with his boyfriend turns out to be equally problematic. Soon after his grandma's funeral, his boyfriend, Windson, decides to break up with him to marry a woman. Windson has been struggling to cope with his attraction to Ivan vis-à-vis his self-identification as a heterosexual man who has dated a woman for a long time. He tells Ivan that, even though he does not really want to marry a woman, he has reached the age of marriage to fulfill his filial responsibility as the only son in his

Figure 2.2 Ivan and his fake girlfriend visiting his grandmother in *Permanent Residence*

family. After the breakup, Ivan tries to end his life in his own apartment, a home-like place where he and Windson have had some great time together. Earlier in the film, Ivan was thrilled when he bought this apartment with hard-earned money after he left his grandmother and started to build a career and establish himself in Hong Kong. This apartment, both a physical shelter and a symbolic home for Ivan and his partner, now becomes a place where he tries to take his own life. Adding to the dramatic narrative, that day is also Ivan's birthday. A celebration of life turns into a heartbreaking breakup and a nerve-wracking suicidal attempt in the very home that he worked hard to build to accommodate his love and his dream.

If homecoming is merely a glorious dream in the troublesome claustrophobic and agoraphobic chronotope of exilic experiences, then queer homemaking is an equally stretched process where home is no more than an ominous utopia for a dream of a *dolce vita* (Berghahn 2006, 151). Ricky and Pascal's small apartment in *Soundless Wind Chime* and Ivan's home in *Permanent Residence* merely function as temporary configurations of their unfulfilled queer love and unsettled exilic life. These "claustrophobic apartments" are not real homes. Rather, they constitute what Marc Augé calls temporary and transient *non-places*—transit points and temporary abodes "surrendered to solitary individuality, to the fleeting, the temporal and the ephemeral"—that offer very little concern with the settlement and development of relations, histories, and identities (1995, 78–79). These non-places are every bit akin to Foucault's "heterotopias of deviation" (1986) that exist in the counter-sites of otherness as effectively enacted utopias to house those undesirable on the margin of the society (queer migrants, in this case). Foucault's theory outlines two types of heterotopia: one is concerned with the accumulation of time and eternality, which I discuss below, and another with time in its most transitory and ephemeral form, as we have seen in Ricky's and Ivan's "non-homes" in Hong Kong. If the impossible homecoming can be understood through the lens of stretched kinship, then these heterotopic non-places also present an exemplar of queer homemaking as a stretched arrangement and formulation of "home" that only accommodates transient queer intimacies and unsettled desires instead of a solid, concrete queer future conditioned by love and hope through a stable and long-term relationship.

Ivan eventually survives the breakup and continues to take care of Windson's mother, who is dying of a terminal illness. He pays for her expensive medical bills and then for her funeral and cemetery after her decease. Windson's mother and Ivan treated each other as family, even though the boys never revealed their intimate relationship to her in this stretched kinship connection. Before long, Windson's father also passes away. Coming out, or coming home, have both become impossible for Ivan and Windson. Six years later, they unexpectedly meet again in Australia. Ivan proposes to Windson, but the latter is still overwhelmed by his lingering attraction to Ivan vis-à-vis his own heterosexual identification and eventually takes his own life. As I have pointed out elsewhere (2012) and as Audrey Yue comments (2015, 289–90), Windson's death is a punishment less for his homosexuality than for his failure as a son who cannot take care of his parents (a failed homecoming) and as a partner who disappointed both his wife and Ivan (a failed homemaking). Despite their various and continuous attempts as queer migrants in the "non-places" to build a life and a future together, Ivan and Windson never really succeeded in making a home of their own.

In this case, both transnational homecoming and homemaking have failed for the duo. From the physical separation from his grandmother to his failed attempts to save Windson's parents and marry Windson, stretched kinship always has an essential role to play throughout Ivan's life as filmmaker Scud's cinematic doppelgänger. Not unlike Ricky's story in *Soundless Wind Chime*, homecoming is ultimately an impossible process for Ivan to complete, while the once-promising homemaking eventually fails. Ivan's troublesome floating life reaches an end in the final scene of the film, where director Scud predicts Ivan's decease in 2047 and imagines an ocean cemetery where coffins float permanently above the motionless Dead Sea.[6] The cast list then begins to roll out on screen, each name pointing to a coffin, indicating a place that Scud/Ivan has chosen for himself and for his film crew. Death is paradoxically the only permanent residence and perhaps the only feasible heterotopic ending for Ivan, who has struggled through his life to find a place and build a home. A cemetery is the *exemplar par excellence* of Foucault's first type of heterotopia, a quasi-eternity in dissolution and disappearance. A never-sinking and permanently floating ocean cemetery in *Permanent Residence* is a rather heterotopic enactment of a permanent "home," where the exhausted queer exiles can finally rest in peace.

This argument further questions and challenges the very idea of "home" in homecoming and homemaking: What is home? Where is home? What does family mean and with whom can people build a family together? Here, "home" is not a notion that we can easily take for granted. The different configurations of home, both in its imagination and realization, often entail and unleash a rather complex intervention and relocation of the body and the memory from the family of origin to the home of one's own. This mobilized journey often goes through various "non-places" as transit points in between the imagined homecoming and the anticipated homemaking that conjointly structure the mythic, heterotopic non-places of transient desires. These non-places as the second type of the Foucauldian heterotopia—supposedly ephemeral and temporary—paradoxically look rather persistent when queer migrants are stuck en route in these non-places along their love-seeking and home-searching journey. For the exilic queer migrants, the regrounding via homecoming and homemaking is as much remote and impossible as the settlement of their exilic and migrant identities. From the permanent ocean cemetery to the transient non-places, "home" as an ontological and symbolic place is always hard to pinpoint in the emplacement and displacement of queer kinship, while the very idea of home and family has often become unstable when the exilic queer migrants keep floating from one place to another without settlement and regrounding.

Here, Ricky's and Ivan's transnational homecoming and homemaking in *Soundless Wind Chime* and *Permanent Residence* have offered two resounding autobiographical notes to the issue of home and kinship. Ricky's and Ivan's respective migration follows a similar route from mainland China to Hong Kong and then to a Western country, each step bringing them new possibilities for their coming of age and coming to terms with their sexualities. While their migrations enable them to further explore and express their attraction to the same sex, their queer desires and intimacies are isolated in a different time and space (a heterotopic non-place) and carefully tucked away from their families of origin. The "coming-out migration" may have afforded both of them a certain level of sexual freedom, but this process has also created a double-stretched kinship connection, first from the homeland of China to Hong Kong, and then from the city-state of Hong Kong to the West.

In these films, mainland China is often depicted through the protagonists' families of origin (aging and dying) as a conservative motherland with very limited tolerance for queer desires, while Hong Kong and the West are queer paradises where Ricky and Ivan (young and desiring) can come out at ease. But this process of "coming out to Hong Kong" and "coming out to the West" also involves certain risks concerning stretched family kinship. Ricky almost lost the chance to say a proper farewell to his mother, while Ivan indeed missed his opportunity when his beloved grandmother passed away. In addition, Ricky's partner died in Hong Kong, while Ivan's boyfriend eventually committed suicide in Australia. Both their homecoming and homemaking as border-crossing and transnational queer migrants have miserably failed. If stretched kinship is a kinship of unease, then the process of migration also involves certain risks and uncertainties that may not lead to positive outcomes, as further demonstrated in the analysis below.

Lost in Migration and Dead on Arrival

I started my discussions on stretched kinship and queer homemaking by casting migration under a generally positive light, arguing that migration often opens up new possibilities for queer people to explore their sexualities, build peer rapport, and become fully independent queer individuals. I saw migration as a process that enables queer homemaking and creates alternative kinship connections for queer people to complete a journey of uprooting from the original families and regrounding into alternative homes. In the film *Permanent Residence*, the protagonist's mobilities have afforded him the opportunities to search for love and a better life; the only "permanent residence" is death—a quasi-eternal heterotopia at the end of migration after many precarious transit points. The end of mobility is the end of change, growth, development, and transformation. The choice of mobility, by contrast, is a savior and a necessity for people like Ivan/Scud to keep alive and active, as it bears the promise of a possible queer future for the hopeless and homeless floating queer exiles. At first look, mobility is life, and mobility is home.

However, this is simultaneously the dark side of mobility. First, migration can end up in death and sorrow, or alienation and disorientation. In addition to love and comfort, the key foci in our considerations of migration experiences, the emotionally embodied process of migration may also involve violence and trauma. Second, for rootless queer migrants, both the homeland and the host society can become an impossible location for settlement. Third, for some people, migration is always a *route*, a never-ending process of becoming, without a final destination or a final chance to put down the *root* to become local. We have seen such complex formulations of queer mobilities in *Soundless Wind Chime* and *Permanent Residence*, while this theme is also salient in Scud's other queer feature films including *Amphetamine* (2010). Although the story in *Amphetamine* is fictional, this film is better understood as a semi-autobiography. Kafka and Daniel, the two protagonists in the film, serve as Scud's doppelgängers whose background stories parallel Scud's own life trajectory: Kafka's family moved to Hong Kong from mainland China; Daniel, a high-achieving Hong Kong elite, immigrated to Australia before coming back to the city-state. I see Kafka as the carrier of Scud's childhood memory and Daniel of his adulthood story.

The embodied emotions of the two characters in *Amphetamine* hold the key to unlock the complex formulations and interventions of home and migration. Kafka Tam, the first protagonist, works as a personal trainer and a model in Hong Kong. His childhood story is not shown in detail, but the movie has left some clues for the audience to complete the jigsaw of Kafka's past. Born in 1982, he probably moved to Hong Kong from mainland China at a young age with his family. His father died when he was a child, and his elder brother has been abusing methamphetamine. His mother, appearing only briefly in Kafka's drug-induced illusions and conversing with him in Mandarin, has been hospitalized and remains unconscious due to an unspecified terminal illness. Growing up in a suburban slum, Kafka had to look after himself and his family. He started to learn martial arts when he was young to become strong, as nobody can protect him but himself. Now a personal trainer with a well-toned body, he provides occasional sex services to gay men in the gym where he works, as depicted at the beginning of the film.

Not unlike Ricky and Pascal in *Soundless Wind Chime*, people like Kafka are seldom allowed the chance for a proper settlement in the host place. Unskilled and undereducated, they often reside in the lowest level of the social hierarchy, laboring hard to make a living where capitalism ranks human dignity based on people's economic values. Facing homophobia and xenophobia, they either return to their homeland with a shattered dream (e.g., Ricky) or die as immigrants at a young age (e.g., Pascal as well as Kafka, as we will see later in the film). For them, settlement often appears temporary and transient, while the migrant identity is rather persistent and permanent. The film *Amphetamine* has a Chinese title, *An Fei Ta Ming*, which is both a transliteration of the drug's name and an archaic way to say "settlement is not his fate." Disadvantaged and underprivileged, people like Kafka are often soon forgotten by the host states and missing in both official history and migration scholarship, as Nayan Shah (2012, 3–9) points out in a different context.

For Kafka, his disadvantaged immigrant family offers little support and protection for him, and he has to rely on himself. However, his physical-bodily strength cannot solve every problem. His family still lives in poverty and his mother dies of illness halfway through the film. More important, his physical power also fails to protect him, as shown in a traumatic flashback in the movie. When Kafka saw a mainland Chinese woman harassed by a gang, he stepped up to save her and fought the gangsters single-handedly. Outnumbered, he was beaten up and then violently gang-raped. Since then, he has become addicted to amphetamine to both ease the lingering physical pain in his body and escape from the long-lasting mental wound. He starts to hallucinate, partially due to the side effects of the drug, where his memory with his mother resurfaces in a painful way. He cries and blames himself for not being able to save his mother from illness and for not having provided her with a happy and affluent life. The woman he saved from the gang arguably serves as a reminder of his mother, a female immigrant from mainland China facing local people's abuse and hostility in Hong Kong. This young woman has then become his girlfriend, out of gratitude for his heroic (yet tragic) sacrifice, but this relationship does not last long.

Here, the migrating queer body—defined by mobility scholar Andrew Gorman-Murray as "the site of sexual identity-formation and the vector of movement" (2007, 106)—is significant in understanding the emotionally embodied queer migration. After all, sexuality lies primarily in the body and its pleasure, remarks Gorman-Murray (2009, 443) after Michel Foucault (1978), and the body itself presents "a more appropriate *scale* for analyzing the complexity of queer migration" (original emphasis), if we were to recast the grand narrative of the national and the transnational to the migration experience per se (Gorman-Murray, 444). But, in *Amphetamine*, Kafka's body is less a carrier of pleasure than a traumatized endurer of the rapist and localist penetrations; his sexuality lies primarily in the body and its wounds. At any rate, the body is the forefront carrier of feelings and desires in the imagination and enactment of mobility; for border-crossing immigrants like Kafka, it is the physical pain and mental trauma carried by the body that constitute and structure the exilic experience of migration.

Traveling back to mainland China, Kafka conceals a small amount of amphetamine in a bottle of chewing gum, which results in him and Daniel, his boyfriend, being arrested at a security checkpoint. In a dark and claustrophobic interrogation room, both Kafka and Daniel are stripped naked and thoroughly body-searched for any possible drugs concealed. The duo is portrayed in absolute helplessness, going through anal probes in full nudity by a group of police officers. This scene sharply resembles the flashback in which Kafka was violently gang-raped in what seems to be a suburban wasteland in Hong Kong. That is to say, both sides of the law (gangsters and cops) and both sides of the border (Hong Kong and mainland China) have abused him equally brutally. Daniel is released thereafter because he has an Australian passport. Kafka, however, is detained in mainland China until Daniel rescues him with the help of a lawyer. The interrogation room and the detention center—the abysmal non-places that interrupt the migrating routes—have further traumatized Kafka's already wounded body and mind.

As a result of the brutal and violent rapist penetrations, first by the gang and then by the police, Kafka has developed problems for sexual intercourse. On the first night he sleeps with Daniel, as seen in an early scene, he is unable to have sex with him at all. He has a terrible nightmare that Daniel forced him for sex and he fought back by throwing Daniel out the window using his martial arts skills; out of immediate regret and guilt, he jumped after Daniel and ended up killing both his boyfriend and himself. Awakening from this nightmare, he suffers a severe nervous breakdown and shouts to Daniel that he will never be able to perform sexually with a man. If completing the journey to perform and confirm one's sexuality inevitably involves "getting laid" (Maddison 2002, 157), then the body and its pleasure must determine (and are determined by) one's ability to actualize his sexuality. Kafka's inability to act on his sexual desire and on his intimacy with Daniel significantly curtails his comfort-seeking and love-seeking migration journey. He tells Daniel that everyone who loved him has left him, from his mother to his girlfriend he saved from the gang, while Daniel reassures Kafka that he will never leave him alone. However, Kafka's dysfunctional body only leads to a disorientation regarding his attraction to men and his struggle over his sexuality. He cannot explain why he is wholeheartedly in love with Daniel but his body failed miserably. His emotional intimacy with Daniel is deeply frustrated by his incapability of building a physical-bodily connection with the object of his attraction and desire, and his sexuality is hopelessly detached from his feelings of love and intimacy (Figure 2.3).

Kafka, a tragic queer figure, represents those migrants whose emotional embodiment is deeply troubled along the migrating routes. His first migration, from mainland China to Hong Kong, only resulted in a broken family and a life in struggle and poverty, in addition to his traumatic experience at the hands of the gangsters. His second migration, temporarily from Hong Kong back to the Mainland, resulted in an equally traumatic and violent experience at the mercy

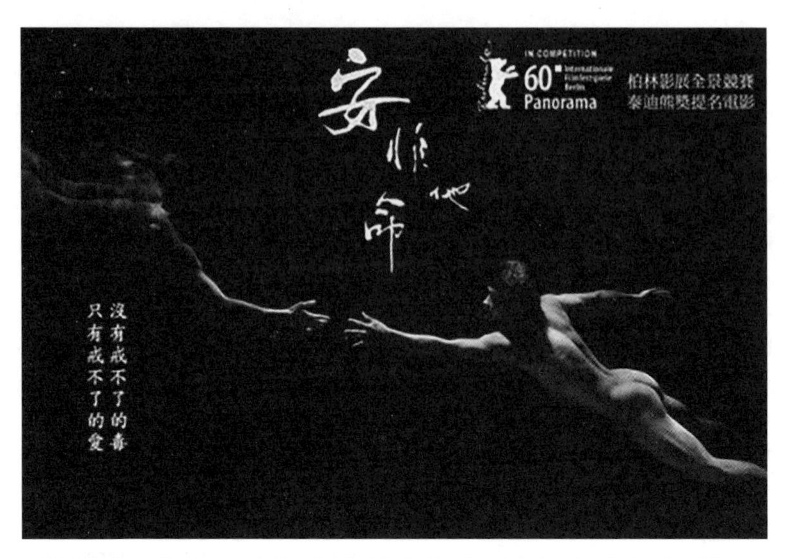

Figure 2.3 Kafka tries to reach Daniel in his hallucination in *Amphetamine* (film poster)

of the authorities. In the host city, Kafka is treated as a mere object for sexual consumption (in the gym) and rapist penetration (in the slum); in the home state, he is seen as a drug addict carrying the highly restricted amphetamine. He is neither embraced by Hong Kong nor tolerated by the Chinese motherland. Just like the collapse of his family and the death of his mother, his personal sense of home-like belonging is never fully settled. Instead of the emotionally embodied love and comfort made possible through migration, Kafka is embodied with trauma and violence along his migration routes. As I have pointed out, his body is less a carrier of pleasure than an endurer of pain in the enactments of mobilities.

Even his name, Kafka, serves as a metaphor of a traumatized embodiment. This name comes from Haruki Murakami's acclaimed novel *Kafka on the Shore* (2002), in which the 15-year-old protagonist leaves home and embarks on an exilic journey in order to escape from an oedipal curse that he would murder his father to marry his mother and his sister. The Kafka in the film, seen reading Murakami's novel, apparently resembles and considers himself the same exilic queer figure as the Kafka in the fiction. In both cases, Kafka is not a real name but a reference to the writer Franz Kafka and his classic novel *The Metamorphosis* (1915). In the film, Daniel points to the poster of a local theatrical adaptation of *The Metamorphosis* and asks Kafka whether he has read this masterpiece. In Franz Kafka's story, a traveling salesman (i.e., another reference to mobility and exilic body) mysteriously metamorphoses into a monstrous insect-like creature, a queer and uncanny embodiment resented by his own family. His feelings and emotions (as a human) are detached from his physical appearance (as a non-human), which serves as a reference to the inhuman treatment of Kafka in

Amphetamine. The Kafka in the film carries a double-embodied metaphor as both Murakami's and Franz Kafka's exilic and estranged characters, who are either mentally traumatized or bodily deformed, left to the mercy of the indifferent and abusive family and society.

Body-painted with feather wings attached to his torso, Kafka jumps off the roof of Daniel's apartment towards the end of the film, probably under the hallucinating effect of amphetamine. His "flying" is depicted as apparently suicidal, before the camera reveals a balcony on the lower level of the building that Kafka lands on and avoids death. Shot in slow motion and edited into different parts throughout the film, this flying scene has some uncanny resemblance to Alan Parker's film *Birdy* (1984). In *Birdy*, a war veteran suffering from post-traumatic stress disorder believes that he can fly like a bird and jumps off the rooftop. Seemingly suicidal, he also lands safely on the lower level of a mansion. Here, the imagination and the enactment of flying/mobility in both films function as the protagonists' escape from their respective trauma: if humans have hurt them more than anything else has, then the dehumanization and bird-like embodiments become a highly legitimate transgression for them to move on from the past wounds that were caused by no other than their fellow human beings.

This traumatized and dehumanized emotional embodiment of Kafka further implies the plight facing queer immigrants like him. When Daniel first meets Kafka, he describes Kafka as "the loneliest person," who does not seem to belong to this world at all. Unlike Daniel, who immigrated to Australia from Hong Kong and returned as a high-flying financial advisor, Kafka is stuck at the bottom of Hong Kong's capitalist society with little chance for upward social mobility. He is an outcast in this regional financial center, straddling the legal and illegal borders in his identities (immigrant and drug addict) and in his professions (personal trainer and sex worker). Self-reflexively, Kafka tells Daniel that he was once cast in a local film, *Illegal Border-Crossing* (*Feifa Rujing*), which is in fact Scud's early film, *Permanent Residence*. His self-mocking implies his dislocated identity and deep-buried anxiety in between the inaccessible homeland (homecoming) and the unattainable love (homemaking) in the host city. His desire for acceptance and anchorage remains unsettled, as it lacks material-bodily and psychosexual fulfillment as well as basic socioeconomic grounding.

In *Amphetamine*, furthermore, one of the major shooting locations is an unfinished harbor bridge under construction. Built from both sides of the harbor, the bridge is waiting to be connected in the middle. Daniel tells Kafka that the day the bridge is connected will be the time they close the gap between them to build a long-lasting relationship. The bridge is a promise for both connectivity and mobility, in the sense that it connects the two separate lands across the harbor and enables movements between them. But this bridge is never connected in the film, and Daniel and Kafka have never built a stable relationship when the latter struggles with his drug problem and his disconnected body and emotion.

The behind-the-scenes footage included in the DVD release of the movie reveals that the working title of the film was *Love of the Broken Bridge* (*Duan Qiao Zhi Lian*), which symbolizes a broken queer romance without a future and an interrupted migration journey without home and settlement. Not unlike the nomadic gay cowboys in *Brokeback Mountain* (Ang Lee, 2005), both Kafka and Daniel in *Amphetamine* are passengers, instead of settlers, in the home-searching and love-seeking migration journeys. Their encounters cannot but look temporary and transient.

Kafka dies from an amphetamine overdose towards the end of the film, aged 26, with an unfulfilled dream of love and home. If the promise of settlement is only provided by the host state to a select few, then the promise of a better life through migration is also a dream that does not always come true. For many exilic queer migrants, "home" is inaccessible either as the origin or as the destination, while the promise of mobilities barely offers them the comfort of love and anchorage. When homemaking is as impossible as homecoming, they are caught up and stretched across various heterotopic non-places, trying to find a non-existent home place through a never-settled process of movements. In Kafka's case, migrations turn out to have only replaced his old sufferings with new agony and added new trauma to his old wounds. If migration is a trip searching for home, love, and a future, then it may well end up in a trek that is homeless, loveless, and futureless. For some, they are lost in migration and dead on arrival. Migration is always an uncertain and uncanny queer journey, hopeful as much as hopeless.

From the impossible home to the unattainable love, the autobiographical and cinematic migration stories examined in this chapter demonstrate queer people's emotionally embodied experiences of mobilities under the intermingled forces of development (migrating for a better life) and familism (isolating queer desires from the original home). The unfulfilled homecoming and homemaking and the unsettled bodies and desires in the long process of uprooting—with or without the chance to put down the roots for regrounding—inevitably become constituent of and productive of the stretched kinship structure that I have discussed earlier in this book. If mobilities often bear a sense of hope for a better tomorrow and hence appear attractive to queer people, then we should also bear in mind that mobilities come with significant contingencies that may become unbearable for many. In fact, migration often entails certain economic capital (e.g., financial resources for survival) and cultural capital (e.g., knowledge and skills for employment) to reestablish oneself and negotiate an identity and a sense of belonging between the homeland and the host society. In this sense, the enactment of migration and the process of post-migration settlement are deeply conditioned and structured by one's cultural and social mobilities, which this book further considers in subsequent chapters.

3
Sinophone Mobilities

If the stretched kinship of unease and the turbulent process of homecoming and homemaking constitute the ineluctable outcomes of the development-induced migrations, then this underpinning geographical mobility per se should be further scrutinized in the broader context of queer Chinese-language cultures and mobilities. This chapter considers the intermingled cultural mobility and geographical mobility as equally important and mutually generating forces in the imagination and enactment of movements that are further conditioned by social mobility and immobility. Using "Sinophone mobilities" as an expansive, heuristic category, I look at queer mobilities through the lens of "Sinophone" and question and queer Sinophone theories and ontologies by scrutinizing various forms of mobilities. These include (1) the conditions and consequences of migration and the post-migration settlement and localization; (2) the issue of cultural mobilities in the form of queer Sinophone cultural productions and cultural flows between China and Sinophone societies and communities; and (3) the underlying issue of social mobility behind migration and settlement and behind the formation of Sinophone cultures. As this project germinated from my research in mainland China through which I gained access to queer Sinophone cultures and migrants, the case studies included here have either a direct engagement with China (as the origin and the destination of migration) or a significant stake in China (as a site for Sinophone cultural productions).

Mobilities/Sinophonicities

Before the birth of Sinophone theories, two predominant approaches were evident in the consideration and conceptualization of queer Asian cultures: the first is to recuperate the significance of the local, vis-à-vis the US-/West-dominated global, and the second is a postcolonial critique of queer Western centrism (Wilson 2006, 6–7). The former has often been criticized for nativism and its essentialist view of culture, and the latter for its curtailed ability to provincialize the West. Ara Wilson thus calls for a "critical queer regionalism" as a conceptual reframing that transcends these two approaches and situates Asia in "complex modernities and transnational flows in a global context shaped by political economic asymmetries" (11). After all, East/West and Asia/America are not purely imagined categories (which imply a borderless world where queer cultures circulate without local resistance), nor are they fixed classifications based merely on geolocation (which appear too rigid and sedentary). Such binaries as "queer Asia/America" and "local/global queer" are established upon, but not bound up with, the geolocations and geopolitics of Asia and America, and the East and the West. These locales are significantly shaped by their own histories and cultures, as well as by the intermingled local and global forces of modernity and sexuality that are often more complicated than the local/global dualism could adequately capture.[1]

This is why the notion of "Sinophone" offers a promising lens through which we can better reframe the territorial and conceptual locations and dislocations of various Chinese societies that previous queer regionalism was striving and struggling to address. The notion of "Sinophone" delineates a linguistic, cultural, historical, and political stance that aims to bring diaspora Chinese communities and marginalized Chinese cultures under a single framework. This concept is often attributed to Shu-mei Shih for her coinage and development of Sinophone theories (2004, 2007, 2010a, 2010b, 2011, 2014). Shih's framework prioritizes localized and heterogenized Sinitic-language cultures of Chinese immigrants who have put down their roots for several generations in their new home to become more eligible as "local" and less eligible as "diaspora." Sinophone studies offer a paradigm-shift from diaspora studies (with its strong nostalgic attachment to the ancestral homeland of origin) to a linguistic-historical understanding of cultures and people (that is sensitive and subject to the spatiotemporal resettlement and localization of Chinese-speaking immigrants). The propagation of Sinophone theories seeks to rationalize and reinstall those peripheral, "post-diasporic" communities as equally authentic and significant Sinitic-language cultures that have long been articulating their own voices through film, literature, and other cultural outputs.

Facing China's rise on the global stage, "Sinophone" enables a conscious and timely breakup from the China-centrism that often sees the continental mainland China as the superior Chinese society and the single origin of authentic Chinese cultures. Such China-centrism often neglects different constructions and articulations of "Chineseness" in other Sinitic-language areas. Here, the resistance against China's international expansion and power assertion does not necessarily come from the West but instead from overseas Chinese communities. Thus, excluding China has become a priori in the theorization of Sinophone, while pushing China to the margin is less a consequence than a condition for "Sinophone" to gain its theoretical and ontological legitimacy. In Shu-mei Shih's version of Sinophone,

China and other Sinitic-language communities do not share an umbilical relationship as the motherland and her diasporic children; rather, China is rendered from the ancestral mother to a complete other. This otherness has generated much debate about the notion of Sinophone. For Sheldon Lu (2008) and Emilie Yeh (2012), the Sinophone concept is epistemologically limiting in the sense that it creates a dichotomy between China and the rest of the Sinitic-language world. Sinophone is also deeply rooted in postcolonialism (Yeh, 77) through its "phone" connection with other "phone spheres" like Francophone and Anglophone (Lu, 23). With Lu and Yeh's invocation of the idea of "Sinophone cinema" in 2005, Lu further develops the notion of Sinophone along his own lines to include rather than exclude mainland China in the Sinophone nexus. This results in two variants of "Sinophone" that differ in rejecting or embracing China.

Although Sinophone theories (in both Shih's and Lu's versions) remain inadequate in addressing non-Sinitic-language cultures created by diasporic Chinese artists and filmmakers (Chan and Willis 2012, 2014), the notion of Sinophone possesses a "more flexible position in regard to national identity and cultural affiliation" compared to the national and transnational metanarratives (Lu 2007). That is to say, the Sinophone framework offers a promising lens to examine Chinese cultures and communities across the globe and makes possible a less rigid approach compared to the geopolitical nationalism and regionalism previously favored by those in Asian studies and queer studies. In Shih's development of Sinophone, she gradually makes clear that Sinophone studies are concerned with Chinese cultures and communities "on the margins of China and Chineseness" (2010a, 29) and "on the margins of geopolitical nation-states and their hegemonic productions" (2011, 710). Sinophone studies are hence read by Ari Heinrich as "an inherently queer project" (2014, 3) that, not unlike queer theory, prioritize marginalized cultures while constantly questioning the identitarian essentialism (of sexuality, of Chineseness).

The conceptual connections between Sinophone studies and queer studies thus enable a new theoretical approach and methodological positioning described as *queer Sinophonicity* by Howard Chiang (2014a, 19–24) and Andrea Bachner (2014, 201–2). First, both "queer" and "Sinophone" draw our attention to the fluidity, diversity, and complexity of sexualities and cultures. They hence both offer enough conceptual flexibility for us to scrutinize the ever-changing sexual practices and contestations in Chinese cultures as "processes of becoming" rather than "states of being" (Bachner, 202). Second, queer Sinophonicity is a much more nuanced negotiation of the territorial-conceptual locations and dislocations of "queer Asia" and "queer regionalism," insomuch as it is based on linguistic-historical (rather than geographical and geopolitical) understandings of cultures and sexualities. Third, the marriage between queer theories and Sinophone theories empowers marginalized sexualities and communities in a common ground on the verge of heteronormativity and China-centrism.

Therefore, queer Sinophonicity offers a "minor-to-minor alliance" in both theory and methodology, to borrow Shih's (2014, 223) comments on the consideration and conceptualization of queer Sinophone cultures.

In this sense, mobility studies and Sinophone studies have found a mutual ground through queer theory in challenging and destabilizing the static and immobile views of geopolitical boundaries and categories as well as gender and sexuality. More important, the issue of migration and mobility is central to Sinophone's theories and ontologies, insomuch as Sinophone societies and communities are established upon historical mobilities that shifted Chinese émigrés and cultures from China to its diaspora. It is therefore inevitable to look at Sinophone cultures through the lens of mobilities and to consider queer Chinese cultural flows through the lens of Sinophone. Similar to my qualification of queer mobilities, "Sinophone mobilities" offers an expansive and flexible category through which we can better understand various forms of mobilities across geolocations, cultures, and social classes. However, the major concern of Sinophone theories is post-diasporic Chinese cultures and societies where immigrants have put down their roots to become local and their diaspora identity has expired and evaporated. That is to say, Sinophone theories are noticeably obsessed with settlement and rootedness, or when migrating routes have become post-migration roots (Shih 2010a, 46). This obsession with settlement in Sinophone theories and ontologies needs to be further questioned and queered (i.e., mobilized and destabilized) through the lens of queer mobilities.

In the previous chapter, I considered stretched kinship and homecoming and homemaking through autobiographical migration stories between mainland China and Sinophone Hong Kong. In the film *Amphetamine*, for example, Kafka and his family serve as a microcosm of mainland Chinese immigrants exiled to Hong Kong from the communist regime since the mid-twentieth century. Some of them had successfully settled in the then-British colony, whose descendants have become post-diasporic and local-born Sinophone Hongkongers. In contrast, many immigrants have remained at the bottom of the society, unable to fit in, secure a decent job, or achieve a full settlement to become local residents. A lot of them, as legal or illegal immigrants, have to struggle under the localist indifference and resentment. Unwanted in their homeland and unwelcome in the host society, people like Kafka never have a chance for settlement; alienated in the localist social (and sexual) hierarchy, they remain en route with a hope too slim to put down a permanent root. In the long journey to become post-diasporic Sinophone, they are also lost in migration and dead on arrival.

From this perspective, mobility is essentially a privilege that entails certain socioeconomic capital for the enactment of migration to be less risky. Recent scholarship has exhausted how mobilities come to represent inequality and exclusion across race, class, age, gender, power, and the very ability to move,[2] which conjointly mark the deeply entangled "politics of mobilities" that are concerned with the production and distribution of power through movement and migration (Cresswell 2010). The enactment of migration and the desire for settlement often entail and involve a certain level of social mobility that warrants settlement and residency. For those who arrived with little social, cultural, and economic capital, it is challenging to reestablish themselves and build or sustain a family. Even if they have survived the migration route, the regrounding process itself can be even more costly in the host society, given that the state and social support for immigrants are often limited and selective, if not negligent and indifferent. The promise of settlement through mobility may well be hindered by the lack of social mobility.

Through this lens, if the notion of "Sinophone mobilities" can help us make sense of China-originated migration and post-diasporic localization, then we must acknowledge that the social *immobility* has already precluded many disadvantaged migrants from settlement in the first place. The current Sinophone theories emphasize settlement and localization as the assumed outcome of mobility; however, I consider the routes and the processes of migration equally meaningful sites of queer cultural expressions and productions, especially given that many migrants never reached the point of settlement and residency in the host societies. This is why I am also skeptical about current mobility scholarship: even though social analysts in mobility studies acknowledge both positive and negative experiences in the emotionally embodied processes of movement, their scholarship tends to focus on those who have succeeded in migration. Those who have failed, returned, or died along the way and those who have been lost, wounded, or traumatized often do not have the chance to articulate their story and make their voice heard in the host societies. The failed or interrupted migrations have not caught enough attention in current mobility studies and Sinophone studies.

Thus, I argue that both Sinophone scholarship and mobility scholarship should further turn the spotlight to the contested and complicated migrating *routes* (motions and emotions, and pleasure and pain) in addition to the regrounded *roots* (settlement and localization), so as to enable a much richer and fuller appropriation of mobility experiences. In uprooting and regrounding, failures in mobilities are too well shadowed by successes. Not every migrant has reached the point of permanent settlement, but the unsettled bodies and desires have nonetheless generated unique and heterogeneous voices along their migration journeys. Routes and roads are equally important sites as home and destination in the productions of migrant cultures and emotional embodiments; rootlessness is no less salient than rootedness in the experiences and examinations of mobilities.[3] Between home and host societies, there exists a plurality of histories and stories, constituencies and contingencies, and experiences and expressions that are as powerful and meaningful in the nexus of geographical, cultural, and social mobilities. Non-settlement migrations like what we have seen in the autobiographical Sinophone Hong Kong films should be further examined and embraced in the atlas of "Sinophone mobilities."

To that end, let us not forget that "home" itself is never a fixed structure or entity but a contingent passage between the rooted conservatism and the endless faring of movement (Chambers 2001, 26, 188). Moving and mooring, uprooting and regrounding, mobility and immobility, and stability and instability all play important roles in the motivation and enactment of migration. The embodied queer emotions and desires are precisely born in the transitions between roots and routes and in the tensions between mobility and immobility. These emotions and desires are also "mobilized," so to speak, along with the bodily carriers of pleasure and pain in migration. In this regard, the very dualistic categories of "roots and routes," "home and host societies," and "origin and destination" should be further questioned and problematized, insomuch as they are mutually conditioned and often convertible in the mobilized experience of migration. Here, the appropriation of Sinophone mobilities can shed further light upon the complex formulations and interventions of queer mobilities.

Longing/Belonging

As we have seen in the previous chapter, "coming out to Sinophone Hong Kong" essentially constitutes a coming-out migration from mainland China in search of a more queer-friendly environment. In this sense, becoming Hong Kong, or becoming Sinophone, is a process to pursue sexual modernity and freedom that may not be available back in the homeland of China. The Sinophone sphere thus becomes the object of China's (queer) desire. However, not every Sinophone society is more tolerant and friendly towards queer sexualities and cultural expressions. Here I focus on the case of Sinophone Malaysia, where queer Chinese immigrants and descendants are both racial and sexual minorities, unlike other Sinophone societies like Singapore where the Chinese constitute the dominant ethnic group. Malaysia hence offers a strong case for us to understand Sinophone mobilities when queer cultures are compressed between racial and sexual inequalities and between the ancestral motherland and the post-diasporic home. I focus on the migration story and the cultural productions of Ti Bing-yen, an emerging filmmaker who has directed and distributed digital queer films across China and Malaysia, to scrutinize queer cultures and mobilities through both Malaysian Sinophonicities and their entanglements and engagements with mainland China.

Born in Kuala Lumpur, Ti completed his tertiary education in film production in Malaysia and China and works as a filmmaker in his hometown. What brings him to attention is *Exchange 2012* (*Tong Chuang Yi Meng*, 2011), a two-part short film that blends his own real-life story and a fantasy of homosexuals becoming the majority. Here, once again, a confessed personal past and a fantasized collective future have conjointly marked a semi-autobiographical queer story. This work won a short-film award at an international art festival in Malaysia and enjoyed an enthusiastic reception in China's cyberspace after Ti came to Beijing. *Exchange 2012* attracted over one million views combined on several Chinese video-sharing websites, and generated more comments from local Chinese viewers than from their Malaysian counterparts, according to a statement posted by Ti (2013b) on queer social media Feizan. He has since directed and released dozens of short films, music videos, short documentaries, docudramas, and advertisements, many of which are queer-related. Most of these visual creations were produced in Malaysia and a few in China, where he was a film student in Beijing. In these works, queer desires often entangle with family and kinship as well as heterosexual relationships, reminiscent of other Chinese-language queer films and digital videos examined in this book.

Ti's films saliently demonstrate a mobilized desire to cross the queer/non-queer boundaries to challenge the state racism and compulsory heteronormativity in Malaysia, as well as an underlying desire to cross the national and geographical boundaries to challenge the dominance of China in transnational Sinophone cultural productions and circulations. *Exchange 2012,* to begin with, imagines that the mass population turns into homosexuals while gays and lesbians become straight on the alleged 2012 Mayan Eschatological Day—hence an "exchange" and a reverse of the heteronormative sexual hierarchy. Ti adds another twist to the storyline: people who were born on that day will not be affected. Therefore, the two male protagonists in the film have retained their original sexual inclinations, respectively toward the same and the opposite sex. The heterosexual man thus suddenly becomes an outcast in the new socio-sexual order, while his best friend and secret lover has become part of the new normal.

The tension between the two unravels and reaches a climax when they confront each other with their innermost feelings. This scene is shot with a jerky hand-held camera on a gloomy day with a thunderstorm looming closer, through which we feel the tensions bursting out of the shaking frame. Only when one character begins to confide his deep-buried private feelings does the camerawork become steady—the confession and self-revelation seem to be a major relief that the camera also cools down to visually find its inner peace and give audiences a few moments to breathe (Figure 3.1). This is, however, not simply a coming-out scene. When the sexual hierarchy between homo- and heterosexuals has been reversed, who is coming out in this scene—the gay man or the straight man? Who is the queered *other* in this film? They are both left over by the exchange when other people have unknowingly switched their sexual preference and both mobilized by this sudden reversal of sexual hierarchy to expose their deep-buried emotions to each other.

This intense scene, furthermore, intercuts between the current confrontation and the flashbacks of their intimate memories before the exchange, where the

Figure 3.1 The confrontation scene in *Exchange 2012* (courtesy of the filmmaker)

boundaries between the past and the present, the normal and the abnormal, and the real and the imagined have been frequently crossed and transgressed. After *Exchange 2012* won the film award, Ti continued to produce a docudrama recounting the behind-the-scenes story of the making of the film. In this docudrama, he plays a minor role (a journalist), whereas the character based on his own real-life prototype is played by another actor. In addition, he is the director of both this docudrama and the film *mise en abîme*. In this case, the borders between the fictional and the non-fictional and between the narrator and the narrated are further blurred, through which an uncanny queer feeling emerges. Ti often opens his films with seemingly heteronormative characters and stories, before taking a dramatic turn to mobilize these characters and overturn their positions in the socio-sexual hierarchy between fantasy and reality and between the seemingly rigid gay-straight dichotomy.

This mobilized desire to transcend fixed sexual boundaries and narrative conventions has frequently manifested throughout Ti's film repertoire. In Ti's later comedy *Valentine's Package* (*Qingren Taocan*, 2013), for example, two heterosexual couples turn out to be two queer couples, while a straight man is mistaken by them as gay. Ti also directed *Same Love* (*Tong Fu Tong Qi*, 2013) in Beijing, a short film based on a video that had gone viral in China's cyberspace. In the original video, a Chinese woman suspected that her husband was cheating on her and tried to catch him and his mistress. She had her friend shoot the whole process with a video camera, and caught her husband cheating on her not with a woman but with a man. A conflict then erupted in front of the camera, and the recording of this real-life drama was uploaded to and widely circulated through local social media and video-sharing websites. This video parallels the increased public awareness and concern of *tong qi*—women who have unknowingly married homosexual men (see Chapter 1). Ti adapts this story in *Same Love* with a twist: a woman catches her husband cheating on her with a man, only to reveal that she herself is a closeted lesbian.

While the original video casts the gay man in a rather negative light as both sexually deviant and morally degraded, Ti's film reverses the story from an intense conflict and confrontation to a process of mutual coming out and mutual understanding. In this film, a seemingly heteronormative marriage turns out to be deeply problematic and a heterosexual couple turns out to be queer; the viewers' heteronormative assumption and expectation are first aroused and then contradicted. Overturned in this film is not only the woman's identity from straight to queer but also the gay man's role from the target of condemnation to an equal victim of compulsory heterosexuality. The real-life conflict thus becomes a bittersweet queer comedy in which homosexuality paradoxically functions as the ultimate salvation to a hopeless heterosexual marriage. From *Exchange 2012* to *Same Love*, the dramatic tension in Ti's films most noticeably derives from a mobilized queer desire to declare that gay and straight are equally normal—as much as equally queer—by destabilizing the boundaries between the two and frequently reversing their roles in the narrative and in the characters' own conceptions of queerness and straightness. Although Ti told me during my interview that he did not have a single theme running through his repertoire, most of his films unmistakably demonstrate a mobilized desire to challenge the dominant, compulsory heteronormativity in China and Malaysia.

Ti's works also demonstrate a strong tendency to write same-sex desires and marriage equality into the rubric of the family. In *Wedding Anniversary* (*Xi*, 2014), the protagonist talked emotionally in a flashback about his struggle and stretched experience that his attraction to men had disappointed his parents. But his grandmother, who had been unconditionally supportive, came to his same-sex wedding where other family members were absent. At his wedding anniversary in 2030 when he has become an old man, he is still very grateful for his grandmother while Malaysia is also turning into a more inclusive country. Here, the past confession and the imaginative future are enabled and connected by a successful queer homemaking, where the anchorage of love finds its structural support of kinship through the grandmother's blessing. The longevity of this fantasized same-sex relationship in turn becomes a vehicle through which the filmmaker actively imagines and calls for a more tolerant and inclusive future.

Ti's signature queer stories parallel his own experiences of migration as a queer Sinophone filmmaker. As a Chinese descendant born in Malaysia, Ti shows a very conscious awareness of a localized Malaysian identity. His self-introduction on the Chinese gay social media platform Feizan begins with "I am Ti Bing-yen, Malaysian" (2013a), while his digital profile also conspicuously states "Malaysian" as the tagline. These practices avoided any possible confusion about his nationality and self-portrayed national identity when he was in China. Along his migrating route between the two countries, Ti demonstrates a very clear post-diasporic identification that Sinophone theories have warmly celebrated—that the label of Chinese diaspora has expired and the Chinese descendants have become fully localized in the new country of residence (without losing the ancestral language). This strong sense of nationalist belonging also runs through Ti's works. Some of his (non-queer) films have a more native Malaysian focus and require local knowledge to understand. *Pray for Beng Hock* (*Quanjiafu*, 2013) is based on the tragic death of journalist and councilman-aide Teoh Beng Hock. Through this film, Ti calls for the Malaysian authorities to further investigate Teoh's suspicious "suicide" in 2009. Another short film, *Young Man* (*Nianqingren*, 2014), was produced in memory of Yasmin Ahmad, a late Malay director whose own films and alleged transgender and intersex past have been put under the spotlight for academic inquiry through the lens of queer Malaysian Sinophonicity (Hee and Heinrich 2014).

Furthermore, to understand Ti's story through queer Sinophone mobilities, we must first understand Malaysian Sinophonicities. Since its independence in 1957 and the establishment of the state religion, Islam, in 1963, Malaysia has witnessed a gradual revival of Islamic doctrine, ethics, and (sex-related) values (Teh 2008). Since then, non-conforming sexualities have been socially and religiously alienated and silenced by the increasingly heightened Islamization (Offord 2013).[4] The religious situation in Sinophone Malaysia is more complicated. The latest census in Malaysia has confirmed the popularity of Buddhism and Daoism, in lieu of Islam, among its Chinese population.[5] However, even though most Sinophone Malaysians are not bound by Islamic law, they are subject to the secular law that punishes homosexuality (Williams 2009, 6–7). For Sinophone Malaysians, queer desires and cultural expressions are still confined under Malaysia's legal and political ceilings.

A former British colony thirty percent of whose population is ethnically Chinese and Indian as a result of historical migrations and transnational mobilities, Malaysia's hybrid ontology arguably marks its plight in defining a monolithic national identity.[6] The state's economic, cultural, and religious policies established since the Sino-Malay sectarian strife in 1969 have been further marginalizing ethnic minorities. Today's Malaysian state shows a strong favoritism of *bumiputera*—literally "sons of the soil"—a political term that privileges Malays and other indigenous Malaysians over ethnic minorities of foreign origin (Yue 2008, 251).[7] In this case, Ti Bing-yen's nationalist identification with the country rather manifests as a Sinophone Malaysian identity, as distinctive from the *bumiputera*-centered state nationalism and racism, in a (supposedly) multicultural Malaysia. In other words, this is less an identity than a position—"a position of in-betweenness," as Kai-man Chang (2015, 255) comments on Sinophone Malaysian queer filmmaker Tsai Ming-Liang.

Malaysian Sinophonicities, as Hee and Heinrich (2014) point out, often take the form of a negotiation and a resistance against the *bumiputera* privilege and the (heteronormative) racial harmony pictured and imagined in state propaganda. In the long history of Chinese immigration to Southeast Asia, Chinese migrants and descendants have been struggling for over a century against a "dual domination," a concept developed by Ling-chi Wang (2006) to address Chinese diaspora. This dual domination comes from both Malaysia's state racism and the Chinese cultural essentialism, and from both the local nation's refusal and the increased pressure from China's rise on regional and global stages (see also Shih 2010a, 48; 2011, 714). Ti's clear nationalist identification with Malaysia and his local focus in filmmaking demonstrate a strong longing and craving for the nation to proclaim local Sinophone filmmakers as equally genuine and socially responsible Malaysian citizens. As Yuen-Beng Lee (2012) reminds us, today's Malaysian digital filmmakers like Ti, who are urban-born and educated overseas at tertiary level, often show a strong willingness to tell local stories and express their discontent about Malaysia's social and sexual inequity. Seldom before seen in the local film history, the ethnic and cultural diversities of the country are directly portrayed in their works (Muthalib 2007). Ti Bing-yen's films, in this context, constitute a site of negotiation and resistance and a clear homonationalist desire towards the nation-state to claim equal ethnic and sexual citizenship—that both ethnic minorities (as Chinese) and sexual minorities (as queer) are equal citizens in Malaysia.

This queer Sinophone longing for a homonationalist belonging potentially destabilizes the *bumiputera* ethnocentrism and heteronormativity to mobilize a queer Sinophone articulation facing Malaysia's state racism and homophobia. Ti's claim for equal love and equal nuptial rights in his films not only voices an activist demand but articulates an implicit call for the state's acceptance (love) and recognition (equality) of ethno-sexual minorities. Today's queer Malaysian Sinophonicities inherently entail a mobility to cross the state-regulated racial and sexual boundaries, as reflected through Ti's works, and to destabilize the rigid ethno-sexual categories for more flexible and inclusive racial and sexual relations. In this case, queerness and Sinophonicities are mutually mobilizing and mobilized, and empowering and empowered, in their "minor-to-minor alliance" born from the in-between position of longing and belonging. Queer Sinophonicities, from this point of view, are essentially a mobilized desire to mediate and mitigate the state discrimination against the local Sinophone community and to challenge the assumed heteronormative racial harmony.

Further, Ti's case has also demonstrated a queer Sinophone mobility to cross the border between Sinophone Malaysia and mainland China to challenge another side of the dual domination: China-centrism. Studying film production in Beijing, Ti not only made the aforementioned *Same Love* with a local team but also brought his Sinophone Malaysian films to China. Many of his digital films are circulated through China's online social media and various queer film festivals and communal screenings, allowing viewers to directly experience queer Sinophone Malaysian cultures on local film screens. The enthusiastic local reception of his films shows that a young filmmaker from a "peripheral" and "marginal" overseas Sinophone community is fully capable of making his voice heard in the ancestral Chinese motherland. Ti's post-diasporic Sinophone root, that is to say, has once again become a mobilized migrating route back to mainland China. China has therefore become a site where mobilized queer Sinophone Malaysian cultures find an audience and generate a voice.

However, such geographical and cultural mobilities through migration and film distribution also reveal a Sinophonic conjuncture and disjuncture that further problematize Sinophone's phonic/linguistic root. According to Ti, Sinophone Malaysians often have trilingual literacy in Malay (the official language), English (a postcolonial residue), and Chinese (a post-diasporic legacy). But "Chinese" as a linguistic category encompasses a large number of different dialects spoken by the Chinese population in Malaysia. In Ti's case, he speaks fluent Mandarin along with basic Cantonese and Hokkien, two major Chinese dialects common in Southeast Asia.[8] The Romanization of his name ("Ti Bing-yen") is based on the Hokkien pronunciation, while in China his name is spelled and pronounced differently as Zheng Binyan in Standard Mandarin (Putonghua). This presents the first indication of a Sinophonic disjuncture in transnational migrations and queer cultural flows between China and the Southeast Asian Sinophone sphere.

Furthermore, the language used in most of Ti's films is Malaysian Mandarin, characterized by its unique accent and lexicon that are different from that of Putonghua, the official language in today's PRC. Film viewers in China, me included, sometimes still need subtitles to fully understand the dialogue in Ti's works. While these films were not intentionally produced for an international audience, the mobilized transnational flows of queer Sinophone cultures have brought local content to an international stage, where the shared "Mandarin" linguistic root alone is not enough for audiences in China to decipher Ti's films. Echoing Song Hwee Lim's writing in a relevant context (2008b, 12), the Sinophone Malaysian dialogue in Ti's works sometimes remains "too local" to become decipherable for non-local audiences. On queer social media Feizan and China's prestigious review website Douban, many comments from local viewers focus on the unfamiliar Malaysian-accented Mandarin in Ti's films. In addition, the video-sharing sites in China appear to attract only local viewers commenting in simplified Chinese, the PRC's official writing system, while Ti's audiences on YouTube apparently come from a more diverse linguistic background and have commented in English and both traditional and simplified Chinese.

If the reception of Ti's films outside the PRC demonstrates a multilingual Sinophone mobility across a wide spectrum of "Chinese languages," then the case of mainland China rather presents a monolingual immobility isolated in transnational queer cultural flows. That is to say, Sinophone Malaysian films have become a queer linguistic *other*, easily picked up by Chinese audiences as foreign to China and to the local understanding of Chineseness. This linguistic version of China-centrism is worsened by the cyber-isolationism enforced by the Chinese state and strongly contrasts Ti's own multilingual Sinitic-language proficiency and YouTube viewers' diverse linguistic backgrounds.[9] In this regard, this phonic disjuncture potentially destabilizes China's strong monolingual dominance and its monolithic construction of Chineseness. The Sinophonic language (Malaysian Mandarin) in Ti's films challenges and mobilizes both the Malay/English dominance in Malaysia and the Putonghua dominance in China.

However, Ti's multilingual background and the online comments on his films written in different languages also demonstrate that the Sinophone sphere itself is full of such phonic/linguistic contradictions and displacements among various Chinese dialects and accents. Beng Huat Chua (2012, 35) pointedly asks, while Francophone refers to French and Anglophone to English, which Sinitic language does the "Sino" in "Sinophone" refer to—Mandarin, Cantonese, Hokkien, or other Chinese dialects?[10] Moreover, to what extent can the Sino/phonic conjuncture and disjuncture transcend the "indecipherable localism" (Lim 2008b) in transnational cultural flows? In "The Voice of the Sinophone," Lim further questions the very linguistic centering in the theorizations of Sinophone and calls for a more inclusive scope (verbal and non-verbal, diegetic and non-diegetic, and aural and visual) in the study of Sinophone cultures (2014, 72–74). In so doing, argues Lim, we are able to undo the "Sino" linguistic root in the Sinophone to further embrace today's transnational queer migrations and cultural mobilities, as seen in Ti's case.

But Sinophone theories still face a linguistic crisis, as seen in my interview with Ti, completed in English and Mandarin. The translation and understanding (as well as possible mistranslation and misunderstanding) between us reveal an even more deep-rooted dilemma in Sinophone studies. Regardless of the languages that Ti has adopted for film production and I have chosen for interview, every finding of this research and every piece of information under scrutiny have to be presented in English, should I publish this research in "international" academia. The very concept of Sinophone is theorized and developed in English, not in any Chinese languages that Sinophone as a conceptual category encompasses. Sinophone studies as a discipline often presents itself in Anglophone scholarship and hence casts itself out from its own linguistic territory. It has largely failed to mobilize and destabilize the "English-language hegemony" (Wilson 2006, 2) in Asian studies and queer studies, nor does it make Chinese-language cultures more presentable on the international stage in their own voices.

Nonetheless, the marriage between Sinophone theories and queer theories enables a unique lens to scrutinize migrations and mobilized cultural flows, as seen in Ti Bing-yen's case.[11] As a non-Malay Malaysian filmmaker and a non-Chinese Chinese descendant, Ti speaks up with his hybrid and mobilized identity against both sides of the dual domination: the *bumiputera* ethnocentrism and heteronormativity in Malaysia and the China-centrism that often neglects Chinese cultures and languages outside the PRC. Situated between longing and belonging, and between mainland China and Sinophone Malaysia, the geographical and cultural mobilities shown through Ti's case add a Sinophonic note to our considerations of queer mobilities. Here, the concept of Sinophone mobilities has enabled a lens through which we can consider the generation and circulation of queer cultures out of and in between national and transnational identities, as well as how the "post-diasporic" Sinophone cultures and descendants have become once again mobilized to engage both the local state and the ancestral Chinese motherland. In this case, the real and imagined boundaries between mainland China and the Sinophone sphere have been increasingly destabilized by the post-diasporic Sinophone mobilities, when the descendants of historical Chinese émigrés move back to China and choose the latter as a site for queer cultural production and articulation.

Cultural Flows/Counterflows

To better understand and make sense of today's Sinophone mobilities, we need to turn the spotlight away from the traditional, one-dimensional understanding of migration and cultural flows out of China that led to the historical formations of overseas Sinophone cultures. We should instead focus on the multidimensional mobilities including migration and cultural flows from Sinophone communities back to China—a kind of "counterflows" of Sinophone cultures, so to speak, back to their ancestral origin. Through this lens, China itself becomes a site and a platform for Sinophone cultural productions, as seen in Ti Bing-yen's case above, as well as in a Taiwanese gay-friendly coffee house and film club in the center of Beijing. In this case, the film club itself has turned into a place that encompasses mobilized Sinophone cultural flows and counterflows, which further blurs the boundaries between mainland China and the Sinophone sphere. Such an urban queer enclave accordingly becomes a queer public space that is conditioned and structured by various types of mobilities.

Named Two-City Café (*Shuang Cheng Kafei*), this coffee house and film club was established in 2012 by Ah-Jer (Lai Jeng-jer) and Yeh-tzu (Yeh Chien-te). The story of Two-City Café evolved from almost two decades ago when *tongzhi* activism and other social movements concerned with identity, lifestyle, and culture blossomed in Taiwan (Sang 2014, 52–53). Ah-Jer and Yeh-tzu traveled from Taiwan to the US in the late 1990s to visit the local gay scenes and indulge themselves in American gay cultures. Inspired by a gay bookshop in New York, Ah-Jer returned to Taiwan and founded the iconic Gin-Gin Bookstore in 1999, the first LGBT bookshop in the Chinese world, and remained in charge until early 2011. Yeh-tzu went to graduate school and then opened a restaurant but also left his business in 2011. The duo decided to continue the around-the-world trip that they had left behind over a decade before, which eventually brought them to Beijing. Their global and cross-strait mobilities led to today's Sinophone Taiwanese cultural articulation and reproduction in mainland China.

Yeh-tzu had visited Beijing twice at the turn of the twenty-first century and was impressed by how fast China was growing. He also learned that Beijing had gone through significant transformations since the 2008 Olympic Games and was eager to see the city again. When I interviewed Yeh-tzu and talked with Ah-Jer in their tastefully decorated coffee house, Yeh-tzu thought China's unprecedented growth provided a once-in-a-lifetime opportunity that attracted people like them for temporary or permanent settlement. In addition, since the Chinese Nationalist Party regained leadership in Taiwan's 2008 election and began to ameliorate its relationship with mainland China, the two sides have reached a number of agreements to facilitate cross-strait flows of capital and people.[12] These are the underlying reasons for the "sudden" interest of Ah-Jer and Yeh-tzu in mainland China. They made their decision to stay in Beijing and opened the coffee house with weekly film screenings and other communal activities in late 2012. Here, the issue of mobilities surrounding Two-City Café is multifold: first, it has mobilized and engaged queer and non-queer desires in its inclusive space-making; second, it makes possible a community of intimate strangers in a public space situated in the center of intra-city and inter-city mobilities; on top of that, it connects the flows of people and cultures between mainland China and Sinophone Taiwan and opens up new avenues to renegotiate the often sedentary conceptions of settlement and localization.

The inclusiveness of Two-City Café, to begin with, has distinguished this coffee house from other queer spaces and film clubs in Beijing. Yeh-tzu made it clear during my interview that he and Ah-Jer intended to follow the "continental European tradition" to establish a salon-style and inclusive public space, as coffee houses traditionally played an important role in public intellectual discussions and in the formation of public spheres in Europe. Having a background respectively in urban planning and architecture, Yeh-tzu and Ah-Jer collaborated with a Taiwanese interior designer who used to work in Europe to design the coffee house (Figure 3.2). They have been promoting the coffee house as gay-friendly but not gay-exclusive. There is no sign whatsoever inside and outside Two-City Café that announces its connection to queer cultures; people in Beijing's gay circles have either heard about the coffee house through word of mouth or learned about its film screenings through queer social media such as Feizan and ZANK. In addition, as a commercial space, its survival still largely depends on its ability to make a stable profit from a wider range of customers, not only from a relatively narrow gay market. Compared to other queer film clubs located in small NGO offices hidden in residential compounds, a commercial coffee house

Figure 3.2 The interior of Two-City Café in Beijing

like this also offers a more relaxing and enjoyable space for dating and social networking.

Yeh-tzu shared with me a story about a local gay man who proposed to his boyfriend in this coffee house. He asked Ah-Jer and Yeh-tzu for help beforehand, and together they designed and rehearsed a romantic proposal. Then, during the discussion after a film screening session in the coffee house, Ah-Jer asked him and his boyfriend to share their stories. The man then proposed to his boyfriend, while Ah-Jer started to play a love song and served a cake to the couple, and this intimate story had a happy ending. Ah-Jer also asked other customers on-site to share their feelings of this romantic proposal and offer their good wishes for the gay couple. Some people were invited in advance, while others happened to be in the coffee house that night. Hosts and guests, participants and onlookers, and the invited and the unsolicited—all of them to various degrees became involved in the scene to jointly create and witness a live queer narrative:

> Yeh-tzu: *We do not promote our café as a* "tongzhi *coffee house" . . . Public spaces should remain public . . . When this [the proposal] was happening, we had other*

> *customers walking into the coffee house—some of them were gay and some were not—and they were watching [with interest] . . . Together we created a utopian public space for social interactions.*

It is precisely from this perspective that I argue it may not be adequate, or indeed relevant, to understand queer film clubs like Two-City Café as counterpublic queer spaces. The notion of counterpublics, or "where members of subordinated social groups invent and circulate counterdiscourses" (Fraser 1992, 123), designates a subordinate and oppositional status of queer publics that marks themselves off from the mainstream cultural horizon (Warner 2002, 119). This understanding firmly pinpoints queer publics in an inferior and somewhat sedentary position, offering little room for them to transgress and transcend the queer/non-queer boundaries to extend and engage, and interact and intersect, with mainstream cultures beyond the so-called "counterdiscourses." Similarly, in early mobility studies and humanistic geographies, public queer spaces were also upheld in this kind of tandem, oppositional binary between queer spatial right and heterosexual spatial privilege (see Bell and Valentine 1995; Binnie 1997; Valentine 2002). Queer spaces are hence often inadequately understood as counterpublic battlefields where sexual minorities claim territories from straight people's colonization and occupancy.

However, this liberalist consideration of queer space as counterpublic space has left intact a normative and oppositional model of heterosexuality versus homosexuality, leading to a rigid and immobile understanding of queer publics as subordinate and minoritarian vis-à-vis the dominant heterosexual spatial entitlement. This "normative opposition" fails to catch "queer contestations and transgressions as always potentially fleeting, recuperated and fluid" (Browne 2006, 888). If space has a sexualized identity, then such identity should not be seen as simply a struggle between the subordinate/alternative and the dominant/mainstream (Hubbard 2000, 211). At any rate, the conceptualization of queer space as "dissident space, resistant space, progressive space, colonized space or claimed space" is essentializing and essentialized by an assumed counterpublic queer opposition against the mainstream (Oswin 2008, 91). If sexual norms do much more than marginalizing homosexuals, then it is important to "challenge the notion that homosexualities are always and everywhere 'alternative' as it is to challenge the perception of heterosexualities as always and everywhere 'dominant'" (98). This is more attentive to the public construction of queer space in understanding the entangled spatialities and sexualities through the material realities of places and spaces (Oswin 2010, 129; 2012, 1627).

Therefore, I propose to consider queer space-making through the dual lens of spatialities and mobilities, when such queer spaces as Two-City Café are hardly subordinate or countercultural but instead at the forefront of geographical and cultural mobilities. This approach questions the sedentary conception of queer space and calls into attention the mobilized fluidity and flexibility in the cultural politics of space-making. I see queer public spaces as spatiotemporal entities that mobilize the encompassed and embodied emotions and intimacies through cultural intersections and transgressions. This understanding is attentive to both spatiotemporal migration and movement as well as cultural mobilities and cultural flows that help reproduce and enrich the meaning of queer public spaces. Through this lens, a queer space like Two-City Café is inherently a public space embodied with and conditioned by different types of mobilities. Here, it is not only that the physical space itself serves as a rendezvous point in a network of intra-city and inter-city mobilities that bring together local customers and Taiwanese visitors; rather, the fixity of the film club as a material space and the mobility of its participants are mutually conditioned to conjointly structure the mobilization of the embodied desires and intimacies.

More specifically, a public space functions as an intersectional point of queer mobilities in a migrant city like Beijing, whose value lies primarily in its contribution to building an intimate space and "a community of intimate strangers" (Wilken 2010; Shah 2012). A sense of intimate belonging often emerges in this film club that enables a special kind of social bonding, however ad hoc and volatile, among the participants who share the common experience of migration and face the localist indifference in this host city. In the screening sessions I attended, the discussions often extended from comments on films to our own memories and stories of movements. My field notes from October 2014, for instance, have recorded how the embodied experiences of mobilities have been shared and articulated in this queer space:

> We started to talk about Beijing's localist discrimination against migrants from other places . . . We opened up to share our experiences, both good and bad, and the discussion became a transient yet intimate moment before we left the film club at the end of the night. Many of us would probably never see each other again, but our heart and soul came together and our memories became integrated. We caught a glimpse of each other's life and at the same time became part of it through our encounters.

That is to say, participants of urban queer film clubs like Two-City Café often come from different walks of life with different geographical origins, whose paths otherwise barely cross and roads seldom intersect. The film club effectively brings these strangers together, through which a queer sense of intimacy emerges that we do not know each other but are nonetheless intimate and connected through our shared experiences and emotions. We are all passengers traveling through this queer space yet carrying the embodied memories and intimacies that are often mutually recognizable and identifiable. From long-term participants to casual visitors and customers, our connections are constantly forged and forgotten, built and rebuilt, grouped and regrouped, visited and revisited—and hence mobilized rather than fixed and stable—in this intimate urban enclave.

A mobility-embodied and mobility-enriched public space like this offers both a physical and an emotional space for the frequent and yet ad hoc encounters. It may never be a destination but provides an all-important place to temporarily accommodate and connect our past and present stories, memories, and intimacies. While the material space offers precarious groundings for the traveling bodies as carriers of emotions and experiences, it is the underlying relentless mobilities that bring people to and from this space, through which a community of intimate strangers comes into being. Echoing my earlier argument in this book, settlement and grounding often appear temporary for queer migrants, while mobility rather looks persistent when they keep floating between the impossible homemaking and the impossible homecoming. A queer public space, in this regard, presents an everywhere important "home"—or an alternative kinship circle as I have discussed—to house and host the unsettled and mobilized bodies and desires between the home of origin and the home of destination. If Sinophone mobilities are situated in an in-between position, then a queer public space like this also situates in an intimate network of strangers as a heterotopic non-place that may be ephemeral but nonetheless important.

Echoing my analysis is Yeh-Tzu's account that the coffee house is brought to life by the random encounters as well as the stories and intimacies born from within. This is apparently different from other queer film clubs in Beijing such as Concentric Circle (that resembles a counseling group; see Chapter 1) and the Fellowship of *Tongzhi* Film-Lovers (that predominantly focuses on cinematic art; see Chapter 5).[13] A queer public space like this serves as a platform for intimate encounters, both queer and non-queer, and for the establishment and extension of human connections, both long and transient. Two-City Café hence enables a space where such encounters keep flowing. It harbors diverse migrating and traveling bodies and emotions in a city like Beijing with a large floating population and many temporary visitors and residents. It is these mobilized encounters and interactions that have been constantly rewriting and redefining the meaning of this queer space. In Yeh-tzu's words:

> *We hope to provide a space supported by the people and the stories behind it . . . If we have more spaces like this in the city, or if they become prevalent, then people can rethink themselves and* others *from a new perspective [Yeh-tzu said "*others*" in English]. These* others *could be* tongzhi, *could be women, and could be marginalized urban dwellers. We hope this [rethinking] can be materialized in our space.*
>
> *Against the backdrop of globalization, inter-city mobilities have become a common experience . . . Different people come to our space with different embodiments. The "city" is a metaphor and in itself an organic body. Different bodies come from different cities, communicating with each other, and competing and collaborating with each other, entangled and stretched in shared love [and intimacies].*[14]

This is where emotions and embodiments become preponderant in the experiences and expressions of mobilities (Gorman-Murray 2009, 2012) and in the formations of intimate spaces beyond the mere queer and non-queer opposition (Oswin 2008, 2012). A public space as an ad hoc community of intimate strangers is deeply engaged with the emotionally embodied mobility and fluidity across time and space when the city itself is embodied with a diverse range of experiences, identities, and desires, thanks to the increasingly frequent migrations and cultural flows underlined by China's rapid development. These newly emerged intimate spaces and networks are conditioned and contextualized by the larger social transformations when China is turning from "a society of acquaintances" to "a society of strangers," as formerly established social connections have been reconfigured by the neoliberal privatization of the economy, family, individual life, and social network. This is redolent of the surged popularity of online and mobile queer social media where social relations and interactions often start from strangers and become mobilized by unexpected encounters. Individuals freed from fixed and established social connections and institutions thus become more active in exercising their agency to choose and join in different cultural and consumer spaces to forge new and more flexible communities and networks. An intimate public space like the coffee house becomes a place that accommodates and connects these individual strangers who are attracted to each other partially because they are strangers bearing different emotions and embodiments. The meaning of queer spatialities is hence constantly renegotiated and redefined through queer mobilities in collective queer space-making.

On top of that, where Sinophone mobilities are concerned, Two-City Café has been developing around a Taiwanese theme and collaborating with a range of businesses and individuals to promote Taiwanese cultures. Ah-Jer and Yeh-tzu not only serve Taiwanese coffee and drinks as well as large numbers of Taiwanese books and magazines for the local customers, but also invite scholars and artists from Taiwan for seminars and exhibitions, sometimes with a focus on gender and sexuality. Many movies they have chosen to show in the film club were also made in Taiwan, while the differences and similarities between Beijing's and Taipei's queer cultures often become a focal point in post-screening discussions. It is also in this sense that the coffee house and film club become deeply involved in the increasingly mobilized cross-strait cultural flows and counterflows that further destabilize the boundaries and mobilize the connections between the two locales. Ah-Jer and Yeh-tzu hold the belief that mainland China and Sinophone Taiwan can mutually empower each other in developing, mobilizing, and constructing a more inclusive future that overcomes their rivalry beyond historical isolation. Here, cross-strait migrations and cultural flows have and will continue to play an important role in connecting the two societies in an intimate network of mobilities, where the two sides are also "intimate strangers" based on their historical and ongoing connection and separation, as well as their resemblance and difference.

As a queer public space that connects Beijing and Taipei in a cultural network, Two-City Café itself becomes a site for Sinophone Taiwanese cultural articulation and reproduction—a small but nonetheless important outlet that engenders and empowers "minoritarian" queer Sinophonicities in the heart of mainland China. Meanwhile, the café also turns into an object of China's gaze and desire when local customers come to the coffee house with an active consumerist appetite for Taiwanese cultures and products. Marketed as "the closest window to Taiwan" for local customers and "the first stop of Taiwanese visitors to Beijing" for travelers, Two-City Café has become a popular transfer station and transit point for migrants and tourists alike. Itself an outcome of Sinophone mobilities, the coffee house as an intimate public space has connected the two cities and the two sides across the strait in a network of mobilities, which in turn constitutes part of the larger Sinophone cultural nexus and transnational East Asian migrations and cultural flows.[15]

Furthermore, for the two coffee-house owners, queer issues and geopolitics often conjointly mark a minoritarian identity that differentiates queer Taiwanese Sinophonicities from queer people and queer cultures in continental China:

> Yeh-tzu: *Taiwan has been on the cultural margin since ancient times and never in the geopolitical center . . . The marginality of Taiwan and the marginality of* tongzhi *at some point become intersected—a double marginality of identity. For a* tongzhi *from Taiwan, it is this [double] marginality that allows him to see things differently.*

Contrary to the PRC's large continental territory and geopolitical power, Taiwan has long been a marginalized island on the periphery of the Asia-Pacific. The marginality of Taiwan mirrors the marginalized queer people and queer cultures—a "minor-to-minor alliance" in Sinophone mobilities, if we once again borrow Shu-mei Shih's words (2014). Yeh-tzu also thoughtfully contemplated that, although Taiwanese people were often seen as "others" by local Beijing residents, if he fell in love with Beijing and settled in this city, would he become "local"?

This echoes my critique of the obsession of Sinophone theories with spatiotemporal settlement and localization in the formulation of the Sinophone cultural sphere. Specifically, how "local" is local enough to count as "localized," and how long is long enough to qualify as "post diasporic"? Shih argues that Sinophone studies, albeit comparative and transnational, are "everywhere attentive to the specificity of time-and-place" (2010a, 29). However, I wonder whether temporal and spatial markers alone are sufficient in legitimating an imagined Sinophone sphere. For Shu-mei Shih, the diaspora has an end date, which is vaguely pinned down at the second or the third generation, when the descendants of the immigrants have become localized but still speak their ancestor tongues (45). That means, paradoxically, this localization process does not allow a complete linguistic localization. This hence confines Sinophone theories and ontologies in a rather narrow scope, constituted only by those who have erased their diaspora identity but not their diasporic language. Once the descendants stop speaking the ancestral tongues, they no longer qualify as "Sinophone." Then how do we conceptualize and scrutinize their struggles and stories, when they are not fully diaspora, not linguistically Sinophone, and not ethnically local? Moreover, do those who have returned to and settled in mainland China still count as "Sinophone," or perhaps "counter-Sinophone" or "post-Sinophone"?

In addition, the "local/non-local" and the "diasporic/post-diasporic" seldom constitute homogeneous categories. In Taiwan, for example, it has long been debated which languages count as "ancestral tongues" (Ho-lo/Taiwanese Hakka, Taiwanese Hokkien, Taiwanese Mandarin, etc.) as well as who qualifies as "local" in Taiwan's hybrid ontology (*benshengren, waishengren, yuanzhumin, xinzhumin*, etc.). Throughout this chapter, I have adopted "Sinophonicity" in its plural form, since there does not exist a single point of arrival of heterogeneous languages and cultures, even within a given Sinophone society. Here, the notion of Sinophonicities and that of Sinophone mobilities (1) better address the ever-changing and increasingly mobile queer cultures, (2) further embrace the instabilities and contradictions embedded in migrations and cultural flows, and (3) offer more conceptual flexibility in scrutinizing Sinophone cultures in their complex and strategic entanglements with China and "Chineseness." If the concept of queer Sinophonicities offers "a different genealogy that challenges Chinese studies (with its China-centrism) and queer studies (with its Western-centrism)" (Shih 2014, 223), then such marginalized positioning itself testifies for the geopolitical power asymmetries and the uneven cultural flows between China and the Sinophone sphere and between the West and the East. A "minor-to-minor alliance" of queer studies and Sinophone studies does not necessarily guarantee a stronger methodology, if we do not embrace the embedded mobilities to challenge and problematize the sedentary conceptions of settlement and localization.

Moreover, the theorization of queer Sinophonicities still faces an internal dilemma: if procreation is a precondition of Sinophone theories and ontologies that are only attentive to the second/third-generation immigrants, then "queer" and "Sinophone" are inherently contradictory, insomuch as queer non-procreation is unproductive of and irrelevant to the multigenerational formation of Sinophone communities that necessitates heterosexual reproduction. In this sense, queer Sinophonicities still present an incomplete project. More important, Sinophone theories have so far failed to account for the localization process of first-generation immigrants, even though some of them have become "localized enough" and no longer consider themselves migrants or diaspora. The same can be said for those proficient in local languages and no longer relying on Chinese in everyday life, as shown in Hongwei Bao's autoethnography (2013) that resonates with Ien Ang's *On Not Speaking Chinese* (2001). This is reminiscent of Chan and Willis's critique that Sinophone theories fail to address diaspora Chinese cultures produced and articulated not in Chinese languages (2012, 2014).

That is to say, there still exist some missing pieces in the formulations of Sinophone theories and ontologies that are inattentive to the many diverse forms of cultures and mobilities that have been precluded from the imagined Sinophone sphere. Here, I do not mean that "Sinophone" has to become an umbrella term that accounts for all possible types of mobilities before and after historical immigrations and settlements; rather, for Sinophone theories to become a meaningful conceptual and methodological framework, we need to know its contingent boundaries and in what sense and to what degree such boundaries can be crossed and destabilized. This is particularly important when the unsettling and unpredictable mobilities of queer desires contribute to refiguring the sedentary default of settlement and localization. The Sinophone framework, in other words, needs to be more critically examined and problematized through the lens of queer mobilities.

Furthermore, positioning a diverse range of Sinitic cultures and languages into a single conceptual framework risks building an "imagined community" (Anderson [1983] 2006, 6–7; Walsh 1996, 5–17). This risk emerges at two levels. At the global level, as Arjun Appadurai (1996, 40) comments in a different context, the sense of nationhood, or that of common belonging, is increasingly transcending state boundaries when the scattered and stretched identities of a transnational diaspora have been activated to imagine a community. At the level of individual societies, each Sinophone society is not a monolithic entity but full of contested and mobilized cultures and experiences. That is to say, while Sinophone theories insightfully break up from the monolithic view of Chineseness to empower the marginalized Chinese cultures beyond state boundaries, its overarching coverage of scattered and stretched Sinitic-language cultures may also construct a Sinophone sphere in the form of an imagined community.

The position of China in this imagined Sinophone sphere is also under debate. While Shu-mei Shih has included ethnic minorities in Han-dominated China in the Sinophone (2011), Audrey Yue suggests that the often-marginalized queer cultures inside China should be synthesized into the Sinophone sphere as well (2012a). In any case, the cultural heterogeneity within China and the minority cultures inside the country can be equally empowered by Sinophone theories. Indeed, there is little point in debating China's position in the Sinophone sphere if we treat China as a monolithic entity, since in so doing we are trapped in the same geographical and geopolitical essentialism that Sinophone theories aim to transcend in the first place. At any rate, China is also the beneficiary of global queer cultural flows from other regions (Yue and Khoo 2012, 9–13), while the counterflows of cultures and people from Sinophone societies back to China further problematize China's role in the nexus of geographical and cultural mobilities. In "Transnational Queer Sinophone Cultures," Fran Martin pointedly argues that mainland China has been increasingly interlinked into the transnational Sinophone cultural network; therefore, "in a practical sense, it becomes harder than ever to conceive of mainland Chinese queer cultural life as sealed off from that of Sinophone queer communities outside China" (2015, 43). Both in theory and in practice, it is counterproductive to completely detach Sinophone cultures from mainland China, or China from the Sinophone sphere, when they are deeply connected not only in histories but also in a growing intimate network of mobilities.

Overall, from Sinophone Malaysia to Sinophone Taiwan, the queer migrations and cultural mobilities discussed in this chapter have bridged the oppositional, dualistic categories of queer and non-queer, local and non-local, and China and the Sinophone to make them once again mobilized and intimate to engage and interact with each other. Sinophone theories, despite various internal and contextual limits, offer a productive instrument for our investigation of queer cultures through the conceptual lens of queer Sinophonicities and Sinophone mobilities. Here, the very dichotomy of "flows" and "counterflows" should be further challenged, when the spatiotemporal movements of people and cultures have become increasingly frequent and fluid as well as multidimensional. Cultural mobilities, as inseparable constituents of the queer mobilities under scrutiny, saliently transcend the real and imagined geographical and geopolitical boundaries in the emotionally embodied experiences and expressions of migrations. The imbricated geographical and cultural mobilities are further conditioned and structured by social mobilities and immobilities, which this book further considers in the next two chapters.

4
The Myth of Quality

When kinship is often stretched by the emotionally embodied migrations in the intermingled geographical and cultural mobilities, one underlying question remains unanswered: who can afford such mobilities and what drives them to move? In this case, the rhetoric of *suzhi*/quality led by the party-state in the PRC and its lingering social influence may help us understand the pursuit of individual human capital and class migration in today's post-socialist queer China. If the desire for personal quality and upward social mobility is what drives people to leave the family and embark on migration journeys, then those who come from socially advantaged backgrounds are more likely to succeed in and continue for such social mobilization. In the case of China, its strong and continued economic growth in the recent decades has also produced a large rising and aspirational middle class. Here, the myth of *suzhi*/quality not only underlies and underlines queer migrations and stretched kinship but also reproduces larger social stratification and class hierarchy among sexual minorities, which is central to the understanding of today's queer Chinese cultures, communities, and mobilities.

Post-*suzhi* Human Capital

Loosely translated as "quality," the term *suzhi* has long been a major subject in the study of post-socialist China. In Lisa Rofel's early ethnography of Beijing's gay community (1999), she notes that urban gay men used the term *suzhi* to distinguish themselves from rural-to-urban migrant "money boys" (gay prostitutes). The prostitutes were often degraded as low-*suzhi*/low-quality migrants who "polluted" Beijing's gay scene and gay culture (Rofel, 466–67; see also Kong 2011b). Since then, the myth of *suzhi* has become a ghostly discourse haunting the studies of China's queer cultures and communities as seen in Bao (2011a, 135), Ho (2010, 89–97), Rofel (2007, 85–110; 2010, 453), and more recently Chiang (2014b, 364). However, as Goodman (2014, 109) points out after Anagnost (2004), the term *suzhi* is hard to define given its wide use in various social and political domains with changing connotations and unstable boundaries.

The portmanteau term *suzhi* has a long history in the Chinese lexicon. *Su* refers to a white or light color, often connoting purity and originality, and *zhi* means texture or quality. A famous example of *suzhi* is seen in ancient poet Du Fu's verse *White Silk* (*Bai Si Xing*) in which he mourns that, once silk is dyed with color, it will lose its original whiteness and pureness, or what he calls *suzhi*. His lament is directed not only towards dyed silk but also to people who have lost their natural "purity" in the corrupted society. In this sense, *suzhi* refers to the original quality of a person or a thing that has not been altered, dyed, or polluted.[1] This meaning of *suzhi* was still evident in Maoist and post-Mao eugenics for "better reproduction and better upbringing" (*yousheng youyu*) to create higher-*suzhi* citizens (Yan 2008, 114), where "quality" was seen as firstly inborn and then subject to nurture and upbringing.

The meaning of *suzhi* continued to change towards the end of the twentieth century. During the Seventh Five-Year Plan for Economic Development from 1986 to 1990, *suzhi* was a prominent concept across two related domains of governance: morality and ethics (*jingshen wenming*) and family planning (*jihua shengyu*). On 28 September 1986, the Chinese Communist Party (CCP) released a resolution on socialist morality and ethics, where "ideological and moral *suzhi*" (*sixiang daode suzhi*) and "scientific and cultural *suzhi*" (*kexue wenhua suzhi*) appeared hand in hand as key factors in improving the quality of China's population.[2] In an analysis of census data published in 1991 by Yimin Shen, then-head of the Census Center at the National Bureau of Statistics, it is stated that China's population control should continue to focus on and further raise the public awareness of "population quality improvement" (*tigao renkou suzhi*). In both cases, *suzhi* is attributed to the "quality" of people that needed a vertical and upward lift for improvement and enhancement.

Furthermore, the state documents in the 1980s attributed China's previous failure in modernizing the country to the general "low *suzhi*" (low quality) of its large population (Anagnost 2004). That is to say, *suzhi* was conjoined with the country's population issue during the post-socialist economic reform, where the discourse of "population quality" shifted the state policy from regulating birth to improving *suzhi* in the general population—hence "a shift from quantity to quality" (Anagnost, 190). At that time, *suzhi* was often a descriptor of the overall population, yet not as pervasive and flexible to apply to individuals as we have seen later (Yan 2008, 75). The term's rising popularity since the 1980s was followed by a sharp increase in the use of "*suzhi* education" (*suzhi jiaoyu*) when schools and universities started to revise and improve their curricula in 1995 (Kipnis 2006, 299–300; Yan 2008, 117; see also Bakken 2000). The *suzhi* rhetoric reached the peak of its discursive power in 1997, when the landmark Fifteenth Central Committee of the CCP elevated the country's private sector to the same level as the state sector in conjointly building a "socialist market economy" through cultivating a large and "high-*suzhi*" labor force (Yan, 112–14).

In other words, *suzhi* has to a significant extent lost its meaning of "unaltered natural quality" in the PRC's sociopolitical discourse and become something that one can and must acquire and improve through upbringing, schooling, and training. The emergence of this *suzhi* discourse has led to a new social system to rank-order people based on their value (worth) for the country's socioeconomic revival and growth, compelling a conception of human subjects as "lacking" and in need of constant improvement and readjustment in the booming capitalist knowledge economy as well as the neoliberal market and governmentality (Yan 2008, 137–38). In post-reform China, argues Anagnost (2004, 192), this new valuation system manifests primarily in (1) rural-to-urban migrants who are lured to the city where acquiring *suzhi* is an escape from rurality and (2) the urban middle classes who heavily invest in their children's education. The former is often seen as lacking and needing *suzhi*, while the latter is at the forefront of China's neoliberal subject production by building quality into the new generation. The differences between these two social groups most noticeably mark the boundaries in the cultural imagination and public stereotype of low-*suzhi* versus high-*suzhi* populations. As such, "*suzhi* defines strategies for social mobility" (Anagnost, 192).

This explains why people in China often associate high-*suzhi*/quality with urban upbringing, advanced education, a decent job and income, exquisite cultural taste, tidy and clean appearance, and fluency in Putonghua. In contrast, rural-born, undereducated, unemployed or poorly employed, culturally dubious, unkempt, and accented men and women are often labeled "low *suzhi*" with a deplorable lack of quality (cf. Tang 2013, 70). Moreover, relocating *suzhi* from inborn qualities to nurtured human development is essentially repositioning it from the primitive nature to the symbolic culture. *Suzhi* has hence become increasingly associated with "educational credentials, high culture, science and technology, modernity, and progress" (Hsu 2007, 21). In a queer context, while *culture* is something that can be learned and cultivated, *sexuality* often appears primitive and unrefined. The untamed and unregulated biological-sexual desires and practices are hence firmly pinpointed in the opposite direction of "cultivated quality." The stigma around socially and sexually active gay men in the so-called *quanzi* ("circles"), a popular slang term in China's queer communities, partially owes to the fact that unregulated sexualities fall off this *suzhi* discourse in producing sexually self-governed "high-quality" citizens. Through such self-regulation, the state has effectively transformed direct governance into a kind of autonomized governance at a distance (Anagnost 2014, 200) that helps maintain a desirable and stable social order during China's ongoing social transformations.

More important, while *suzhi* has become a ranking system mainly based on nurture and culture, the issue of quality has increasingly become an individual problem. Being "low-quality" or *di suzhi* implies that one has failed in self-development through education and training and hence lacks "culture" (*mei wenhua*); being "high-quality" or *gao suzhi*, in contrast, shows a person's hard work and success in self-improvement and enculturation (*you wenhua*).[3] *Suzhi* is hence often used to "legitimate social exclusions and inequalities engineered by the Chinese state" (Bao 2011a, 135; see also Goodman 2014, 109–10), even though differences in individual qualities are often caused by larger systematic problems such as imbalanced developments and uneven distributions of educational resources. This has led to a robust *suzhi* hierarchy and a new articulation and understanding of human value in China's reform and development, which marks a moral distinction between the high and the low that is of social and national importance (Hsu 2007, 157–80; Kipnis 2006, 297; Yan 2008, 137).

However, recently, the term *suzhi* has been losing its popularity in various social registers, especially among the rising and ever-expanding (queer) middle classes. This word is still often used in discussing education or public etiquette but is largely out of favor in describing individuals or specific social groups. At any rate, *suzhi* already sounds slightly obsolete in daily parlance and too judgmental and cynical in everyday conversation regarding social (and sexual) practices. The term *suzhi* itself has to some extent expired, the reason for which I further consider later in this chapter, but the logic behind it still plays a significant role in today's queer cultures, only at a deeper and more implicit level. The general understanding of "quality" in today's China is less akin to the previous state propaganda of *suzhi* but increasingly towards a neoliberal self-investment in pursuing and accumulating various forms of human capital, especially the class-structuring cultural capital.

In his classical study *Distinction: A Social Critique of the Judgement of Taste* ([1984] 2010), sociologist Pierre Bourdieu has shown how and why cultural taste functions as a strong indicator of social class. Economic capital is often conjoined by "cultural capital," or class-specific knowledge and training, in the social hierarchy where cultural products and practices are "classified and classifying, rank-ordered and rank-ordering" (218). As such, cultural capital is accumulated and augmented particularly through the process of upbringing and education—a "cultural pedigree" (55) to various levels of nobility and seniority. Of particular importance is the concept of "habitus" that is situated between "the capacity to produce classifiable practices and works" and "the capacity to differentiate and appreciate these practices and products (taste)" (164). Here, habitus is a Latin term meaning a habitual or typical condition, or a set of general principles instilled by our life experiences, that structure and underline our cultural taste—or "why we like what we like"—in our everyday thinking and decision-making (Stewart 2014, 58–59). Habitus is thus a "structuring structure," so to speak, of cultural taste and judgment; it functions as the very system of classification of cultural practices in both cultural production and appreciation (see Maton 2014; Costa and Murphy 2015).

Since Bourdieu, material wealth is no longer understood by sociologists as the sole marker of class; cultural capital often plays a more important role in today's class analysis.[4] Meanwhile, social analysts have begun to challenge Bourdieu's findings, arguing that today's consumers of high-brow cultures often show less aversion towards and more interest in middle-brow or popular cultures and hence become less "snobbish" and more "omnivorous" in cultural tastes.[5] As the inaugural "cultural omnivore" theorist Richard A. Peterson points out in an early article with Kern (1996), the likely reason behind these changes lies in an overall increase in educational, geographical, and social mobilities and in the massification, industrialization, and liberalization of arts and cultures (905–6). This echoes Beverley Skeggs's critique in *Class, Self, and Culture* (2004) that recent scholarship on class conflicts and social stratification often retreats behind the discussions of mobilities and individualism in neoliberal economies (47–61). Nevertheless, capitalist market forces have swept through the whole cultural hierarchy from mass to elite levels, where arts and aesthetics often become accessible with a price tag attached in their production, consumption, and appreciation. Bourdieu's own *market* metaphor of cultural *capital* therefore continues to shed light on today's social and cultural theories and practices, leading to the birth of two new conceptual categories in sexuality studies: sexual capital and erotic capital.

An early use of "sexual capital" can be found in Robert T. Michael's (2004) discussion of sexual health. Martin and George (2006) have further theorized "sexual capital" along Bourdieu's thoughts, echoing Gonzales and Rolison's (2005) and Koshy's (2004) respective discussions of sexual capital among African- and Asian Americans. Adam Green (2008a, 2008b, 2014) further popularizes this sex/market metaphor with more emphasis on the issue of "sexual field," another term derived from Bourdieu's theory. The notion of sexual capital also finds its global resonances in academic investigations of, for example, cross-racial sexuality in Shanghai (Farrer 2010) and sex workers in Southeast China (Ding and Ho 2012). Defined as "a person's resources, competencies and endowments that provide status as sexual agents within a field" (Farrer, 75), sexual capital or "sexual currencies" encompass bodily beauty and performativity, sexual and emotional sophistication, and sex-related knowledge and skills (Ding and Ho, 50).

The so-called "erotic capital," by contrast, derives from recent scholarship on sexuality and social class. Siobhan Brooks adopts this term in *Unequal Desires* (2010) but appears to use "erotic capital" as merely an equivalent to "sexual capital." Meanwhile, British sociologist Catherine Hakim has presented a full theorization of erotic capital as a fourth personal asset in addition to economic, cultural, and social capital (2010). This has led to Hakim's subsequent publication of two highly controversial books: *Erotic Capital: The Power of Attraction in the Boardroom and the Bedroom* (2011a) and *Honey Money: The Power of Erotic Capital* (2011b). Working along and against Bourdieu, she argues that erotic capital has long been overlooked because "the elite cannot monopolize it, so it is in their interest to marginalize it" and degrade those who employ it (2011a, 17). Hakim sees erotic capital as independent from the class origin (and cultural pedigree) and hence a potentially equalizing tool that enables people to cash in their individual erotic assets to exchange other forms of capital and climb up the social ladder. Erotic capital, in this sense, is *convertible* to and *exchangeable* with economic, cultural, and social capital in social mobilities.

However, the idea of erotic capital has not fully grown into a well-grounded body of scholarship. First, Hakim's blueprint of erotic capital overlaps with the existing category of sexual capital. She defines erotic capital as a broader category encompassing both sexual and social habitus and sees sexual capital as a narrower concept confined in the realm of sexuality (2011a, 129–30, 253). However, sexual capital is in fact also deeply situated in wider socioeconomic conditions and practices, recognizable and convertible through social exchange. Second, Hakim overtly states that her project focuses only on the "heterosexual majority" (129) and has not been tested and examined in queer studies or any non-Western contexts. Third, she believes that women generally "have more erotic capital than men because they work harder at it" and "are well placed to exploit their erotic capital" (2010, 499), which pinpoints women as both the subjects and the ideal objects of erotic exploitation. In this book, I define sexual capital as both physical (beauty and strength) and symbolic (sex-related knowledge and values) that can be integrated into the social and cultural domains; I treat erotic capital as a particular form of sexual capital that explicitly presents sexual attraction and provokes erotic desires.

Overall, Bourdieu's concept of human capital provides a certain insight into the myth of quality in a Chinese context. Tang (2013), for example, sees *suzhi*/quality as a Chinese variation of Bourdieu's cultural capital (69–70), while Anagnost (2008) refers the discursive figure of *suzhi* to "the formation of human capital" (512) in class aspiration, cultural taste, educational attainments, consumer consciousness, and urban residence in gated communities (509). Here, I define *suzhi*/quality as a class-structured and class-structuring human capital that is inherited and invested through upbringing and education in pursuing upward social mobility. This *suzhi*/quality mostly manifests in the form of cultural capital (what we know) that is inseparable from and often convertible to economic capital (how much we own), social capital (whom we know), and sexual capital (how attractive we are) in the state-engineered reproductions of class-related advantages and privileges. In this case, the discourse of quality embodies (1) an institutionalized hierarchy between high and low *suzhi*; (2) an individualized capital that one can cash in for social class mobility in China's neoliberal culture and market; and (3) a state-led social ideal that celebrates quality over quantity and civilized culture over unregulated human nature. By the "myth" of quality, I refer to a lingering popular belief and social discourse of *suzhi* that has been effectively cultivated by the party-state in the past few decades, which has constituted a recurring theme in (queer) Chinese studies that needs further investigation in the twenty-first century.

Furthermore, since 2002, the Chinese state has recognized the emerging middle classes as a growing force for China's economic progress and social stability (Goodman 2016, 4–5). This has been conjoined by the national higher education expansion (*kuozhao*) admitting tens of millions more tertiary students since the turn of the twenty-first century (7), which has significantly boosted education-oriented geographical and social class migrations among the young generation (and contributed to the stretched kinship structure that I have discussed earlier). An increasing number of educated urban and urbanized queer people have emerged as part of the rising and aspirational middle classes in today's China. Although research-based estimations of the size of China's middle classes vary significantly (9), the ongoing middle-class expansion closely overlaps with the state-engineered pursuit of *suzhi*/quality in reproducing self-governed citizens and upward social mobilization.[6] Here, the Chinese middle classes in question designate

> a large, loosely defined social group that shares the potential or the experience of enhanced access to resources (education, information, and wealth) and rapid upward social mobility and is becoming the object, inspiration, and exemplary yardstick for contemporary governmental discourses of self-improvement. (Tomba 2009, 592)

In this case, the lingering myth of *suzhi* offers a critical lens that helps us understand how and why the desire for and the pursuit of "quality" and upward social mobility continue to shape queer cultures and communities in today's post-socialist and post-*suzhi* China, where the growing urban middle classes have assumed more socioeconomic significance and visibility.

The Rise and Fall of an "Upward" Community

China's online queer communities and social media present an important case for us to understand today's social stratification and queer social mobility, as online social media often bring together a diverse demography across a large span of China's territory where regional development is significantly imbalanced. Lacking sociocultural acceptance and public space, queer people in China heavily rely on the internet for dating and social networking, where larger social inclusions and exclusions are often reproduced in smaller online queer communities. Gay dating and hookup websites emerged in China at the turn of the twenty-first century and some large sites remain popular today. But these dating services are often designed with very simple functions, only allowing users to upload photos with basic information such as age, height, body weight, and location. These online dating sites resemble a supermarket where customers choose unfamiliar products only by the pictures and the small print on the package, while the "quality" of the products remains unknown.

This kind of online dating presents several issues. First, with limited information, finding an ideal date takes a lot of guesswork. Traditional gay dating platforms often carry the stigma of "hookup centers," insomuch as the simple online profiles are only sufficient to identify a casual sex partner but very inadequate to identify a potential soul mate. Second, these sites often have curtailed capability to facilitate online interactions, and users often approach desired targets through mobile phones and Instant Message software outside the dating platforms. Third, with simple web design and very basic functions, most gay dating sites look rather shabby (or "low in quality") compared to today's sophisticatedly designed mainstream social media with rich functionalities. In this context, the emergence of Beijing-based queer social networking service Feizan has caught wide attention. Its story began in the Chinese New Year of 2010, when Ling, the founding owner, traveled overseas with his boyfriend for vacation. They took the chance to browse foreign gay websites and found them generally well designed to a high quality. These foreign sites contrasted sharply with the very shabby online forums and gay dating platforms in China, which motivated Ling to create a high-quality digital community for Chinese queer people. A graduate in computer science from one of the top Chinese universities, Ling soon brought together a team and established Feizan.

This groundbreaking project offers the first well-designed and fully functional social networking service for Chinese gay men. It allows users to create personal profiles, upload and post pictures and articles, follow others and join in interest groups, design and participate in short surveys, as well as organize and publicize social events. Feizan's rich functionality is conjoint with sophisticated and professional web design that presents a concise and clear layout similar to that of Facebook. That is to say, Feizan's technological and aesthetic infrastructures are constructed to a high quality, which marks a major departure from other shabby-looking underground gay sites in China with very limited functions. The early development of Feizan also demonstrated an intensive engagement with Beijing's local queer communities where Ling initiated this online social networking service; this included various queer social events organized by Feizan such as gay dating, film screening, and social sports for local queer people. In the first year, Feizan only saw a slow growth to about 10,000 registered users; in other words, this site first started as a rather small online queer community led by Ling with a local focus on Beijing.

The intimate sense of community was strong in Feizan's early development. When I joined the site in 2011, Ling would leave a message in the newcomers' profiles to welcome them into the community, and we could contact him directly with questions and feedback. In this way, the site members had the chance to contribute to the construction of this virtual queer community. Other than organizing social events in Beijing, Feizan attracted well-known gay public figures to the site. These people have become role models that others can look up to and learn from their experiences in dealing with the common difficulties facing queer people, such as kinship negotiation and marriage arrangements. Interest groups established by the users also covered a wide range of topics from film and music to fashion and sports. Feizan soon became a renowned queer social network, both for its well-designed infrastructures and for the strong sense of community and the high-quality original content actively generated by its users.

To put it another way, the need and desire for quality led to the birth and early development of Feizan as a benchmark of gay social media platforms and online communities in China. In addition, Feizan's success lies not only in its insistence on quality and in its strong sense of community, but also in the culture it aims to cultivate among its members. While early gay websites in the PRC were often permeated with erotic and pornographic content (Ho 2010, 100–109), Feizan differs significantly from its predecessors in establishing and actively enforcing an anti-obscenity policy. One of Feizan's early slogans was "browse Feizan in your office," meaning this site had nothing pornographic and could be viewed even in the workplace. Ling told me during my interview that he designed Feizan for people to showcase diverse *interests* (read: cultural capital) on this platform, instead of sharing erotic content as often seen in other Chinese gay sites. Those sites overloaded with erotic materials often leave an impression, as well as a stigma, that queer people only seek sexual enticement and enjoyment. Facing China's strict censorship, erotic gay sites have to operate in an incognito fashion, such as regularly changing URLs to escape the authorities' crackdown, which further intensifies the stigma that queer desires only belong to a dark, underground world. Feizan, in contrast, aims to prove that vibrant queer cultures can be and should be bathing in the sunlight.

In other words, Feizan breaks away from the underground gay world that often renders people mere sexual objects; it instead promotes a more positive, upward, optimistic, and confident queer image seldom before seen in China's online queer spaces and wider queer communities. The name Feizan consists of flying (*fei*) and compliment and praise (*zan*), connoting a clear departure from the underground gay websites for an upward queer mobility and visibility (Figure 4.1). This upward image fulfills queer people's mobilized desire to break away from the (internalized) shame and stigma in search of a more positive queer community and social presence. Feizan's upward culture has attracted large numbers of "high-quality users" (*gao zhiliang yonghu*), a term favored by

Figure 4.1 Feizan's front-page banners from 2013 to 2015 (high-flying balloons up in the sky have been a major theme)

the Web 2.0 industry to describe social media enthusiasts who actively and spontaneously generate original content and attract new users. These active content contributors constituted a considerable portion of Feizan's early residents.

As Ling put it during my interview, those joining Feizan in its early stage truly "treated people as humans"—respecting each other and willing to contribute to the community, rather than objectifying each other and utilizing this platform for gay porn exchange or cruising for sexual encounters. Feizan's early members rather represent a certain demography with particular cultural interests, taste, and capital in social mobility and individual quality. Ling's personal story as a rural-to-urban gay migrant who graduated from an elite university and pioneered queer social media in China serves as a microscopic example of Feizan's early success. Starting from the local queer communities and the vibrant migrant city of Beijing, Feizan was first established and developed by those who had already succeeded in educational, geographical, and social class migrations against the backdrop of China's thriving economy and development-induced mobilities. This small group of people with relatively advanced social, cultural, economic, and educational capital set the tone for the early development of Feizan. Feizan's upward cultural inclination is both a condition and a consequence of an upwardly mobile queer community, which is in turn embraced and further cultivated by its members.

Writing on *suzhi* and community-building (*shequ jianshe*) in urban China, Luigi Tomba (2009, 592–93) argues that the emerging and rising middle-class communities have reproduced self-regulated subjects who (1) know what they want and actively choose what to consume, (2) have proven capable of governing themselves to build and maintain their own communities, and (3) effectively serve as benchmarks of social aspirations and behaviors and models for individual self-improvement. These qualities extend the state-led production of a "high-*suzhi*" and reliable labor force that can be entrusted with China's capitalist expansion and the great dream of revival. Through this lens, there is little surprise that Feizan's early members have established and developed an autonomous online kingdom to exchange and further augment their newly acquired human capital. These well-educated and self-regulated citizens/netizens are diligent in choosing what to share and to consume, and work along rather than against the lingering *suzhi* hierarchy by displaying and maintaining a higher cultural stance. This practice in community formation and culture construction differentiates and safeguards their online community and culture capital from the low-*suzhi* others and from the dubious underground gay websites overloaded with unregulated and overtly erotic sexual capital.

In a broader context, the role of middle-class communities first lies in upholding and normalizing the current social order. This social order protects the legitimacy and supremacy of the "educated, consuming, and above all 'responsible' urban middle class" who are produced by the state-led developmental strategies as privileged urban workforce and upwardly mobile social elites (Tomba 2009, 596). For these beneficiaries of the nationwide pursuit of *suzhi*/quality, it is in their best interest to maintain their well-trained and mobility-embodied status (592–93). At the same time, the middle classes are held to be the most responsible citizens who, by virtue of their higher *suzhi*, will help maintain "social and political stability in a time of growing economic inequality and social complexity" (593). Thus, they have a moral obligation to be role models and be accountable for their behaviors. If being queer is a transgression from the responsible sexual citizenship where heterosexual procreation is pivotal to China's social stability and future growth and prosperity, then the pressure for the middle-class queers to regulate and discipline their (already deviant) sexualities is even stronger. In this sense, excluding overt display and circulation of erotic capital is both a marker of high *suzhi* and social status and a moral obligation intrinsic to upholding a responsible middle-class image. Therefore, showcasing one's cultural capital in lieu of purely erotic capital in queer social interactions has become a new queer middle-class habitus warmly embraced and celebrated in China's "upward" queer communities like Feizan, underlined by the lingering myth of quality that separates and quarantines the cultivated culture from the primitive nature.

As Allan Bérubé (1997) comments in a different context, the so-called queer communities and politics are often built by middle-class and college-educated (white) gay males "around a belief that homosexuality could and should stand alone as the organizing principle" (60), effectively overshadowing their own underlying social, educational, and class privilege. Interviewing Ling in late 2014 about Feizan's upward inclination in community-building and upmarket cultural taste in digital video productions, I raised the question that this might lead to an "elitism" that reproduced and reinforced larger social exclusions:

> Ling: *Many people love our products . . . Refined and higher-quality* tongzhi *products are still scarce. Once we have them, people will come and see them.*
>
> Author: *But the pursuit of high quality may potentially exclude audiences in the lower cultural hierarchy* (di wenhua cengci guanzhong)*?*
>
> Ling: *No. I mean we all love good-quality* (youzhi) *products, so our products need to have quality* (you pinzhi).
>
> Author: *Will that more or less convey a sense of elitist* tongzhi *culture?*
>
> Ling: *I think today's* tongzhi *is not in the position to talk about elitism at all—we should already be thankful if we have decent-quality* (xiangyangde) *products.*

Throughout my interview, Ling indicated that queer media and cultural products in China generally remained "low in quality," compared to their Western counterparts, and hence it was too early to talk about "elitism" when the basic needs for quality were still unsatisfied. As I have discussed earlier in this book, I became interested in and gained access to Feizan and urban film clubs because of my own past success in cultural, educational, and social mobilities that equipped me with the cultural capital as entry tickets to these communities. I am concerned that Ling's and my preferences for "quality" may have put us in a privileged (if not elitist) position that limits our understandings of how queer cultures are reproductive of social class and stratification. After all, we are both "products" of the state-engineered nationwide pursuit of *suzhi* in our own geographical and social migrations, during which we have both significantly benefited from the existing hierarchy of quality.

Ling's emphasis on quality is first and foremost a (conscious or unconscious) strategy to accommodate an urban middle-class demography and augment class-specific capital represented by Feizan's early members. Its departure from erotic underground gay sites in building an "upward" queer community inevitably entails online exchanges of cultural capital among its members. These exchanges often take the form of shared pictures, articles, status updates, and interest groups generated and established by the users. In addition to personal pictures, for example, large numbers of culturally themed photo albums have been created by the members that conspicuously indicate their broad cultural interests beyond the exchange of primitive sexual currencies.[7] The diverse ("omnivorous") range of picture collections on Feizan sharply contrasts with the oversupply of seductive and erotic photos on other gay sites in China; members of Feizan are hence allowed a much fuller self-portrayal through a wide range of cultural interests beyond the singularity of the sex-driven online display of physical attractiveness and erotic capital.

Feizan also allows and encourages members to post long articles, including self-introduction, opinion essays, social comment, film and music reviews, fiction, real-life stories, poems, as well as other genres. Each day, the articles that have attracted most comments will be automatically ranked in the "hot topic" list on Feizan's member-facing internal front page. Moreover, every time a member uploads a picture or posts an article, or "likes" or comments on other people's content, the system will automatically generate a status update on the front page as well as in the user's own profile. This further facilitates and accelerates the flows and exchanges of cultural capital through user-generated and shared content. People can also choose on the front page to view status updates from those they have followed or those in the same geographical area, so as to identify potential dates and partners with shared interests and tastes—essentially those with similar cultural capital and associated social status.

In a larger context, the augmentation of cultural capital caters to the growing appetite of an aspirational middle class who crave "culture" and "quality" through education and self-development to continue their upward social migration and legitimate their current social position (Anagnost 2004). To claim membership in Feizan's community, in other words, one has to possess and provide some cultural capital for exchange. If other gay websites in China invite and incentivize users to cash in erotic capital for hookup and casual sex, then Feizan makes it possible for people to cash in cultural capital for dating and relationship building. But this does not mean that Feizan is a desexualized space; on the contrary, sexual capital is often in high demand and in high supply in this queer community. The circulation and exchange of sexual capital on Feizan often take a more refined form, such as medical knowledge on sexual health, techniques and skills to enhance the pleasure of sexual intercourse, and tips for skin care and gym exercise to improve one's physical beauty and bodily strength. Personal pictures indicating one's sexual assets (e.g., youthfulness and fitness) are also popular on Feizan.

In this case, public displays of sexual capital often take an enculturated form on Feizan that "elevates" the primitive, biological nature to the symbolic culture, while explicitly erotic content is often reported by the users and then removed by the administrator. Sexual capital is thus often deployed and exchanged in a more self-regulated form as sex-related knowledge, reminiscent of the myth of quality in reproducing self-governed and health-conscious good sexual citizens.[8] Here, the excessive supply of pornographic content that was common in China's online queer space has been replaced by a surplus of high-quality, original, and omnivorous cultural capital as well as refined sexual capital in cultural forms. Unsurprisingly, this coincides with the state regulation and censorship of obscene content in maintaining and strengthening a civilized society whose exemplar members in urban (and online) middle-class communities can be entrusted for autonomous governance at a distance. By virtue of their habitus in pursuing culture and quality, the docile and self-censoring middle classes are ideal citizens in an ethical and moral society carefully engineered by the state.

But Feizan has since then expanded to a large empire. Despite its slow growth in the first year, Feizan's reputation as an upward gay community has boosted the snowball effect and led to a hundredfold increase in the number of registered users to over one million as of late 2014, as Ling confirmed during my interview. Invited or unsolicited, numerous LGBT organizations and social groups from gay choirs and bookshops to queer film clubs and coffee houses have all landed on Feizan to publicize their services, businesses, and social events. No longer able to organize communal activities on its own for a large and diverse user-base scattered across the country and around the world, Ling's team behind Feizan has redefined the role of this website from a small online community to a large social network through which various individuals, businesses, queer NGOs, and social groups can coordinate and publicize their own social and communal activities.

Accordingly, the growth of Feizan has dramatically changed its demography from a community of socially advantaged and culturally exquisite middle-class users to a more inclusive and culturally diverse mini-society. The conglomeration of cultural capital in Feizan's early community has been largely diluted by its changing demography. As a result, Feizan's attempt to maintain a high-quality queer community free from erotic content is no longer equally respected by the newcomers. Recent years have seen users increasingly challenge the anti-obscenity policy by uploading explicit content. Because of such user-generated content, Feizan has been blocked several times in the 3G/4G cellular networks operated by China Mobile, a state-owned telecommunication enterprise and the world's largest mobile-phone carrier. After all, the entrusted autonomous self-governance cannot challenge the predefined state policy and existing social order, while the emerging middle classes are only autonomous in choosing what they consume when they remain "responsible enough to actively contribute to the maintenance of social order" (Tomba 2009, 592). With its expansive scale, Feizan can no longer fly under the radar as a small middle-class online community. Instead, it has to enforce stronger self-censorship to ensure the very survival of this social network and reinforce its culturally enriched upward image distinctive from primitive sexual temptations. Some users have shown a strong and consistent support for the anti-obscenity strategy to keep Feizan safe as a high-quality and "pollution-free" paradise, while many others who cannot fit in have been driven away from Feizan.

Social Distinction vs. Individual Choice

As shown in Feizan's case, the distinction between cultural and erotic orientations has led to a major divide between those who actively pursue cultural capital and those who care more about erotic capital. This divide is not entirely new and not exclusive to Feizan; to a significant extent it has sculpted and structured China's gay communities and social interactions that I have observed and empirically experienced in the past fifteen years or so both online and on the ground. This major divide reveals a deep-buried question about *suzhi* and human capital in China: why have the desire for erotic capital and that for cultural capital generated two distinctive queer discourses often at each other's throat? One explanation lies in the prevalent futurelessness of queer love in China that I first discussed in Chapter 1: people often have to break up with their same-sex partners to fulfill their social and filial responsibilities through heterosexual marriage and reproduction to continue the family line. This has led to two different approaches in negotiating one's social, cultural, and sexual identities that indicate the underlying issues of social mobility and immobility, and inclusion and exclusion, in queer social life.

On the one hand, displaying and capitalizing on cultural capital in social interactions indicates one's desire and determination to commit to a long-term relationship established upon the relatively more stable and long-lasting cultural interests. In this case, high cultural capital may also imply more advanced socioeconomic status; showcasing non-erotic cultural tastes and interests thus indicates one's social position and further demonstrates one's ability in augmenting human capital and climbing up the social ladder. People in these categories are more desirable, insomuch as higher economic, educational, social, and cultural capital often lead to more recourses to expand life options and deal with the common challenges facing queer people. Stretched kinship negotiation, overseas gay marriage and migration, international surrogacy and adoption, and other problems in long-term queer relationships all entail advanced knowledge, financial resources, and social connections to mitigate and resolve. The ability to display such qualities thus testifies to one's potential in maintaining a queer life and building a possible queer future out of the heteronormative closet.

On the other hand, those who only exploit erotic capital often carry the stigma in today's queer Chinese communities that they have nothing to show except their body. The exclusive self-portrayal of physical attractiveness often connotes a desire for casual sexual encounters without commitment, as opposed to showcasing a range of cultural interests that indicates one's willingness *and* ability for a stable relationship. Over-capitalizing on erotic capital often implies that the person lacks sufficient resources to maintain a long-term queer relationship and hence eagerly capitalizes on the body for as much sexual pleasure as possible before he reaches the age and has to obey the family for a hetero-reproductive marriage. In a relevant scenario, those heavily exploiting their erotic selves may have already chosen a heterosexual marriage and hence only socialize with other queer people for extramarital sex as an outlet for their same-sex desire, in which case their sexual selves must be separated from any public display of their social and cultural identities. That means those who carry on the habitus from erotic gay sites and continue intensively sharing erotic content on Feizan appear to have failed in cultivating cultural capital and pursuing upward mobility that can potentially afford them a better chance for a long-lasting queer relationship and a promising queer life.

To put it another way, the type of human capital that one is able to display and capitalize upon implicitly indicates one's potential ability to choose between a queer future and a hopeless and futureless hetero-reproductive closet. In this sense, the most cherished "quality" in queer Chinese communities is not cultural taste per se, but the very ability to build a long-term relationship and maintain a queer life in a country like China under compulsory heterosexuality and familism. This ability has little to do with one's physical appearance and erotic attractiveness; rather, it is mainly enabled and enhanced by the possession of advanced cultural, social, educational, and economic wealth in the pursuit of individual quality and social mobility. It is this kind of "quality" that has deeply divided queer people on Feizan and in larger queer Chinese communities: while erotic capital caters to sexual desires, other forms of human capital determine the possibility and opportunity of creating a queer future outside heteronormative marriage and kinship. In this sense, the display and exchange of cultural capital on Feizan is essentially a filtering/screening process—a mechanism that turns away "low-quality" queers and attracts people with similar levels of cultural capital and social status—which effectively reduces the *quantity* to identify and match potential dates and partners with desirable *quality*.

Here, the problem of compulsory familism and heterosexual procreation has been channeled into the imperative process of development and self-improvement in pursuing quality and capital. In other words, the growth-induced upward social mobility and upward cultural mobility have offered a sense of hope for some queer people facing the prevalent problem of kinship and reproduction. As Katherine Sender reminds us, often those with more social privilege can afford to indulge in greater sexual transgression (2004, 222), while others are more subject to public scrutiny and more constrained by their limited resources to expand life options under the heteronormative productions of social and familial structures. Queer sexualities are never only about sexual desires and deviance but deeply intermingled with the issues of class and privilege in the larger sociocultural hierarchy that have been reproduced in queer communities. In this case, as far as queer mobilities are concerned, migration ("moving out") is often driven by a strong and pervasive desire for upward cultural mobility and upward social mobilization ("moving up"). If migration is a process of horizontal movement, then cultural capital accumulation as a form of cultural mobility constitutes and entails a vertical process over time that is often folded into and inseparable from upward social migration.

In addition, when early online queer spaces were permeated with erotic content, the overflow of erotic capital led to a public stigma that offered little help to improve the social position and public image of queer people. When queer social activism has been developing in China during recent years and sexual minorities generally enjoy more social visibility, a growing concern over sex-related queer morality and public image is shown both on Feizan and in wider queer Chinese communities online and offline. In any case, stigmatized social groups are more likely to raise their social position with high "moral capital" by investing in and producing positive and often desexualized public images (Sender 2004, 222). This to some degree compensates for their transgressive sexualities that have fallen off the public consent of good sexual citizenship. For the rising and aspirational queer middle classes in China, "culture" is a much better card to play than transgressive erotic desires to legitimate their success and privilege in social mobilization. Both inside and outside Feizan, a growing advocacy has been calling for a higher standard of sex-related morality so as to compensate for the already degraded public image of queer people. This factor has further contributed to the deep divide and the ongoing debate over refined cultural tastes versus expressive erotic desires that continue to classify and rank-order different forms of human capital in structuring queer Chinese communities online and on the ground.

But this divide between cultural and erotic pursuits has been increasingly challenged, especially in online queer communities where participants of one large social network often come from a wide spectrum of social backgrounds with different class status. From 2012 to 2015, for example, network-wide debates frequently broke out on Feizan regarding the importance and appropriateness of cultural capital and erotic capital in both individual choices of same-sex partners and the collective social visibility and public impression of queer people. One side of the debate strongly advocated for an upward queer public image through self-improvement and self-discipline as well as a public demonstration of queer people's commitment to building responsible and long-term relationships.

Meanwhile, another side unapologetically proclaimed physical attraction, sexual emancipation, and individual choice as unalienable rights in the negotiations and practices of non-conforming sexualities. Similar to my observations and experiences in other queer Chinese communities, neither side of this long-lasting debate could fully convince the other.

Here, the debates on Feizan indicate some recent developments in the lingering *suzhi* discourse and in the measurement of individual quality, as suggested by those who favor the display of erotic capital in China's queer communities. They argue that erotic capital is an integral part of human beings and hence a valuable and inseparable asset in individual quality. More important, the physical appearance that one was born with also needs careful "cultivation" (e.g., through skin care and fitness routines) that entails money, knowledge, self-education, determination, and hard work. If the cultivated cultural capital is cherished, then the erotic capital accumulated through individual efforts should be equally acknowledged and celebrated. In addition, a hookup for casual sex may well initiate a serious relationship where a casual exchange of erotic capital may turn into a long-term commitment. On top of that, displaying cultural or erotic interests (or both) is ultimately an *individual choice*, which neither the state nor other people have the right to judge whatsoever.

In China's neoliberal culture and market, the mobilized desire to define one's identity and sexuality through the liberal discourses of individual choice and unalienable rights is precisely why the term *suzhi* has lost its popularity in many social registers. Nowadays, talking too much about *suzhi* paradoxically shows low *suzhi*—pointing moralistic fingers towards other people's "personal choice." Chinese people have to various degrees benefited from the country's strong economic growth in more than four consecutive decades and enjoyed increased social mobilities through education and migration. That is to say, *suzhi*/quality is becoming less a privilege than a more prevalent condition experienced by an ever-growing population, especially the rising urban middle classes, although the ability to inherit and cultivate human capital still varies significantly among different individuals and families. When the overall "quality" (economic and cultural capital) of the population is increasing, speaking too much about *suzhi* once again shows low *suzhi*—thinking too highly of oneself as if other people have not or cannot improve their quality.

In the recent decade, *suzhi* has increasingly turned into an arrogant accusation and a vehicle of moralistic naming and shaming; queer moral capital in the name of *suzhi* has often become a negative moralistic (or immoral) capital that is increasingly unwelcome in today's queer communities. *Suzhi* is still in use as part of a long-lasting social vernacular but no longer appears as the first choice among today's urban middle-class queers and other social actors. On the other hand, the very increase in social mobility and "population quality" has extended the *suzhi*-style social exclusion and class stratification. The discourse of *individual choice*, for example, strongly parallels the rise of the increasingly individualized and privacy-conscious middle classes in China who are themselves produced by the state-led privatizations of the economy and individual life (Liu 2014, 142; So 2013, 162).[9] The rising and aspirational middle-class queers increasingly demand sexual privacy free from public scrutiny; if they do not want their own individual lifestyle to be judged, then they can no longer judge others in the name of *suzhi*, at least not publicly. What has changed is not the class-structured and class-structuring distinction between the symbolic culture and the sexual nature, but a middle-class habitus and politeness to keep one's opinions to oneself to show respect towards other people's lifestyle and individual choice—which itself demonstrates a "high quality."

However, privacy is a privilege, as I argued above based on Sender's observation. It is not that the rising middle-class queers care less about erotic capital but that they possess the class-specific privilege to exchange erotic capital behind closed doors. As Skeggs (2004, 60) resoundingly argues, while class is being displaced by theories and claims of mobility and individualization, it is simultaneously being institutionalized and reproduced as "a re-legitimation and justification of the habitus of the middle-class that does not want to name itself, be recognized or accept responsibility for its own power." The silence of middle-class queers on their privilege implicitly attributes social distinctions to "individual choice," as if such choice is not constrained by social stratification and segregation. The very ability to make choices *as* individuals first and foremost owes to the possession of certain class-specific human capital and social privilege. The discourse of individualization is ultimately a (not so) new middle-class excuse to continue justifying existing social exclusion along the lingering myth of "individual quality," albeit no longer in the moralistic name of *suzhi*. Rejecting the language of class is to effectively manage the newly stratified society by articulating inequalities as "options"; the so-called "individual choice" is inherently a class privilege articulated by those who have it or those who want it.

During recent years, arguments concerning individualization and social distinction have frequently surfaced and resurfaced on Feizan under the themes of education, migration, cultural taste, and commitment in same-sex relationships. This social networking platform itself has often become a battlefield where people holding different opinions attack each other and defend their own stance. In this process, many previously active users, including some of my informants, have left Feizan because the quality of the discussions has dropped to a disordered level of verbal fights, while constructive insights (read, once again, cultural capital) are increasingly scarce. The early sense of intimate community has largely disappeared along with Feizan's changing demography and rapid growth—*quality* has been diluted by *quantity*, in short. With fewer users contributing high-quality original content, Feizan has lost its appeal among queer Chinese people. When I expressed these concerns during my interview with

Ling about the withdrawal of active users from Feizan, he acknowledged the problem but had yet to come up with a solution:

> Author: *I notice that many early users have been complaining about the increase in Feizan's user-base but the decline in its quality. Some early members have left or stopped updating their profiles.*
>
> Ling: *Yes. I think this might be a common problem facing communities. Well . . . what can we do?* [Both of us laughed.]
>
> . . .
>
> Author: *Can I put it this way? Early Feizan had a stronger sense of community and we felt that we all belonged to this place [as a whole].*
>
> Ling: *This resembles the difference between small towns and large cities . . . I grew up in a village . . . where we all knew each other and shared a close relationship. But Beijing has more than 20 million residents—how oblivious and indifferent it feels [living here]! . . . A community is the same: when it's small, we pour our heart and soul into it; when it becomes larger, people also become indifferent. This is the pathology of large cities and perhaps the pathology of large websites [i.e., online communities].*

In 2013 and 2014, Feizan also suffered from a series of long-lasting malicious attacks: automatic robot programs registered thousands of new accounts every day and generated countless status updates to submerge the content generated by real users. From February to March 2014, Feizan was hit by a database malfunction that took the website offline for several days, during which a large number of users lost their profile data. These incidents recorded Feizan's struggle to redefine itself from a small community led by Ling to one of the largest online queer social networks in China. Feizan used to be commercial-free but has incorporated ad banners and started collaborations with gay-friendly businesses to cover the growing operational costs. For Ling, however, Feizan has never been fully commercialized, especially compared to the company's later mobile dating application ZANK that fully operates on venture capital. The rise of the location-aware mobile queer social media like ZANK has also diverted a large number of users from the web-based Feizan to locative mobile dating apps.

Ling's team has been working mostly on ZANK since its release in April 2013, while Feizan has been largely left alone on its own with very limited support. Technical glitches started to emerge on the website and have become increasingly frequent since then; the web design now also appears obsolete compared to the rapidly growing and fast-changing mainstream social media. In other words, the quality of this platform per se is declining. Discontent is noticeably growing among the users, which has caused more people to leave Feizan. Many LGBT organizations (including the film clubs discussed in this book) have also withdrawn from Feizan and turned to mainstream social media and mobile queer social networking services. User-generated content has continued to decrease, and even those who remain on Feizan have begun to complain about the decline of its quality and popularity. In 2017, Feizan's domain name became unresolvable for several months, during which the website was allegedly hosted on a temporary domain unbeknownst to many of its remaining members who had lost access. Since 2018, Feizan has closed its doors to new users unless they have a referral link from an existing member to register. At this point, Feizan is dying.

From a small online community to the largest queer social network in China and then to today's fallen empire, Feizan has left a unique trajectory in its development and contribution to queer Chinese cultures and communities in the early twenty-first century. The rise and fall of this virtual online community have reflected and reproduced the changing social discourses on *suzhi*/quality and the rising middle classes in the larger society. What we have learned by examining Feizan is how the structured and structuring forces of class-related human capital, especially cultural capital, have reshaped and reproduced queer people's consideration and articulation of quality and social mobility under compulsory familism and compulsory development. In the rapidly changing queer cultural landscape, web-based social networking platforms have gradually faded into history and made way for the emergence and popularity of locative mobile social media. The geolocation-based mobile social networking services have become the new frontier in the productions of queer cultures and mobilities, where social inclusion and exclusion continue to shape and reshape people's lived experiences and sociocultural practices under the lingering myth of quality. These will be further examined and discussed in the next chapter.

5
Gated Communities

The myth of quality continues to structure and underline queer social interactions on locative mobile media, especially on gay dating and hookup applications. In the past few years, ZANK and Blue'd have become two large mobile dating services in China for same-sex attracted men. ZANK reached ten million users, before it was shut down by the authorities in April 2017 with other mobile live-streaming and heterosexual dating apps that had "obscene content." Blue'd (pronounced Blue D) proclaims itself the world's largest mobile gay social network with thirty million users worldwide, as seen on Google Play and Apple's App Store in late 2018. Both ZANK and Blue'd attracted several rounds of venture capital investments, respectively published reports on China's "queer economy" in 2014, and invested in digital video and short film productions to promote their services. Other mobile queer social networks that I came across in this project include: Grindr (one of the most popular mobile gay apps in the world), Jack'd (based in the US and popular in China), Aloha (created in Beijing and allowing registration from selected countries), G-You (a less-known gay app in China), Tofu (a China-based mobile app for "rotten girls"—female fans of inter-male romance), and various lesbian dating apps based in China (LaLa, The L, LesPark, and LeDo).

Also known as location-aware or location-based services (LBS), locative mobile social media function on users' geolocational data. Mobile dating apps like ZANK and Blue'd automatically read the GPS data on the smartphone and list nearby users on screen in a grid format based on geolocational proximity—the nearest ones on top followed by others in descending order. Locative mobile media have caught wide academic attention and a substantial amount of research on mobile gay dating apps, especially Grindr, has erupted in English-language scholarship across media studies, cultural critiques, as well as HIV/AIDS prevention and mental health.[1] Here, I consider mobile queer cultures and social practices through China-based locative mobile gay dating and hookup apps, where the technology-aided geolocational mobilities are deeply structured and further complicated by the development-induced social mobility and immobility through the myth of quality. This extends to the problem of social inclusion and exclusion in the form of "gated communities"—from online queer communities and mobile social media to urban queer film clubs—that are produced by and productive of the wider social stratification and segregation in today's China.

Politics of Proximity

Locative mobile media are embodied spaces of proximity and intimacy through which social reciprocity emerges (Farman 2012, 67), insomuch as the broadcasted location often indicates one's social relation and constitutes one's identity (57–58). In the introduction to *Politics of Proximity: Mobility and Immobility in Practice*, Giuseppina Pellegrino defines proximity as physical co-presence and feelings of closeness enhanced by virtual and communicative flows of information via social and relational connections (notwithstanding possible disruptions; 2011, 7). A "mobile intimacy" thus comes into being through proximity that is conditioned by material-geographical and electronic-social mobilities and fluidities across time and space (Hjorth and Arnold 2013, 6–14; also see Raiti 2007). Rainie and Wellman (2012) famously describe such co-presence and closeness mobilized and reinforced by the revolution of digital technology as "networked individualism." They argue that people function more as connected individuals and less as embedded group members in mediated day-to-day social interactions through social media (12). The politics of proximity and intimacy entail and unleash a hyper-connectedness that often turns into an "enforced proximity," to borrow John Tomlinson's (2000) observation of communication and media technology before the onset of locative mobile social networking.

Mobile queer social media significantly differ from other LBS mobile networks in several aspects. First, mobile queer dating apps are often designed for users to discover other queer people in geographical proximity. Unlike Facebook, which capitalizes upon existing social relations and connections, mobile queer social networking often starts from strangers instead of acquaintances. Second, queer people, especially those in the closet, often use mobile dating and hookup apps anonymously, hiding from families, friends, roommates, and colleagues; many of them choose not to include face pictures in their profiles to avoid unexpected coming out. Third, in a country like China, mobile queer media are heavily censored and publicly stigmatized by the authorities, which is underlined by the lingering myth of quality in reproducing self-regulated and socially responsible sexual citizens, albeit less in the name of *suzhi* anymore.

On mobile gay dating and hookup apps like ZANK and Blue'd, users can check others' profiles, become their followers, and chat via the apps based on their geolocational proximity. Each of these applications lists and juxtaposes twenty-some users on the small smartphone screen, resulting in an extremely compact display of nearby users with miniaturized photos and minimum personal information (e.g., distance and sexual roles). People on such mobile queer social media are hence reduced, flattened, and miniaturized into tiny gridded icons one-twentieth the size of a smartphone screen. Profiles on mobile social media are often very concise—a large number of users do not bother to fill in any personal information except for age, height, and body weight. Some people may also write up a few taglines indicating dating preferences. Many profiles include (seductive) personal photos, while lots of others have no personal pictures at all. These profiles on mobile screens look like hyper-thrift "lonely hearts" ads ranked dynamically by geo-proximity. That is to say, mobile social media only allow limited space for self-display, as too much information will inundate the small screen.

The miniaturized profiles on mobile social media bring us back to the "supermarket" that I have described earlier, where we choose unfamiliar products based on the pictures and the fine print on the package without knowing their quality. This is a newly emerged mobile marketplace where neoliberal subjects freely choose what they consume and how they consume it, except that the choice of consumption is now based on rather limited information compared to the web-based social networks like Feizan that allow a broad and rich display of human capital. This new marketplace continues the *suzhi*-style structuring of human value that abstracts and fetishizes the agency of human subjects, who actively and spontaneously produce desires for consumption while being self-knowingly consumed as commodities in the dating market. Such reciprocal consumption habitus and capacity further indicate the emergent consumer citizenship and neoliberal human subjectivity in today's China, as queer cultures and social practices have been increasingly channeled through a capitalist and consumerist process and through the ongoing technological advancement.

Or, to borrow Yan's words, all this "abstraction, fragmentation, volatility, and potential of human subjectivity" has been integrated into the productive forces in China's developmental strategies (2008, 138). That is to say, if the all-important *suzhi* discourse helps people realize that the poverty of the country lies in the low population quality and poor human subjectivity, then the process of consumption encourages and reaffirms their autonomous agency to make free choices as producers/consumers and subjects/objects in the neoliberal market, which continues to work as a driving force for China's capital growth and accumulation (136). The venture capital behind ZANK and Blue'd are also capitalizing upon the rising queer middle classes who are above all eager to define and secure autonomous agency and social privilege through reciprocal consumption, where the neoliberal capitalist expansion drives the formulation and intervention of the socioeconomically marked bodies and sexualities on mobile screens.[2]

Moreover, mobile dating and hookup apps like ZANK and Blue'd are designed with a very specific strategy that enables users to identify and approach nearby dates or sexual partners as fast as possible. In other words, these apps capitalize on the co-presence of queer individuals in proximity with a promise to facilitate mobility and connectivity via mobile digital devices. Unless people use special applications to fake locational data on their smartphones, mobile dating and hookup apps only grant users access to queer individuals in a relatively close geographical radius. One's own profile, in addition, will be read mainly by nearby users. It is precisely in this sense that the principle of locative mobile media is governed by and productive of *the politics of enforced proximity*: geolocational closeness has become the fundamental structure that determines who one can see on mobile screens and who is likely to access one's own profile. The enforced proximity pinpoints people in a nexus where spatial closeness and location-based connectedness become the single most defining feature in queer social networking through mobile media.

The politics of enforced proximity evoke and trouble the myth of *suzhi*/quality at multiple imbricated levels. First of all, the enforced principle of proximity has largely replaced the underlying structure of quality in social networking, while proximity alone does not and cannot ensure quality. In other words, the cost of cultural capital to join in mobile queer social platforms is relatively low, as the enforced proximity does not prioritize cultural tastes and interests. This to some extent explains the surge of popularity of mobile dating apps compared with web-based online communities. Users of mobile social media have to reach out and establish contact based on limited and objectifiable information in people's profiles; while finding nearby queer peers is easier than ever, identifying an ideal date and potential partner once again takes some guesswork. Through this lens, the proximity-based mobile apps are more akin to early gay dating websites and have fewer similarities with web-based queer social media like Feizan, where social connections are established upon much fuller self-portrayals of personal interests and cultural tastes.

As previously analyzed, the display of cultural capital on Feizan is essentially a filtering and screening mechanism. On locative mobile social media, such a tactic no longer works. Mobile devices limited by the hardware infrastructures (e.g., small screens without a full-sized keyboard for text input) have little room to accommodate in-depth cultural and intellectual exchange through well-crafted articles or other substantive textual information. Instead, mobile social media are more suitable for fast circulations of sexual capital such as selfies shot with smartphones and shared through the increasingly ubiquitous Wi-Fi and 3G/4G networks. On mobile dating apps, "quality" is once again submerged by the overflows and surplus of mobilized sexual capital in large quantity. From this perspective, web-based queer social networks (e.g., Feizan) and proximity-based mobile social media (e.g., ZANK and Blue'd) are unlikely to replace each other, because they have distinctive roles to serve and different needs to fulfill.

But this does not mean that mobile social media completely function outside the domain of cultural capital and social distinctions. Rather, cultural capital often circulates in a more nuanced way through, for example, shared photos and selfies that indicate people's cultural tastes and underlying socioeconomic status—a point to which I will return below. In this case, the content shared on mobile screens once again functions as a filtering and screening mechanism to identify and match nearby users with similar cultural tastes and social status. More important, location broadcasting through mobile apps often implicitly indicates one's social position. If location is part of identity, as Farman (2012, 57) argues, then it is also part of individual "quality." Living in which part of the city, dining in what kind of café and restaurant, and spending leisure time in what type of cultural or commercial space all demonstrate one's cultural interest and class affiliation. Further, the principle of enforced proximity potentially connects people in the same neighborhoods such as university campuses or affluent urban residential compounds, the residency in which often entails and indicates certain levels of class-related capital. Thus, the broadcasted locations on mobile social media not only define one's *social relation* but also indicate one's *social position*. It is in this sense that locative mobile media continue to reinforce the social distinctions of "quality" through the politics of proximity. Even when people move or travel to a different place, the location-tagged pictures stored in their profiles will leave a trace, however fragmented, that indicates one's lifestyle, class affiliation, cultural taste, and social position—even though geolocational proximity can be temporarily altered or interrupted by mobility.

The Privilege of Mobility

Users of some mobile social media (e.g., Aloha) are known in China's gay communities for extensively sharing travel photos and selfies in their profiles, including exotic landscapes and breathtakingly beautiful scenery, upmarket fine-dining restaurants, luxurious hotels and resorts, and even first-class/business-class airline cabins and airport lounges. These carefully chosen locations and spaces for the display of the body and the deployment of sexual capital are conspicuously marked by one's socioeconomic status and cultural pursuits to expand life experiences, indicating these traveling bodies belong to the so-called *youxian jieji*, or literally "leisure class." This rather ambiguous term in Chinese people's daily parlance designates those who have extra resources (time and money) to regularly spend on lifestyle expenses such as tourism. Here, the descriptor of "leisure" attributes social success and material wealth less to a clearly marked and objectifiable socioeconomic status than to a lifestyle characterized by mobility and consumerism. That means a more visible middle-class consumer citizenship no longer needs to rely on the moral hierarchy of *suzhi*/quality to articulate its legitimacy, insomuch as such social privilege can be directly shown and seen through a highly mobile lifestyle recorded and circulated through the increasingly ubiquitous social media.

On 25 August 2016, the company behind Blue'd circulated an article online that mocked Aloha users as "*ming yuan*"—social butterflies and internet celebrities provided with and spoiled by the privilege of a hyperactive lifestyle.[3] The article described Aloha users as those who do not need to work to support themselves but instead spend all their time traveling, as indicated by their habitus of intensively sharing travel photos and selfies. Aloha directly fought back via multiple social media channels: "thank you for your kind words—every Aloha user is a life winner!" (Figure 5.1, left). "Life winner," or *rensheng yingjia*, indicates a triumphant social position proudly occupied and declared by those who are doing better than others are in the state-engineered middle-class expansion and upward social mobilization. Such public declarations of social success and class privilege soon turned into an open dispute between Blue'd and Aloha that caught wide attention across the queer communities and mainstream media in China. Blue'd subsequently released a poster that "everyone can be a life winner" while Aloha changed its poster to "being honest and being yourself is the life winner" (Figure 5.1, middle and right). This battle on what counts as "winning" and who qualifies as "winner" in social mobilities continues the lingering myth of *suzhi*/quality in rank-ordering those who have won and those who have lost in China's socioeconomic growth and widening social inequality.

While the designation of China's middle classes still lacks consistency in academic literature, a growing set of scholarship calls for our attention to the intra-class stratification and class-based social comparison that have become increasingly visible since the early twenty-first century. At least two different social strata exist in Chinese people's understanding and conscious experience of "middle classness" that mark a noticeable intra-class distinction (Miao 2017). The lower stratum is the so-called "salaried stratum" or "wage stratum" (*gongxin*

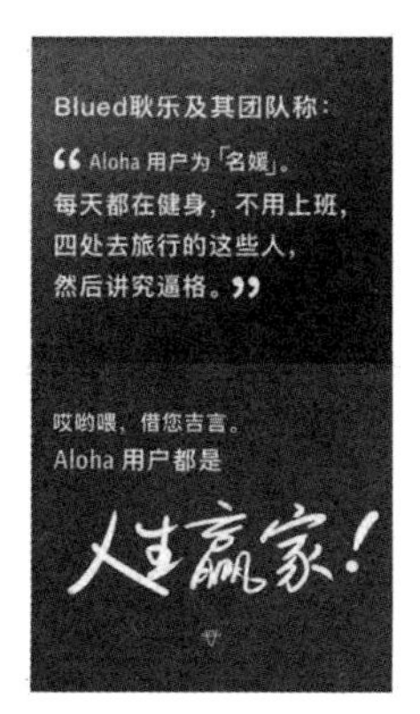

Figure 5.1 Dispute over "life winners" between Aloha and Blue'd

jieceng) that, despite their higher-than-average salary, lack alternative income sources and investment channels. They often live with "a sense of relative deprivation," lacking both money and time to spare as the increasingly expensive urban life often drains their decent but relatively limited financial resources and earning power. This social stratum thus focuses more on the material gain in social success and class privilege. Another stratum, in contrast, has adopted a rather consistent middle-stratum (*zhongchan jieceng*) identity and noticeably placed a greater emphasis on the cultural indicators of class, thanks to their more diverse income sources and financial power that afford them more economic freedom to expand life experiences. This often leads to a cultured and mannered lifestyle that separates them from regular "wage earners."

This analysis extends my argument about the deep divide within the rising queer middle classes in today's China. Although objective factors such as income, occupation, and education designate these people in a single and ever-expanding "middle class," the intra-class distinctions and contradictions are noticeably growing and have produced a plurality of de facto "middle classes" in people's lived experiences of social distinctions. While the mismatch between a mid-range income and the lack of a high-earning lifestyle pronounces a "deprived" but nonetheless "middle" position of wage earners, it is the ability to leisurely choose what to consume and how to spend time and money that marks a "winning" and probably "upper" middle-classness. Thus,

> it is not a simple question of whether the individual could afford the goods and services, but rather whether they could afford them *as part of a lifestyle*, which in turn *feeds into class identity* . . . the ability to afford a certain level of *enjoyment of life* and *leisure pursuits* is seen as important . . . The common denominator in all of the factors was the *quality of life* a middle class person is supposed to enjoy—*above and beyond* what is needed to survive in the city, but including all the extras that would enrich one's *life experience*, thus positively affecting one's mannerisms and behavior. (Miao 2017, 639–41; all italics mine)

The "life winners" on Aloha (which now looks more like a "lifestyle" mobile app in addition to a gay dating platform) have apparently cultivated the habitus of taking and sharing travel pictures and selfies as indicators of their "leisure-class" identities. In today's urban China, leisure pursuits have become a middle-class ideal both desired by average wage earners and showcased by those with more financial freedom and cultural incentive to expand their life experiences and afford a healthy work-life balance.[4] The leisure class is essentially a class bestowed with the relative privilege of social, cultural, and geographical mobilities, whose previous and ongoing success in upward social migration becomes evident in and productive of a highly mobile lifestyle.

In this case, furthermore, the enforced proximity on locative mobile apps like Aloha is contingent on both mobilities and immobilities. Proximity designates a relative geolocational closeness that constantly changes in accordance with the changing distance among people. The principle of proximity thus functions as a dynamic process of becoming through various forms of movements from daily commuting to migration and tourism (mobility), as well as a relative stability when people often live and work in the same place for a prolonged time (immobility). Aloha users appear to be more enthusiastic in sharing their entitled mobile lifestyle as the rising and aspirational "life winners" who can afford the privilege of mobility. In contrast, the immobility—living and working in the same place as a banal, mundane routine—does not fit in this self-portrayed and selectively curated image of middle-class life and consumer citizenship and hence has to be excluded from their profiles.

More important, if a mid-range working wage can lead to an average lifestyle, then "being middle class requires something more: the financial stability of having extra sources of income that are not dependent upon one's day-to-day work" (Miao 2017, 643). Through this lens, showcasing a highly mobile lifestyle indicates either a desire for upward social mobility or an already materialized entitlement to the leisure-class privilege that is less bound up to a single workplace and a single source of income. The desire for and the entitlement to mobility (over immobility) have hence become a celebrated quality and triumphant individual capital circulated through the location-tagged and socioeconomically marked pictures and selfies on mobile screens. This helps explain the astonishment of Blue'd that Aloha users "do not need to work" and instead relentlessly share their hyperactive and hypermobile lifestyle.[5] In this public dispute, the difference in individual quality between "winning" and "losing" was saliently articulated and debated through the lens of mobilities instead of the language of *suzhi*. Mobility, in this case, is both a condition and a conscious choice of the "life winners" to proudly announce their newly acquired capital and financial freedom facing China's ongoing development and rising inequality.

Writing on gender and neoliberal capitalism, Nancy Fraser shows a weakening link between sexuality and surplus value accumulation in the West (2013, cited in Rao 2015, 44). Exactly the opposite is true in today's China: social and sexual mobilities are largely monopolized as a direct function of who has access to capital. Still in an ongoing process of capital accumulation, China's newly emerged middle classes have to establish sexual transgression and potential emancipation on a development-based material foundation, through which a privatized and consumption-orientated homonormative culture and lifestyle become imperative. While the general lack of social recognition draws a rather hopeless picture for queer people, the pursuit of social mobility and the competition for capital have instilled a preoccupation with social class privilege in people's everyday life where a queer future may have become hinged upon. That said, neoliberalism's promise of "inclusive" resource allocation does not solve the more fundamental problem of maldistribution that underlines existing and ongoing social injustice and exclusion, nor does it directly address the sociocultural misrecognition of gender and sexual mobilization.

Furthermore, the enforced principle of proximity in mobile social networks further troubles the myth of quality in structuring and conditioning mobile intimacies. "Bluntly stated," writes Max Fox, mobile dating apps are mainly used by gay men "to find guys to fuck" (2014, 19). Whether one cheers for its relentless supply of erotic capital or impugns it as a disordered market of seductive part-objects (Hartman 2013, 45), it does not change the fact that locative mobile dating apps are pervasively used for "pseudonymous sexual encounters between gay strangers" (Licoppe, Rivière, and Morel 2016, 2540). These mobile apps are meant to "preclude repeat encounters and relational development, so that the protagonists are supposedly left unaffected, emotionally, relationally and socially, by such encounters" (2555). The enforced proximity, in this sense, only facilitates short and transient sexual encounters for quick exchanges of erotic capital but to a much less extent forges meaningful and long-lasting social and relational closeness. In this case, the promise of "mobile intimacies" mostly produces erotic intimacy, while queer people's need for deep sociocultural connections is often left unattended, let alone their longing for love and anchorage.

This explains why mobile apps like Grindr in the West and Blue'd in China carry the stigma as superficial hookup tools. In Chinese gay slang, these newly emerged hookup apps are known as *yuepao shenqi* or literally "holy tools for fuck-buddies." What is condemned is never sex per se but that the enforced proximity on mobile platforms offers too little for the exchange of cultural capital and too much for erotic encounters. This is why Ling's company launched ZANK as a mobile service for interest-based dating, as distinctive from sex-based dating and hookup. ZANK carries on Feizan's early strategy to augment cultural rather than erotic capital, with an eye-catching slogan "dating starts from interests" (*yuehui cong xingqu kaishi*), which essentially says "dating starts from similar cultural pursuits and habitus." But the proximity-centered design of ZANK, not unlike its various predecessors and competitors, has continued the enforced principle of geolocational closeness and hence significantly limited its potential in capitalizing non-erotic forms of human capital.

ZANK's strategy for interest-based dating has soon been challenged by the users' resistant tactics. While some people initiate dating in restaurants, cinemas, sports centers, bookshops, and film clubs, others use the same feature in the app for dating in hotel rooms—an indirect call for hookup and casual sex. ZANK has to some extent become yet another "holy tool" on mobile screens. Driven by venture capital, Ling's company also has a financial obligation to its investors and needs to promote ZANK to as wide a market as possible. In other words, quality has to make way for quantity. After all, ZANK's strong cultural focus inherited from Feizan appears insufficient to cater to venture capital's growing appetite, nor does it meet people's demand for rapid and mobilized circulations of sexual capital in the age of hyper-connectivity and digital mobility. This is most evident in the somewhat lukewarm popularity of ZANK in China's gay communities and its relatively small user-base compared to that of Blue'd.

Loyal members of Feizan and ZANK tend to believe that the cultural approach helps differentiate ZANK from other hookup apps in targeting a niche market (cultural snobs and omnivores) within an already niche gay market. Apparently, this will not satisfy ZANK and the venture capital behind it for a larger market share. In addition to incorporating online shopping in the mobile app in 2015, ZANK started to follow other queer and heterosexual dating apps to include "live streaming" (*zhi bo*) in 2016. From mainstream video-sharing websites to mobile dating apps, *zhi bo* has proven extremely popular among young Chinese people and has led to the emergence of many grassroots internet celebrities. However, such live streaming may include content that is erotic in nature. Although websites and mobile streaming apps in China censor and encourage users to report erotic content, it is not easy to control what the users choose to live-stream via mobile phones to a small group of followers. Mobile dating apps hence also turn into "holy tools" for live-streamers and viewers.

These newly emerged "holy tools" have been publicly condemned by the authorities on national television. On 13 February 2015, the influential crime-fighting TV show *Legal Report* (*Jinri Shuofa*) aired an episode titled *Dangerous Relationship* (*Weixian Guanxi*), depicting drug-enforcement agents catching gay men red-handed with methamphetamine and in promiscuous group sex—both illegal in China. The agents found that these people were complete strangers and initiated an investigation into how they hooked up through locative mobile apps for drugs and sex. The investigation concluded in what was depicted as a major triumph that saw dozens of drug-using gay men detained in compulsory rehabilitation centers. However, this episode focused less on drugs than on gay hookup apps. The show described in detail what they called mobile application B (Blue'd) and mentioned another popular platform J (Jack'd). Several drug-using and HIV-positive gay men were interviewed in the rehabilitation centers, talking about the "high percentage" (i.e., the large *quantity*) of drug users and HIV-positive men on mobile gay hookup platforms. A high-ranking national drug-enforcement officer specifically pointed out in the show that the B app had millions of users—and was hence a major threat to social stability and "population quality." Although several detained gay men described the apps as "*tongzhi* social networking software," the fact that these apps were designed and used for dating was completely neglected by the show.

Group sex and drug abuse clearly ran against the lingering myth of quality engineered by the state in producing self-regulated and health-conscious middle-class citizens. Once again, nobody in the show used the term *suzhi*; rather, both the senior drug-enforcement officer and the field agents specifically emphasized that they would not judge "personal choice" (i.e., homosexual orientation).

This further underlines my previous argument that the *suzhi* rhetoric has been replaced by the discourse of individualization that continues to justify social exclusion, where social hierarchy is hidden behind "individual choice" regardless of who has the privilege to make such choices free from public scrutiny. When mobile gay social media have proven effective in bringing together nearby strangers for sex-driven and drug-infused activities under the radar of state regulation, the authorities started to panic and brought up the issue on national TV for a new round of naming and shaming. It soon generated a chilling effect among locative gay app users and reinforced the common stigma around these "holy tools" inside and beyond China's queer communities. Since then, ZANK has automatically displayed a message whenever a user started to chat with others ("keep yourself safe—no porn or drugs") as a way to further encourage self-governance and self-censorship on this mobile dating platform.

The politics of enforced proximity further disturb the myth of quality in fostering a "networked individualism" among the users of locative mobile social media. Mobile dating apps facilitate digitally mediated and transient social connections; once a person travels to another location, the apps will show a different set of users in proximity. What mobile social media have to offer is less a *community* than a *platform* that travelers and commuters pass through and search for quick and ad hoc encounters instead of residency. The early marketing slogan of ZANK, "dating starts from interests," has also been replaced by "no longer lonely with you." The new slogan indicates a promise to save people from loneliness by facilitating location-based social networking and dating via mobile technology. This echoes the slogan of another mobile gay dating and hookup app, G-You: "in lonely cities, there is always a group of people like you." Here the "group" refers to both sexual minorities and lonely urban dwellers and migrants who often turn to mobile apps to find company.

To put it another way, the politics of enforced proximity capitalize on *an economy of loneliness* through mobile queer social networking platforms. In the pursuit of quality and upward social mobility through education and employment, frequent internal/international migrations have often detached people from their original families and social circles and relocated them into new places and environments. Tight and intimate social connections established in one's early life have therefore been replaced by new communities and networks of strangers, from where a loneliness in the localist host cities has emerged and become prevalent. In other words, the discourse of *suzhi*/quality has reproduced not only an aspirational middle-classness but also a post-development urban loneliness that the locative mobile apps have promised to mitigate. However, social mingling through mobile apps often appears as "a repetition of similar encounters among a wealth of potential new partners" and occurs between unknown strangers "who are attractive in part because they are strangers" (Licoppe, Rivière, and Morel 2016, 2541). The promise of the enforced proximity thus becomes questionable, when its strategy to save people from loneliness is to facilitate often short-lived encounters between strangers instead of nurturing and cultivating long-term and deep social and relational connections. This is why the enforced principle of proximity has only reproduced a "lonely crowd" (Fox 2014) on mobile dating platforms where solitudes are plural and users are "alone together" (Turkle 2011).

The idea of the lonely crowd was first developed by David Riesman ([1950] 2001) in his classical sociological research of the "other-oriented" American middle class who rely on a social "radar" to look at others for conformity. Riesman's "radar" metaphor finds a new manifestation in locative mobile media in the twenty-first century—the early version of ZANK, for example, had a function to search for nearby users by showing a radar (a "gaydar") on screen. Writing on networked individualism, Rainie and Wellman (2012) argue that in the recent century every generation has come up with something like "lonely crowd" to sound an alarm about the increase in social isolation and urban loneliness and the decline in community and authentic in-person relationships (117–18). They believe that such changes in human relationships along with the development of social media are not a shift toward social isolation but rather toward "flexible autonomy" (124–25). Neoliberal individuals increasingly play the role of abled agents in making their own choices in social interactions and act less as committed members in fixed groups. They are not lonely—loneliness exists only in isolated cases—but rather have more choices to invest their time across various networks and communities and devote themselves to social reciprocity in more selective ways.

However, what they call "autonomy" is precisely what I have described as a class-specific privilege of mobility that enables certain socially advantaged people for autonomous decision-making and individual self-governance to move freely among different networks and social groups. Those down the social ladder may not have the opportunities to be equally "selective" in queer social interactions and transgressive sexual practices. For sexual minorities, especially the closeted ones, their commitment to queer social networks is often isolated and separated from real-life connections with families, friends, and co-workers. That is to say, even if they can choose from a wide range of networks and groups to join, their transgressive sexual and cultural expressions are only allowed in self-confined queer communities online and offline, particularly in a country like China. These people already live in social isolation, while proximity-based locative media only relocate them into networks of strangers. To that end, the principle of proximity has limited capacity in facilitating queer social networking and collective homemaking to establish intimate communities or alternative families, as we have seen in the cases of early Feizan and the Concentric Circle film club.

In this sense, the guaranteed proximity does not solve the problem of queer people's social isolation, nor does it provide a solution to the loneliness facing urban queer migrants and residents. Mobile dating and hookup apps at best offer a complement, not a replacement, to queer people's needs for social connectivity and relational reciprocity. While Dennis Altman (2014, 6) believes in the equalizing power of mobile queer social media where everyone can come out and join in, these mobile platforms may not be the places that queer people fully belong to, not to mention that this "equalizing power" is deeply structured by social stratification and the unequal access to capital. It hence becomes questionable whether the networked individualism can really connect "everyone." Here, who has been excluded is arguably a more important question than who has become mobilized and networked. Above all, the exchange of sexual capital through mobile dating services offers little structural support for people's stretched experience of kinship and little help for their struggles in building a possible future. Many mobile social media users are still left single and lonely after their transient encounters, longing even more for love and anchorage that are hard to realize through such "mobile intimacies."

Furthermore, mobile queer social media users continue to clash with the authorities in China. In April 2017, the tightened crackdown on "obscene content" in social networking services saw ZANK and other live-streaming apps being removed from the app stores and their associated web portals shut down permanently. Soon after, Feizan also became inaccessible, until it was restored several months later. Those who stayed on Feizan believed that live streaming was the last straw that brought down ZANK, which was struggling in an awkward position to redefine itself from an interest-based dating platform to a mobile shopping portal and a live-streaming center. Initially, live streaming was incorporated in ZANK to attract users and compete against other mobile gay apps with this popular function; however, this made ZANK a target of the tightened state censorship and regulation and eventually led to its termination by the authorities. As far as the party-state is concerned, "networked individuals" through online and mobile social media are only entrusted with "autonomy" when they can contribute to maintaining China's existing social order. Any major deviation or transgression from the blueprint of consumer citizenship and responsible self-governance will be seen as subversive of social stability, at which point they will be effectively terminated by the state and the entrusted autonomy confiscated.

Gated Communities

From Feizan and Aloha to urban film clubs in China, today's queer communities online and offline are *gated communities* separated and segregated by class-specific capital and cultural taste in the lingering myth of quality. Mobilized by

China's capitalist expansion and continued growth, those who have succeeded in social migration and those who desire such success have dominated these queer communities and social networks. My argument of gated communities derives from the scholarship on China's housing reform and urban middle-class positioning. Housing in urban China often takes the form of high-rise residential buildings in individually gated residential compounds, referred to as *xiaoqu*. Most people are living in these condominium estates, not individual houses as often seen in the West. Previously, such an urban living arrangement was based on the *danwei*—"work-unit" or place of employment as both economic and social governing units in China (Bray 2005; Lü and Perry 1997). That means people who worked in the same *danwei* would likely live in the same gated residential compound, where neighbors were also co-workers and the sense of community was strong. As a result of the rapid privatization of state-owned enterprises and the commercialization of the real estate market, the *danwei*-based housing arrangement has significantly declined and has been replaced by private real-estate developments (see Pow 2009; Tang 2013; Tomba 2004, 2014; Wu 2005; Zhang 2010).

In other words, the urban housing sector has transformed from communities of colleagues and acquaintances to private urban enclaves of strangers, which has contributed to the previously discussed urban loneliness and an emergent "society of strangers" in today's China. These urban enclaves often take the form of gated communities where spatial enclosure ensures privacy, higher social status, high-level community services, a high-quality lifestyle, and spatial and social segregation from "low-*suzhi*" groups such as the urban poor and rural-to-urban peasant migrant workers. In today's urban China, people living in the same residential compound and even in the same building do not necessarily know each other, and the sense of community is rather weak. Also, when housing has become increasingly unaffordable in China's major urban centers, many residential properties have turned into rental apartments and shared households of strangers. Frequent changes of tenants in these shared rental apartments are not uncommon in the urban areas where "floating populations" like migrant workers and students abound. Established social connections in these temporary places of abode are hence frequently interrupted by mobilities.

Furthermore, many queer film clubs and LGBT organizations in China are hidden in such gated urban neighborhoods; part of my field research experience was walking through the gates (often guarded by property managers) to visit the queer enclaves and attend the social events in these gated communities. The office of Feizan/ZANK was also hidden in a gated residential compound in central Beijing, and I was questioned for a few minutes by a community guard (*bao'an*, often hired by property management companies) before I was allowed to enter the building. As Luigi Tomba comments,

> regulations have been passed that have encouraged those with private resources to build walls and hire guards in their residential compounds to insulate residents from the increasing dangers of urban life. This, in turn, has produced mixed (public-private) forms of neighborhood governance . . . in the strategies of middle-class positioning. (2009, 598)

These private players—property managers and community guards—have started to take charge of the safety and security of the gated urban communities as newly established forms of self-governed organizations (2009, 599). Following the party-state's vision of "harmonious society" (*hexie shehui*) since 2004,[6] gating and guarding the country's wealthier sectors of the urban middle classes can be easily justified as a precaution to maintain "harmonious communities" (*hexie shequ*) against potential urban unrest caused by the ongoing rural-to-urban migration and the growing social inequality. Gating as a social vehicle thus contributes to maintaining social stability during China's development and transformations.

It is from these fieldwork experiences and reflections that I have developed the metaphor of *gated communities* to designate today's social inclusion and exclusion *of* queer people in the wider society as well as *within* the queer communities themselves. I argue that today's queer communities in China are segmented into different social clusters, or small gated communities, the entry to which entails certain "qualities" determined by various forms of human capital specific to one's social position and class affiliation. Among the film clubs that I visited during my fieldwork, the Fellowship of *Tongzhi* Film-Lovers (*Huo Ying Tong Ren*, hereafter the "Fellowship") presents an *exemplar par excellence* of gated urban queer communities. As the oldest queer film club in China established in early 2009, the Fellowship derived from the Beijing LGBT Center that had held occasional queer film screenings since mid-2008. Lu Tai, a young film lover traveling to Beijing for job search, participated in a few sessions and then took up the challenge to establish a regular film club for the LGBT Center. The club gradually became independent in subsequent years, only in collaboration with the center to use its office as the screening venue. The Fellowship has online profiles on popular film websites Douban and Mtime and then on Feizan and mainstream social media Weibo and WeChat, with over 30,000 followers combined. As of early 2016, this film club had organized more than 300 weekly screenings in seven consecutive years, only with sporadic interruptions, and some early sessions each attracted as many as eighty participants in a small screening venue.[7] These achievements reflect the Fellowship's unparalleled success and influence in the local queer community.

The Fellowship has a strong and distinctive cinephilic taste and inclination. The films shown in this club are worldwide art-house cinematic classics including both queer and non-queer films, with very few commercial blockbusters. Each time, one or more guest speakers will be invited to the screening and will prepare a slideshow presentation to share their reflections on the film; sometimes Lu Tai himself will deliver a talk after the screening (Figure 5.2). During my field research from 2013 to 2014 that included participatory observation in the Fellowship, most post-screening discussions were led by either a veteran cineaste or a young filmmaker or film student; these people exclusively demonstrated an impressive knowledge of and a deep passion for cinematic art. Moreover, the discussions often developed closely around the films and could be completely irrelevant to queer issues. Sometimes the participants only talked about the characters and the stories, or generally about love and intimacy without specific reference to transgressive queer desires, even though most of them were gay men (with a few lesbian women). Both the guest speakers' devotion to and the participants' enthusiasm in cinematic art have been frequently and saliently hailed as a unique quality of this film club through its online publicity across mainstream and queer social media. The distinctive cinephilic focus of the Fellowship, queer or not, separates this film club from its competitors such as the counseling-style Concentric Circle, the gay-friendly coffee house and film club Two-City Café, as well as the more entertaining film clubs in Shanghai and Guangzhou that I visited during my research.

Figure 5.2 Lu Tai introducing French actress Isabelle Adjani to the film club participants (photo by author with Lu Tai's permission)

However, this artistic taste and obsession with cinematic art may potentially alienate the participants whose passion for film is not as strong. When I interviewed Lu Tai in late 2014, together with a regular participant and a volunteer working in the club since its foundation in 2009, the distinctive cinephilic orientation of the club and the film-focused organizing style were central concerns in our conversation. During my observational study in this club, I noticed that there were always some attendees who were less active in the post-screening discussions. They often showed less interest in the films and were more likely to drop out from participation after their first session. At any rate, a two- or three-hour screening of an art-house film followed by a one-hour discussion can be exhausting, if not disappointing, for those who only came to mingle with their queer peers and look for potential dates and partners:

> Author: *Some participants seem to come here for dating and networking?*
>
> Lu Tai: *It's possible. Many people might be like that. Probably fewer people come to the film club purely for film screening.*
>
> Xiao (long-term volunteer): *One-third—I'm in charge of* qiandao *[taking and keeping records of attendance] and roughly one-third of them are regular participants for film screenings.*
>
> Author: *So roughly one-third regular participants, one-third casual visitors, and one-third "one-timers"?*
>
> Lu Tai: *That's probably right. Some people couldn't fit in* ("bu he pai"). *People have different thoughts and personalities, as well as different interests.*

In this case, the focus on cinematic art of the Fellowship arguably functions as an underlying classifying mechanism that engenders potential inclusions and exclusions. As I have argued after Pierre Bourdieu, taste in art is automatically rank-ordered and rank-ordering, while the pursuits of certain cultural capital and upward social mobility are tokens of the rising and aspirational middle classes in urban China. Lu Tai's personal experience—migrating to Beijing and building both his own business and the queer film club from scratch—presents a successful story of social mobility and "class escape" (Bérubé 1997, 44–45) from the left-behind rurality and poverty in China's less-developed area. Such social class mobility empowers people in coming out as successful urban gay migrants from disadvantaged geographical and social positions. However, as my previous analyses have shown, only a select few are able to put down their roots in the host city, while those failed in geographical *and* social class migrations are often soon forgotten and reduced to silence. In this case, the taste in art-house cinema and the knowledge of film cultures shared by the members of the Fellowship not only symbolize advanced cultural capital but indicate their previous success in social mobilization. Both their geographical relocations and their cultural pursuits have constituted an upward lifting of their social position and class affiliation.

It is in this sense that I argue today's queer communities in China are gated and segmented by class-specific qualities and cultural tastes both embedded within and enabled through upward social mobilization. The Fellowship, for example, functions as a small queer community gated by the relatively highbrow taste of art-house film, a luxurious cultural capital not often affordable for those down the social ladder. Concentric Circle, with its focus on psychotherapy and mental health, also reproduces self-governed "high-quality" citizens by regulating transgressive psychosexual desires through the modern science of psychology.[8] Furthermore, a commercial coffee house like Two-City Café caters particularly to the consumerist desire of the rising urban middle classes, while "coffee" itself has been a symbol of a Western lifestyle and a token of middle-classness in today's China. Although the term *suzhi* seldom surfaced during our post-screening discussions in these queer spaces, the foci on middle-class consumer citizenship and subjectivity and on self-development through science and culture have unmistakably extended the *suzhi* discourse of building "quality" into people, which in turn produces and justifies social distinctions. These queer film clubs, in other words, are gated and walled by class-specific qualities, the entry to which is not often granted to those with less cultural and economic wealth.

They are, in short, gated queer communities. In this case, the "gating" process ensures both physical/spatial and social/cultural segregations. At the physical and spatial level, gating and walling present both a condition and a consequence underlining the emergence of China's middle-class communities. The fact that these queer film clubs exclusively locate in large urban areas (or satellite university towns near major metropolises) has in itself limited the access to urban residents and successful rural-to-urban migrants. Such spatial gating and zoning, argues Tomba (2009), effectively limit self-governance and autonomous participation "by the physical and administrative boundaries of the community" (559). The geographical locations and borders of these communities—which initially came into being through social mobilization and middle-class expansion—have now begun to define new urban boundaries and segments that potentially consolidate existing social stratifications led by those who already gained their social-economic privilege. Anagnost (2004) describes this as a "stunningly concretized" urban gatedness that separates the newly emerged middle classes from less wealthy and lower-quality urban slums scattered around the cities and the areas between cities and villages (190–91). Gates and walls hence work as both inclusive and exclusive technologies that, by virtue of their segregating and border-defining functions, create physical enclaves and social spaces while limiting the membership to clearly delineated social groups (Tomba, 599).

At the societal level, this marks a new middle-class "territoriality" that offers the promise of a good life for the socially mobilized, better educated, and reasonably wealthy populations (Pow 2009). This territoriality has emerged in a time when China's deprived past and pre-reform social upheavals still haunt its elder citizens, as I have discussed earlier in this book, who have often passed on to the new generation a sense of insufficiency of material wealth and inadequacy of social welfare—and hence a strong desire for security and stability through such vehicles as housing and gating. The formation of this territoriality also owes to "the rapid social change and dramatic improvement of some social groups' lifestyles, together with the widened inequality gap between different social groups" (Tang 2013, 66). In this sense, the established spatial and social boundaries effectively protect the rightful material wealth and social privilege of the beneficiaries of China's post-socialist economic miracle.

This line of thought helps explain the value of gating for queer people in a wider social context. The need and desire for security and stability are even stronger among the futureless queer individuals, whose life already lacks the insurance of marriage and reproduction as well as the scaffold of family blessing, social tolerance, state support, and legal recognition. Other than economic and cultural capital, they barely have anything else that can still offer them protection and a sense of longevity and futurity. At any rate, in an authoritarian country where sex-related issues have been heavily regulated and self-regulated as encouraged and enforced by the state, pursuing economic and cultural wealth seems to be the only available and legitimate channel for upward queer social migration. Gating and walling are hence irreplaceable in producing and maintaining a sense of territoriality, however fragile, when queer people have very limited "territory" and social space in the wider society. Their membership in gated communities engenders a relative privilege that to some extent compensates for their transgressive desires that have been precluded from the normalized productions of conforming sexual citizens. Gating also helps protect privacy, to the extent that the exchange of sexual capital can be carried out behind closed gates and erected walls.

It is also in this sense that urban gating and social gating have proven effective in structuring social distinctions *within* China's queer communities both online and on the ground. The very ability to build and maintain a committed and long-term queer relationship is a privilege that many people still cannot afford in today's China; advanced social position and individual capital thus indicate a better chance for a good life and a possible queer future. Therefore, gating effectively brings together people with similar social status and cultural tastes, which ensures and extends the effective exchange of human capital and helps facilitate queer social interactions and intimacies such as dating and relationship building. After all, cultural taste is a matchmaker and "what brings together things and people that go together" (Bourdieu [1984] 2010, 236–37). If gating on Aloha and early Feizan presents an efficient mechanism for users to filter and screen desirable dates and potential partners based on cultural capital and class-related lifestyles, then social gating in urban queer film clubs and communities also enforces such social distinctions that mark the difference between "winners" and "losers" and their respective abilities in building a queer future out of the heteronormative social and familial structure.[9]

In this case, gating and walling in today's China have also reproduced the state-engineered larger social inclusion and exclusion within urban middle-class communities. People entitled for residency in these gated urban enclaves—both in the physical form as gated residential compounds and in the metaphoric form as queer spaces gated and walled by cultural tastes—are those who have benefited the most from the state policy in improving population quality and in expanding urban middle classes through economic reforms and the higher education expansion. Although these urban communities and cultural spaces are often open to new members, the de facto residency is often granted to those who have enough class-related capital to "cash in" for membership. The beneficiaries of previous social mobilization have silently built walls and closed the doors to their less successful counterparts, further consolidating their privacy and primacy while reinforcing existing social boundaries.

As a filtering and screening mechanism, gating hence offers selective inclusion and exclusion to set the boundaries, map the territory, and regulate entry to maintain the quality of the gated communities. Not unlike the gated and walled "harmonious" urban residential compounds that need property managers and community guards, socially segregated queer communities entail committed members and strong leaders and gatekeepers. In the case of the Fellowship, the organizer decides what films to show, which guest speakers to invite, what kind of media outlets to use for publicity, and what topics to discuss after screenings. The core members of this gated community (long-term participants and volunteers) also contribute to maintaining its organizing style and operational standard. Such a strategy ensures that temporary visitors and would-be residents follow the rules and the examples to uphold the value of this community to maintain its quality and safeguard its cultural and social wealth from any potential "gate crashers." Social gating, in this sense, functions as not only a matchmaking mechanism but also a quality-control process by setting up role models and encouraging and enforcing self-governance within the established boundaries and gated territories.

On top of that, gating helps maintain social distinctions across different types of queer spaces forged by those seeking different types of capital. Such distinctions most saliently manifest in the assumed differences between gay bars and film clubs in the lingering *suzhi* hierarchy. In my interviews with the founder of the Fellowship and the organizers of the Concentric Circle film club, they made the same point separately that those coming to film clubs are essentially a very different type of people from those frequenting gay bars. This echoes my observation that many people in China's gay communities online and offline have shown a distinctive aversion to cruising spaces like gay bars and nightclubs in favor of cultural spaces like film clubs:

> Author: *What is the value and meaning of the Fellowship for you?*
>
> Lu Tai: *People come to watch film and then have a chat together—they often enjoy themselves, which makes me happy as well . . . For networking, I also prefer to meet new friends in this way. I don't like Blue'd and Jack'd and don't like visiting [gay] bars. I met my friends and acquaintances all in this way [through the film club].*
>
> Author: *Then what's in it for the participants?*
>
> Yao (pseudonym, frequent participant): *It feels like we have "found it" [a place we belong to]. . . . coming here, we are all the same, and sometimes what people say can get deep into your heart. We watch a lot of films—*tongzhi, *art-house—and I like them all.*

Similarly, in the case of Concentric Circle, the filmic-therapeutic experience with a focus on mental development (*xinling chengzhang*) is valued and hailed by the organizers as "much more beneficial" for queer people than is the experience of visiting cruising spaces like gay bars (see Chapter 1). Here, bars and nightclubs are in themselves highly contradictory places. On the one hand, bar culture in China is a fashion coming from the West after the opening up of the country, and some early gay bars were established with the assistance of Western gay and lesbian activists. In this sense, gay bars are "modern, urban, and Western," leading to an increasingly popular lifestyle enjoyed by today's young consumers and urban dwellers. On the other hand, a strong stigma has been surrounding these places as "disordered, unregulated, and lacking meaning and value" for queer people, indicating a rather negative stereotype that these places are mainly used as cruising spaces to hunt for sex.

If we see gay bars and nightclubs as gated urban queer enclaves, then such gating maps their territory along two types of boundaries: sexual capital and economic capital. Along the first line, physical attractiveness and sexual vivaciousness often determine one's popularity in gay bars. In this sense, cruising spaces like gay bars and nightclubs are gated and marked mainly by sexual attraction and bodily appeal, where the aged and the unkempt are often excluded from these gated urban venues. Here, the surplus of sexual capital in these cruising places is still seen by many in a tandem opposition to the upward cultural pursuits that provide a better chance for a committed same-sex relationship. In the stratified and segregated queer communities, this line of thoughts extends the *suzhi*-style social distinction that renders gay bars towards the lower end of the hierarchy of quality as shallow and superficial cruising spaces gated and walled not by cultural pursuits but by erotic desires.

More important, while sexual capital tends to decline when people age, cultural and economic capital often increase when people get older; if the former is precarious, then the latter rather needs gradual accumulation over time and hence bears a sense of longevity. For queer people, as I have discussed, anything that offers a sense of longevity and futurity as well as security and stability will be warmly embraced and celebrated, given that their sexualities still lack proper support and protection across a range of social institutions. Also, middle-class queers increasingly crave committed same-sex love and long-term relationships, as other aspects of their life have already been dramatically improved and better supported during China's rapid development and social transformations. The longevity of queer love is the last missing piece and the most challenging part to acquire and secure, as many people will have to break up with their same-sex partners for heterosexual marriage and reproduction to fulfill their filial responsibility under compulsory familism. This marks an ongoing mismatch between the unsustainable queer love and the relentless progression of other life conditions in people's lived experiences of transgressive desires.

That is to say, when cruising spaces are often stigmatized as inattentive to people's longing for love and anchorage, other social groups such as film clubs have emerged as new and "higher-quality" social circles for dating and networking: both the focus of Concentric Circle on self-development and the cultural taste of the Fellowship function as more reliable matchmaking mechanisms that offer a sense of longevity. If cruising connotes a *horizontal* flow of erotic desires between young urban queers driven by an urge to cash out their sexual capital when they still can, then frequenting cultural spaces rather indicates a desire and determination for a queer future driven by the process of *vertical* self-development and capital accumulation through upward cultural pursuits and social mobilization. If the former primarily focuses on present enjoyment, then only the latter—the condition and the consequence of an upward social mobility—can be a savior of the already precarious queer love that significantly lacks social recognition and family support.

Further, gay bars and nightclubs are also gated and walled by economic capital, which appears even more problematic. "Cruising" aside, people often see gay bars as consumer spaces for those with more financial freedom to sustain an active lifestyle, the entry to which will not be granted to the less wealthy others such as the urban poor. However, in today's post-*suzhi* society, not every kind of individual quality is created and treated equal. China's rapid and unprecedented growth has led to a highly inconsistent formation of the middle classes where mismatches between economic wealth and cultural capital are commonplace. Economic wealth, albeit a material foundation, is sometimes less powerful than cultural capital in marking and justifying social distinctions. If we see gay bars as consumer spaces and film clubs as cultural spaces, then Ying Miao's observation can help us understand their differences:

> having money is not considered enough: only when a person also strives to better him or herself can he or she be considered to have attained superior social status, or in this case, the middle class . . . they are differentiating themselves from those "others" who are perceived as only meeting the economic criteria for middle class. Economic factors might be fundamental to pinning down their own class identity, but simply being similar on a material level was not enough, or indeed relevant, for them to associate with someone as a member of their class. (2017, 639–40)

That means soft and symbolic cultural indicators carry a heavier weight than does hard and objective material wealth in people's perception of social distinctions. While economic capital is a prerequisite to an ideal middle-class life, culture is "the defining point of middle class identity" widely perceived by Chinese people to justify intra-class social distinctions (642–43). Such distinctions often emerge between the culturally superior "winners" and the average others who lack cultural pursuits and hence only possess partial middle-class status, even though socioeconomic data indicate that their de facto income falls in the same middle range.

To that end, gay bars gated by erotic desire and spending power often appear insufficient for dating and relationship building, insofar as these places offer little concern and little relevance to the defining cultural indicators of class status and social belonging. This distinction is every bit as important for today's internally gated and segregated middle classes. Taste, education, mannerism, and behaviors all function as significant determinants of class identity, where quality consumption, aspiration, intellectual pursuits, and cultural interests all indicate a worthwhile lifestyle that distinguishes those who have "won" from those who have money but lack cultural capital (Miao 2017, 633, 641). As a result, "there is a certain level of cultural expectation attached to the concept of middle class" that has been commonly recognized in today's China (641). Hence, the upward cultural pursuits function as not only gating vehicles but also class symbols. After all, urban gay bars and queer film clubs appear to have been gated by different types of human capital that in turn feed into class identities and social distinctions. Although at any rate people can visit both types of queer spaces for recreation and entertainment as well as dating and networking, the distinctions in the assumed differences and gating mechanisms of these queer enclaves indicate a hierarchical structure among today's segregated queer middle classes in a post-*suzhi* society.

From the politics of proximity to the gated queer communities, the lingering myth of quality has continued to underpin the reproductions of social inclusion and exclusion in today's queer communities, although the term *suzhi* has often retreated behind the claims of individual choice, leisure pursuits, and gated territoriality. China's capitalist expansion and development have opened many avenues for social mobilities, often conditioned by the uneven flows and unequal distributions of capital and resources, where the desire for social migration often drives and accompanies geographical relocations and upward cultural pursuits. The search of love and anchorage has to a great extent become structured by the competition for capital and the associated privilege, as well as by the competition for settlement and residency in gated urban communities and social spaces. Meanwhile, these growth-induced mobilities and immobilities have confined gender and sexual diversity in a limited neoliberal process based on individual self-reliance and self-investment, leaving many structural problems to the hands of individual agents.

The neoliberal development and self-improvement may have created many "life winners" and an ever-expanding and ever-desiring middle class, but this process only offers a partial and selective solution to queer people under compulsory familism and heterosexual reproduction. Those who gained their privilege through previous social mobilization have started to build walls and gates to consolidate existing social distinctions, while those failed in and excluded from the development-induced mobilities and middle-class expansion are left with limited choices and resources. The lack of access to capital has largely throttled their dream for a queer future facing the widening social inequality and inter- and intra-class stratifications. While some social groups' gender and sexual mobilities have been folded into the process of neoliberal individualization and human capital accumulation, many others have been alienated who find themselves increasingly deprived of the privilege of mobilities. Social and spatial gating and walling in China's online and urban middle-class communities have functioned as vehicles of social inclusion and exclusion in the country's ongoing post-*suzhi* transformations, which has significantly hindered the once-promising social mobilization and started to concretize existing social stratifications and segregations after four decades of strong growth and development. This will further complicate the issue of social mobilities and immobilities amid the growing socioeconomic uncertainties and complexities, when China marches into its fifth decade of social and economic reform that will continue to shape and reshape queer cultures and queer mobilities.

Closing Remarks

From late 2017 to early 2018, I revisited China when its growth was slowing down (but still topped the world) and the country was undergoing internal economic restructuring. Sitting in a taxi with the radio turned on, I heard a central government official deliver a speech in a high-profile economic forum in Beijing, saying that "China's economic development is changing from high-speed growth (*gaosu zengzhang*) to high-quality growth (*gaozhiliang zengzhang*)." Outside the window and along the highway, established residential compounds were accompanied by construction sites where new apartment buildings were erected. I caught a glimpse of a slogan on a wall that read "improving the level of urban development" (*tigao chengshi fazhan shuiping*). I was told that the local government had temporarily shut down the high-pollution industries to reduce the suffocating smog in winter, although some factories continued production at night under the radar. During my stay, the TV news and current affairs programs made a great deal about China's determination to eliminate poverty within a few years in some of its most impoverished countryside; on the international stage, it was promoting the ambitious Belt and Road Initiative to its neighbors and followers near and far, trying to win support from its allies and critics alike.

These seemingly innocuous moments signaled China's ongoing socioeconomic transformations under the continued developmental agenda—although the focus has been gradually shifted to environmental protection, quality growth, and international expansion. Slogans promoting "change," "development," "rise," and "improvement" were still prevalent in every corner of my hometown, a small inland city overshadowed by and trying to catch up with the affluent coastal areas. In a country with an unprecedented and unparalleled growth rate for several decades, the upward theme of development has indeed permeated all walks of life and all parts of China. Born in the late 1980s and growing up during China's economic miracle and dramatic and profound social transformations, people in my generation have become accustomed to a life dominated by "development" (*fazhan*) and "progression" (*jinbu*)—at both the individual and the societal levels. When everyone is going up and everything is changing at a rapid speed, development and progression have become compulsory, while standing still essentially means lagging behind. Under a deep and strong developmentalism, people do not seem to have the choice or the excuse of not moving forward and upward. Entering the third decade of the twenty-first century, the party-state's confidence in China's power and prosperity through development has reached a new level both internally and externally, gaining a wide nationalist support from its many citizens in spite of various challenges and ineluctable "growing pains" facing it today.

China's case presents a very important lens through which we can better understand and further problematize the issue of gender and sexual modernity and diversity vis-à-vis the liberal-democratic and linear-progressive discourse that appears dominant and imperative in the West. It is also necessary for us to consider China through the lens of gender and sexual mobilities as a compelling case to scrutinize and make sense of its ongoing social change in its determined and single-minded pursuit of the country's great renaissance and revival in the twenty-first century. Along with China's capital-driven expansion and unapologetic power assertion on the global stage, the development-induced mobilities and immobilities will continue channeling queer desires and cultures through a neoliberal capitalist process without a fundamental political reform or a major shift in sex-related social ethos in the foreseeable future. This will further consolidate the stretched kinship structure and the stratified social classes and strata, insofar as compulsory familism and compulsory development are the two pressure points around which Chinese people have been structuring their practices and understandings of transgressive desires. While the diverse and disparate queer social and cultural practices will continue to grow under these shadows, queer people have to work out how to survive under the strong familism and developmentalism when the ongoing neoliberal process never really attends to their underlying longings and sufferings.

The Figure of the Queer Migrant

"The twenty-first century will be the century of the migrant"; political philosopher Thomas Nail opens his book *The Figure of the Migrant* with this declaration (2015, 1). There was movement before there was territory, which effectively mapped the boundaries and created the territories to differentiate clans, communities, societies, and countries. In this sense, argues Nail, migrants are constitutive figures and powers of histories and our current times. Yet in normative liberal paradigms, movement and mobility are overwhelmingly considered secondary and derivative, if not subordinate and invisible, as an aberration to the rules of stable, civilized lifestyles and tight nation-state governance and border control. If the migrant is "the political figure of our time" (235), then it is necessary to refigure the migrant through the lens of kinopolitics (politics of movement) instead of kinetophobia (fear of motion), although movement itself cannot be valorized given the heterogeneous material conditions embodied in migrations (4). The regimes of territorial, social, and cultural motions have been constantly shifting and shaping the figure of the migrant across different types of borders—gates, walls, fences, cells, checkpoints, detention centers, etc.—that are themselves unstable and keep shifting along with geopolitical tensions and conflicts, as Nail further points out in *Theory of the Border* (2016).

Queer Chinese Cultures and Mobilities has considered many different figures of queer migrants: the "sad lonely young men" who are nonetheless self-conscious about their gay migrant/diaspora identities in autobiographical queer films and videos; the young generation who has to face the "annual interrogation" during family reunions; people relocated from *danwei*/workplace-based living arrangements to private residential compounds; co-tenanted queer migrants in shared apartments; the founders, organizers, volunteers, and participants of the urban queer film clubs; regular wage earners and leisure-class queers in various gated communities with different levels of entitlement to a mobile lifestyle; those who have failed and who have succeeded in geographical and social migrations; as well as large numbers of social media users on online and mobile digital platforms who are segregated and stratified by the type of human capital they are displaying and going after. In this sense, the figures and images of queer migrants are far from consistent or homogeneous; rather, they look fragmented and stretched across the complex formulations and interventions of family and kinship, internal and international migrations, and social classes and social strata.

On the other hand, the queer migrants recorded in this book still look rather confined in a small demography of young and educated gay males, while mobilities along the lines of gender/sexuality, ability/disability, and ethnicity/nationality should be further contextualized and examined in relation to China and other Sinophone societies. Studies on lesbian women in Chinese societies are growing under the avid academic interest in gay-male cultures along with emerging scholarship on queer people of age (e.g., Kong 2012) and sexual minorities in rural China (e.g., Koo et al. 2014). However, other marginalized queer people (transgender, bisexual, intersex, asexual, those with disabilities, etc.) in Chinese societies have not caught enough attention. In addition, many agencies based in the West have extended their businesses to China for overseas gay marriage and adoption/surrogacy, when the cost has become more affordable for a growing number of middle-class queer couples. In the years to come, we will see an emerging demography whose same-sex marriage and parent status are recognized in other jurisdictions but not in their home country. These reconfigurations of sexuality and mobility in transnational queer homemaking deserve our attention in the imminent future.

On top of that, as I have discussed earlier in this book, my own image in the research field also appears inconsistent and straddles the East (where I was born) and the West (where I returned from), gay (as all my informants assumed) and not-gay (I never labeled myself as such and never believed in dichotomous sexual categories), desiring and desirable (as young and new to the local gay circles), questioning and questionable (as an ethnographer peeping into the local queer spaces where he was not really a member), as well as backward (growing up in a severely underdeveloped small town and in a regular wage-earner family) and upward (with advanced education at a high-ranked university in the West and a good knowledge of the so-called "high culture"). When I interviewed Yeh-tzu in the Taiwanese Two-City Café in Beijing, he was also curious that I, a researcher growing up in the Mainland, was interested in Taiwanese and other Sinophone cultures on the margin of China and Chineseness. My own contradictory image in the eyes of other queer migrants reflects the heterogeneous formulations and configurations along the very concepts and categories of "queer" and "migrant."

"Migrant" is a strong word. Every time we use this term, we essentially bring up a very complex figure embodied with different constituencies and contingencies as well as different motions and emotions that have been mobilized across geographical and cultural enclaves, borders and boundaries, routes and roots, time and space, body and mind, pain and pleasure, connection and alienation, conformity and non-conformity, social classes and social circles, home of origin and home of choice, and many, many more. Both "queer" and "migrant" are highly complex formulations: nothing other than the conjoint "queer migrant" is more powerful in challenging existing borders and limits, and nothing except for "queer migrant" is more effective in reminding us of existing social norms and conventions. "Queer" and "migrant" are inherently contradictory terms—transgressing and transcending the boundaries, while simultaneously reaffirming the social, cultural, historical, political, and economic conditions that helped reproduce them in the first place. That, at any rate, is the figure of the queer migrant in the twenty-first century.

Gay Circles and Neoliberal Desires

The rise of neoliberal cultures in China in particular, and Asia in general, has raised further questions about the changing queer cultures in the ongoing social transformations in Chinese societies. As a theory of political-economic practices of a free market made possible and safeguarded by the state, neoliberalism appears to have put the "state" in a contradictory position, and it is debatable to what extent neoliberalism entails a strong state and whether democracy is a precondition of a neoliberal economy and society (Bockman 2013; Harvey 2007, 2). Here, I agree with Aihwa Ong that we should consider neoliberalism in its "extreme dynamism, mobility of practices, responsiveness to contingencies, and *strategic entanglements* with politics" (2007, 3; italics mine). This helps make sense of the reproduction of neoliberal structures and agencies in a country without a liberal democracy, such as China, when it is still controversial whether China can be considered a neoliberal economy (Harvey, 139–40; Nonini 2008; Ong 2006, 2007; Ren 2010).

Recent studies (e.g., Rofel 2007) have documented the reproduction of neoliberal subjects and subjectivities in China in such domains as TV drama, museums, and gay bars. Neoliberalism appears to have energized the emergent urban queer cultures that have extended the free-market principles, enabled people to practice and express sexual interests under the banner of liberal individual choice, and to some extent freed social practices and cultural productions of gender and sexuality as well as desire and intimacy from state agencies. This is why Lisa Rofel also makes clear the significance of the expressive desire in the construction of neoliberal agents and the (imagined) gay spheres in such neoliberal spaces as urban gay bars. However, gay bars are not the only "queer publics" in China, and in fact many people have kept a conscious distance from these "cruising" spaces, as shown in my previous discussions. The expressively desiring gay men who are active in gay bars seem to belong to what we call *quanzi* ("circles," literally) in China's gay communities. Loretta Ho (2010) notes the use of the word *quan* among her informants in Beijing (46, 91, 157) and tries to differentiate this concept from what we call "community" in English. *Quanzi* is a slang term frequently used by gay men in mainland China to describe lifestyle-based social circles constituted of socially and sexually active gay men. Those in the "circle" are believed to be more libertine—more likely to seek casual sexual encounters and frequent gay cruising spaces both online and on the ground.

People outside the circle, in contrast, are often less liberal in sexual conduct and especially less active in seeking socio-sexual encounters with strangers. They often see *quanzi* as in a constant state of disorder ("*luan*"; Ho 2010, 46, 91) and criticize those in the circle for their obsession with casual sex and their reluctance to commit. More important, people in the *quanzi* often take the blame that their openness to sex further stereotypes and stigmatizes the entire gay community in the general public, although this so-called "gay community" is in fact a loosely defined entity whose members vary significantly in class, age, education, occupation, and other key demographic parameters. Similarly, *quanzi* is also a loosely defined "imagined community" that lacks clear boundaries. Some people believe that *quanzi* only includes those who are sexually hyperactive, while others think that anyone openly searching for same-sex relationships is also in the *quanzi*, regardless of his attitude toward sex. In addition, "entering the circle" (*ru quan*) and "quitting the circle" (*tui quan*) are not uncommon in the vernacular of same-sex attracted men in China. That is to say, people tend to see *quanzi* as a fluid domain where they can join in or drop out at ease.

"One man's imagined community," to quote Arjun Appadurai out of context, "is another one's political prison" (1996, 32). The desiring neoliberal subjects and subjectivities recorded in previous ethnographies seem to belong to this *quanzi*: the more self-conscious, desiring, liberal/libertine, and expressive gay circles in China. However, their counterparts outside the circles—potentially equally desiring—are often silenced and alienated from this neoliberal euphoria of expressive queer desires. Gay bars as cruising spaces and consumer spaces may be highly productive of expressive desires and desiring neoliberal subjects; however, as I have discussed in this book, they remain inattentive to the process of self-improvement and self-investment for cultural pursuits and social migration through which a queer future may become possible outside the heteronormative closet. The film club organizers in my research maintain a clear distinction between cultural spaces and cruising spaces, and many queer people are very proud that they have never visited such "disordered" places as gay bars and nightclubs, precisely because these so-called neoliberal places and neoliberal desires offer little relevance to their ongoing suffering under compulsory familism and compulsory development, and to their real longing for love and anchorage when many of them still have to marry the opposite sex and live in the closet for life.

The valorization of gay bars and that of neoliberal desires in previous ethnographies hence become problematic. It is not only that we have precluded those outside these places and overlooked other queer social spaces gated by the all-important cultural capital, but that the neoliberal claims have failed to account for what is still at stake for queer people and where their continued sufferings come from under the ongoing and entangled forces of familism and development. In this context, queer film clubs or urban gay bars alone can no longer offer a full picture of today's queer cultures and social practices. Although different queer spaces and enclaves are not mutually exclusive and participants can join in various social circles, these places still entail different forms of human capital in including or excluding different members and participants. In this case, the claims of neoliberal desires and subjects alone are inadequate in addressing and understanding the complex formulations and interventions of queer mobilities and immobilities amid China's rising inequalities and social stratifications in the early twenty-first century.

Searching for China's Middle Classes

Where are the middle classes in today's China? Or, more broadly, how can we qualify (and quantify) the so-called "middle classes" in a Chinese context? Social scientists have been using a range of measurements to delineate this newly emerged social class, from occupation and education to income level, family background, marital status, geographical location, and Communist

Party membership. Yet, the size of China's middle classes has been estimated and calculated at as low as 3.1 percent and as high as 85.5 percent of the overall population, with a very large variation in between (Goodman 2016, 9; Miao 2017, 630–31). More important, objective socioeconomic factors often fail to align with Chinese people's perception of and identification with social class and social status—cultural factors often serve as stronger indicators in today's China where class is concerned, underlined by the lingering myth of individual quality and self-development. There arguably exists a plurality of middle classes in today's China that still lack coherence and consistency in both objective measures and subjective perceptions.

The rising middle classes in China and in other fast-growing countries in Asia have paralleled a resurged interest in class analysis in Euro-American scholarship (Miao 2017, 630), where rigid class categories appear to have been increasingly challenged by more complicated inter- and intra-class stratifications and contradictions and by the intermingled force of social mobilities and immobilities. Class analysis as a method has been developed along two lines in social sciences: the first line focuses on class structure and struggle, following the lineage of Karl Marx and Max Weber; another line—what I have followed in this book—sheds more light on class culture and consciousness, derived from the legacy of Pierre Bourdieu ([1984] 2010) and followed more recently by sociologists such as Beverley Skeggs (2004) and Simon Stewart (2014). Here, class cultures offer a promising lens in today's China (and beyond) through which we can examine the rather inconsistent and heterogeneous formations of the middle classes that are often gated and walled by different cultural tastes and interests, whether queer or not.

Moreover, what I have described as "gated communities" function as the *exemplar par excellence* of Bourdieu's notion of the "field" (*le champ*), or social arenas where habitus operate to structure how we behave and what we like. As Simon Stewart comments in *A Sociology of Culture, Taste and Value* (2014), there exist specific stakes and interests in each field, and the rules and laws of one field may not suit another (64). In short, each field values certain knowledge and celebrates certain forms of capital. From Feizan and Aloha to queer film clubs and urban gay bars, each of these "fields" entails and enforces its own priorities of and preferences for different forms of human capital. In this sense, middle-class communities in today's China are gated and guarded both horizontally by field-specific human capital and vertically by the rank of different habitus in the lingering *suzhi* hierarchy, particularly based on the presence or the absence of upward cultural pursuits that feed into class identities and people's conscious experiences and articulations of social distinctions.

If a stable same-sex relationship and a possible queer future have become somewhat contingent on advanced sociocultural and socioeconomic status, then queer people seem to be left with only two options: moving up to earn a better chance for a happy life or relentlessly cashing out their bodies and desires until the time has come and they have to marry the opposite sex. In reality, there must exist many other choices and practices in between. In perception, however, this bluntly marks the distinction between (1) self-discipline in accumulating class-related capital and earning merits to afford a queer life and (2) giving up on oneself and eventually descending into the dark closet and the heteronormative abyss. These opposite directions in mobilities (moving up or moving down) conspicuously manifest in queer people's selective dating and relationship building—what philosopher and writer Matthew Stewart forthrightly describes as "assortative mating" in a different social context.

In his cover story in the June 2018 issue of *The Atlantic*, Stewart observes through recent socioeconomic data that the rising social inequality effectively decreases the number of wealthy and meritorious candidates on the dating market, which increases the reward for finding one and the penalty for failing to do so. Educational status and other social class indicators hence become significant parameters in selecting and identifying suitable partners. While Stewart is writing about heterosexual couples in the US, his observation echoes another study that provides the first large-scale evidence on the "gay glass ceilings" in the West. Following the neoliberal blueprint of inclusive labor force allocation, the latter study (Aksoy et al. 2018) finds that gay males are significantly under-represented among high-level managers in advanced capitalist economies; even if they can get into these positions, gay men often have more advanced degrees and qualifications compared to their straight counterparts. That is to say, queer people need more educational credentials to overcome the disadvantage in the labor market. In the case of China, the value of educational qualifications and other merits is not confined within the workplace for queer people; rather, they need these credentials to compensate for their transgressions and to survive in a society with low tolerance and low respect for non-reproductive sexualities.

If human capital (especially cultural capital) and the associated social privilege can offer some protection and a sense of longevity for the futureless queer people, then it is not a surprise that many of them heavily invest in self-development and desire high-quality peers as potential dates and partners to build a better queer future. As Ivan tells Windson in the film *Permanent Residence*:

> According to evolutionism, in any large tribe, there is a minority out of the ordinary. They will be repelled and suppressed by the mainstream. *They can survive only if they are more brilliant*. Eventually, their *merits* will spread and become the mainstream. Then a cycle of evolution is complete. (My translation and emphases)

Here, Ivan is referring to sexual minorities that have to be better and smarter than others to survive in a heteronormative society. Along this line, the aspirational queer middle classes—whatever that means in a demographic sense—have to earn "merits" and become "brilliant" life winners as a means to afford transgressive and non-conforming desires.

Indeed, a merit-based system has become prevalent in post-reform China from children's education to government officials' promotion; test scores and report cards have opened up avenues for social mobilities in the past few decades through which a meritocracy has emerged. However, the upward social channels have become increasingly narrow in more recent times. The winning meritocratic class has quietly built gates and walls to safeguard their privilege and silently closed the doors behind them. The once-promising social mobilization has been throttled by the growing social inequality and the increasingly crystalized and concretized social distinctions and class boundaries in today's China. We may find this meritocratic class happily and comfortably hidden under the cover of "middle classes," while their de facto upper-middle status is increasingly difficult for other people to acquire. China's post-reform meritocracy has effectively made itself exclusive and hereditary to manage and protect their wealth and privilege, while those in the middle and lower range of the middle classes are increasingly squeezed. This meritocratic class (or "leisure class" or "upper-middle class") often remains silent and unwilling to acknowledge their roles in the widening social inequality and the rising social immobility, even though many of them acquired their fortune and privilege through previous upward social mobilization in the first place.

If there exists a gay meritocracy in today's China, then the meritorious queer people are understandably prone to choosing partners within the meritocratic club, or at least among those who have shown the potential to become its members. More important, the ability to maintain a same-sex relationship is increasingly seen as a reward in direct relation to one's merits and achievements. This has nothing to do with gay rights or sexual emancipation as we have seen in liberal LGBT activism; rather, this is purely a mechanism for sexual deviants to earn privilege and survive as queers in today's China. At any rate, the *needs* for survival as queer individuals have triumphed over the collective *rights* for sexual and social justice. In this case, it is much easier to trade rights for privileges, especially when the latter can offer a better chance for a promising queer future. The lack of sexual equality seems to have driven people into a frantic pursuit of social privilege as a means to protect their sexual transgression; the social inequality has paradoxically become a salvation of sexual inequality, offering a partial solution for a select few while leaving many struggling under the dual pressure of heteronormativity and post-development social stratification and concretization.

An Economy of Loneliness

In today's China, queer social media companies have actively exploited the post-growth urban loneliness to market their services with the promise of saving people from their single and lonely life. During recent years, the (queer) middle classes in urban China have increasingly discriminated against single people, where *tuo dan* or "escaping from singleness" has become a popular and prominent (and every bit oppressive) discourse separating the winners from the losers based on relationship status. Having a partner almost indicates one's triumphant quality and ability to win in the market, while single people have started mocking themselves as *danshen gou*, or "single dogs," longing for love and attention. This jocular expression has become hyper-visible among the young generation, where self-mocking and self-loathing have turned into a collective, bittersweet valorization of the commonplace singleness and loneliness in today's urban China and Sinophone Asia.

More specifically, the rapid development of the region under global capitalism has put the young generation in a highly competitive market where relationships are expected to be established upon both economic value and cultural capital. Young men and women, both queer and straight, find themselves deprived of resources when the competition for love is increasingly conflated with and appears no less fierce than does the competition for capital. Social mobilities and relationship building have become mutually productive and constituent; those lacking social, economic, cultural, and sexual capital may be further deprived of love and anchorage. Youth loneliness has turned into a problem of social significance under compulsory familism and compulsory development, where single people's longing for romance and affection has led to an ever-growing market and a prospering economy that capitalize upon this pervasive loneliness. This is most noticeably shown by the annual "11.11" shopping frenzy on the 11th of November, China's unofficial Singles' Day as the number "1" symbolizes singularity, when splurging on discounted products is hailed as self-care and self-love for those lacking relational care and support in solitary living. Such self-reward consumption on Singles' Day is apparently contradictory to the common cultural practice of reciprocal gift-giving during traditional holidays. Capitalizing on the prevalent youth loneliness and neoliberal self-reliance, the "double-eleven" shopping spree has become the country's and the world's largest consumerist extravaganza since it was launched by China's e-commerce giant Alibaba in 2009, setting astonishing sales records every year in an economy that increasingly consumes and monetizes singleness and loneliness.

The increasingly prevalent loneliness among urban youth in China and other parts of capitalist Asia has further indicated the neoliberal conditions of human existence under the capitalist reproductions of fragmentary subjects and personhood. As I have discussed in this book, China is changing to a society of strangers, as the formerly strong reciprocal social connections in established institutions have been reshaped by the neoliberal privatization of the labor market and the housing sector. The intimate social circles established in one's early life have also been interrupted by the development-induced mobilities. Urban migrants and residents often find themselves living across various communities of strangers from workplace to home place and everywhere in between. They have to travel through many heterotopic non-places from co-tenanted rental apartments (as temporary homes) and networks of strangers (as alternative families) to online and mobile social media platforms (as gated communities) in the long process of uprooting and regrounding. Many of them have been stretched in a prolonged loneliness when life itself offers little sense of security and stability and little hope for homemaking and homecoming.

The presumption of the economy of loneliness is that single people are lonely and pitiable and hence need to be saved (so there is a market), when the capitalist development has continued to drive single people into family-like structures through romantic and sexual relationships. Contrary to this, the highly institutionalized and compulsory production of relationship and marriage has provoked a resistance among those who have consciously chosen a single life. In any case, living alone has become a growing global trend, as Jamieson and Simpson (2013) report in their research of solo living under globalization. But being single challenges the continuation of the family line and radically deviates from the very Confucianist ideal of reproduction as the centerpiece of filial piety. It also prevents people from establishing families as the basic socioeconomic units that capitalism still relies upon as the central stabilizing entity in today's China. Single people hence face more challenges in everyday life, ranging from public discrimination to peer and parental pressure. Being single, in short, comes with a cost. After all, both cultural capital (interests to pursue while living alone) and a certain level of privacy (that protects individual choice from public scrutiny) are deeply associated with one's social and economic position. If the ability to cash in on human capital to win a partner in the dating market is a token of success, then maintaining a conscious and prolonged single life entails even more social, cultural, and economic resources. It is in this sense that the choice of being single is also a privilege that not everyone can afford under compulsory familism and stretched kinship.

A Resilient Strategy

My coinage of "stretched kinship" was initially inspired by reality TV shows. Long a devoted enthusiast of the cooking show *MasterChef* and its global versions (including the Chinese version), I had watched various contestants kneading and stretching flour dough to make pasta, noodles, and ramen. I also conducted my fieldwork in northern China (Beijing), where people enjoy wheat-based foods, compared to southern China where the culinary style is heavily rice-centered as the climate is not suitable for growing wheat. My hometown is also famous for its local-style ramen made by stretching a small piece of dough many times until the ramen strings become very thin. In other words, the kneaded and stretched flour dough is the common base of our staple foods and deeply embedded in our culture and everyday life, from where my "stretched" metaphor derives and finds its cultural resonance. The term "stretched kinship" hit me when I was watching the films analyzed in this book before I further developed this metaphor together with "homecoming and homemaking," "coming out to the Sinophone," and "alternative kinship" during my fieldwork. This dough-stretching metaphor closely echoes the stretched and stressful experience of kinship negotiations, as well as the elastic and resilient kinship connections when we constantly tighten or loosen the embedded tensions. My theorization of stretched kinship offers a subtle but nonetheless accurate description that closely aligns with the lived experiences of queer people under the dual pressure of compulsory familism and compulsory development.

This metaphor goes further to the process of fermentation. In Chinese, "fermentation" (*fajiao*) often refers metaphorically to a developing and aggravating situation, which reminds us of the usual time constraint in stretched kinship negotiations. The stretched balance often gets tight when the parents lose their patience as their long expectation for the child's marriage has gone unanswered. The aggravation of the situation can be a subtle process where "fermentation" is slowly but surely occurring and building up inside the "dough"—the tension in stretched kinship often quietly aggregates from the inside until one day it becomes too much to bear. This is another layer of my metaphor in considering the temporality of the stretched kinship structure. In addition, when our life becomes increasingly complicated, people need different strategies and tactics in kinship negotiations that fit into their own family situations. As different styles of Chinese bread and noodles need different types of dough with various levels of elasticity and stretchiness, people also need to carefully think about what strategies would fit them and how much tension they can bear in their own circumstances.

Although I contend that there no longer exists a single, universal, one-size-fits-all strategy for coming out to the family, the idea of stretched kinship may shed some light on the issue of kinship negotiation—or even become a resilient strategy itself. The process of "stretching" potentially earns people more time and space to gradually test how much leeway their families may allow for such issues as marriage and reproduction, as today's parents and elder family members may have quite different levels of tolerance for non-conforming sexualities. A confrontational inquiry directly seeking answers to these questions may not yield any meaningful and positive outcomes; instead, these sensitive questions should be implicitly "kneaded" into the most mundane daily conversations and communications with the family. The key is to keep this process slow and steady—like gently stretching flour dough without tearing it apart—which allows the family more time to think about how to respond and leaves more room for subsequent negotiations. One should not give up if the family appears strict and conservative. The essence of stretched kinship is to keep it as an ongoing process of negotiation that is always elastic and dynamic.

Then, once people have enough time and space to carefully figure out where their families draw the line, they can further select suitable strategies they have learned from their queer peers for the next step of negotiation. Some people may come out to their parents in various ways, while others may choose a cooperative quasi-marriage or opt for an incognito heterosexual marriage if the family's tolerance is very low for non-conforming sexualities. Those with more financial resources may turn directly to adoption or surrogacy—this works in some cases when the family cares more about reproduction than about marriage, but may lead to disastrous outcomes in a family where marriage is considered a non-negotiable prerequisite for reproduction. Those who have the opportunity can still try the time-consuming "coming out as coming home" strategy if they do not favor a confrontational declaration of their same-sex relationships, although this has become impossible for many because of the mobility-driven, commonplace separation from the families of origin.

Overall, this resilient strategy is contingent on the stretched spatiotemporal and physical-psychological distance that allows people to gradually observe and test their families' reactions to the issues related to marriage and procreation, and to learn from other queer people's experiences to cope with relevant situations. The core of "stretched kinship as a strategy" is not simply delaying the next step but taking advantage of the separation as an invaluable opportunity to find out the family's leeway and to accumulate enough resources and experiences (read, once again, "capital") to work out the most suitable strategy that matches the actual circumstances. This is also a chance and a process for people to learn more about their families of origin without immediate pressure for hetero-reproductive marriage. If we turn back to the "dough" metaphor, kneading and stretching it is to make the dough elastic and hence even stronger. Exactly the same logic goes into kinship negotiations: stretching the kinship tie is to make it more resilient to sustain the family connection. Overall, "stretched kinship" is likely to continue functioning as an underlying condition in the years and decades to come for those whose sexualities (or other important aspects of the self) fail to align with the family's expectations. A resilient strategy like this may afford them a better chance in kinship negotiations as well as a better tomorrow with the family.

A Queer Sinophone Marxist Critique

Do queer people in China have a future? Can we remain optimistic about a futurity when the hope for social progression seems slim, our life becomes more complicated, and tomorrow turns increasingly uncertain? Haejoang Cho, in her keynote speech at the 2018 Association for Asian Studies Annual Conference, remarked that we are living in an age when capitalism has prevailed over human dignity and everything and everyone is calculated to the benefit of capital. Caught up in these post-development syndromes, today's young people in East Asia have become less idealistic and more pragmatic to heavily and self-consciously invest in self-development. Yet many of them still end up jobless and relationless in the hyper-competitive educational system and labor market where the winner takes it all and everyone must find his or her own way to survive. The question of surviving has replaced that of living, and people no longer expect a future when life is permeated with endless insecurity and anxiety that things will only get worse, not better. The capitalist rationality and the neoliberal marketization of human capital have promised a lot to the young generation but never really come to their salvation. Can we still talk about hope, as Haejoang Cho mused, when young people find themselves compressed between the race for survival and the still strong and ongoing familism in today's Asia?

I share Cho's observations and solicitude, despite her different approaches and contexts. Exhausted by the fierce competition for capital and resources and by the tough competition for love and anchorage, the young generation starts to lose hope when it becomes increasingly difficult to envisage a meaningful future attentive to their real longings and sufferings. The dream of settlement through homemaking and relationship building has often become remote and slim, when the cost of living and the cost of love become unbearable for many capital-deprived urban youths and young migrants struggling to move up and move on. Yet they are still pressured to build a family, start a life, accumulate capital, and pass that on to the next generation to complete the cycle of the great bestowment of life in continuing the family line. Can they—or "we," as this has an impact on many of us—still think about hope when we are compressed between the imperative forces of familism and development? This book, after all, holds its critique against compulsory familism and heteronormativity in one hand, and against imperative development and the dominance of neoliberalism in the other. The former deals with the social and familial misrecognition of non-conforming desires, while the latter addresses the maldistribution of resources. In this sense, we may wonder to what extent and to what end this project may have presented a "queer Sinophone Marxist critique" of the triad of heteronormative familism, China-centrism, and neoliberal capitalism, even though I did not openly engage Marxist thought or follow the Marxist lineage in class analysis, nor did I assemble a conspicuous Marxist/anti-capitalist archive of sociocultural materials.

If this project can be considered a queer Marxist critique as Petrus Liu (2015) has formulated, then this critique probably derives from the following lines: (1) the problem of maldistribution of resources, both material and symbolic, has led to today's socioeconomic stratifications in China and capitalist Asia; (2) the emancipation offered by liberal pluralism is quite limited when it fails to address the underlying structural issues and leaves gender and sexual differences as private matters; (3) the liberalist understanding of gender and sexual mobilities as individual rights does not resonate with or appear relevant to the Confucianist emphasis on reciprocal responsibilities, nor does it relate to the view of the human as a social relation in the Marxist labor theory of value; (4) previous claims of China's neoliberal queer cultures largely missed the still strong familism and the compulsory nature of development, failing to take into account people's struggles under this dual pressure; and (5) the valorization of neoliberal queer agency and subjectivity focuses on people's expressive desires but appears inattentive to their ongoing longings and sufferings under the so-called homocapitalist and homonormative conditions. To that end, these threads have conjointly formed an underlying queer Marxist critique through the case of China and Sinophone Asia against global neoliberal capitalism.

This critique is particularly important when neoliberalism has not only survived but become even stronger since the 2008 GFC (see Mirowski 2013). At any rate, China's capitalist expansion and development have laid the material foundation for and most saliently channeled the emergent formations of queer cultures and economies. The process of compulsory development has produced many "life winners" whose access to capital offers them some protection and compensation for their non-conforming genders and sexualities, but simultaneously alienated many others whose relative lack of capital has limited their options in expanding life experiences and negotiating transgressive desires. In either case, they may end up feeling hopeless and futureless, insomuch as China's capitalist expansion and development do not and cannot address the underlying social, cultural, and political constraints facing queer people. Instead, the neoliberal process leaves structural and systematic problems to the hands of the market and its individual participants, where wider and deeper sociocultural issues become individual responsibilities under the watch of an authoritarian state. The partial remedy offered by the neoliberal process leaves more fundamental issues intact and creates more problems than solutions, where its beneficiaries also fall victim to its imperative agenda.

In other words, neoliberalism's imperative expansion has confined queer people as much as it has mobilized queer desires; it may have enabled certain queer social practices and cultural articulations but also cornered queer cultures and desires in a neoliberal channel. What I have shown in this book is queer people's ineluctable involvement in and obligatory embrace of capital accumulation and neoliberal development, through which I interrogate the values and pitfalls of the neoliberal capitalist process that conditions and structures queer mobilities and immobilities across a wide range of social institutions. Here, my critical lens comes directly from regular queer people who live under global capitalism and both benefit and suffer from the many consequences of its neoliberal expansion. Their focus on self-development and self-regulation as engineered by the state has become increasingly conjoint with a nationalist and ethnocentric mandate for China's revival and dominance, and with a privatized socioeconomic self-reliance that is imperative to the neoliberal process. Today's queer Chinese cultures and mobilities are stretched in a normalizing process by the triad of a familism that mandates heterosexual reproduction, a single-minded China-centrism that dictates the monolithic productions of cultures and sexualities, and a neoliberal capitalist economy that monopolizes the function of capital. The triple lens of queer, Sinophone, and Marxist critiques and that of geographical, cultural, and social mobilities have conjointly disentangled the underlying contingencies and constituencies of gender and sexual modernity, diversity, and mobility in twenty-first-century China and Sinophone Asia.

For a Queer Future

If a gay meritocracy has become a possible modality for a queer future in a country like China, then the more important question is whether the meritorious class can survive at the expense of others who find it increasingly difficult to move up as a means to afford a queer life. The issue of gender and sexual mobilities has been further complicated by that of social immobilities and the concretized social stratifications, where the failure of neoliberalism is equally pronounced in its triumph. Those of us who cannot get into the meritocratic club may find it harder than ever to cross the class boundaries and acquire the socioeconomic and sociocultural capital necessary to establish a queer life and a better tomorrow. Then what choice do we have in building a promising future outside capital accumulation and neoliberal self-reliance? If we can still talk about hope, then where does this hope lie after all? While still exercising their agency, queer people's choices often appear limited and have to be channeled through the structure of family or the process of growth.

One thing that Haejoang Cho did not make clear in her aforementioned speech is which kind of pressure is stronger—compulsory familism or compulsory development—especially for young queer people. Here I can share a brief anecdote from my trip to China in early 2018. I met a particularly talkative driver when I took a "Didi" (the local equivalent of Uber) in my small hometown. The middle-aged male driver unleashed a long verbal attack against me immediately after he learned that I was still single without children. He accused me of not fulfilling my filial piety, being selfish, and not considering my parents' happiness that (he assumed) was hinged upon my procreation. When I got out of the car, he shouted at me "fulfill your filial piety"—or "care for and obey your parents" (*xiaoshun nide fumu*) if we take a more verbatim translation—which is probably the harshest moral accusation one can bear in Confucianist societies.

Here, my career achievement and higher social status were simply brushed off in the face of my singleness and childlessness; based on the latter and nothing but the latter, I was a target of direct moral judgment or what I considered verbal abuse from a complete stranger throughout the ride. After all, going against the familism at the expected age of marriage and procreation is a cardinal sin in Confucianist doctrines. Nothing else—not my cultural and socioeconomic capital—can be my saving grace. In the eyes of the older generation, they hold the moral pinnacle of the traditional values; the liberalist concepts of "privacy," "individual choice," and "treating others as equal with respect" simply did not exist in their vernacular or in their own upbringing decades ago. By that I mean it is culturally appropriate for them to (ab)use the seniority and authority bestowed on them by a strong and rigid Confucianist social hierarchy—they were probably treated in the same way when they were young—which many people in my age group and social circle may find abhorrent. However, admittedly, there are still many young people in China who to various degrees willingly uphold this kind of social hierarchy and will one day become the dominant (senior) part of it, while the low acceptance of transgressive genders and sexualities is also not uncommon among the younger generation today.

What I went through in my hometown offered a striking contrast to my experiences in the West, where taxi drivers are often fascinated by my occupation as a university lecturer with doctoral degrees at a young age—many of them are immigrants themselves and seem glad to see a young immigrant like me who has fared well. I still remember a taxi driver I met in Auckland after completing this research, who literally said it was the "quality" of the passengers that mattered and made him enjoy his job at the end of the day; there was also an Uber driver in Washington, DC, who enthusiastically inquired about my migration journeys and educational credentials throughout the ride. However, back in my hometown, personal merits seem to be rather weightless compared to the fundamental familism as shown through people's single-minded understanding of filial piety as "getting married" and "having children." We can of course argue that what happened to me was an isolated case, or that the older and more conservative generation in China's less-developed areas has not acquired the middle-class politeness that is rather common among today's well-educated younger generation in the country's major metropolises. But I strongly believe that this case offers a microscopic lens through which we can better understand what queer Chinese people are still going through in their day-to-day life and why many of them still feel overwhelmingly helpless and hopeless.

I should note that this incident and my discussion here are highly problematic. On the first level, I have valorized compulsory familism/heterosexual reproduction as a single, predominate problem that renders everything else irrelevant. Second, I might have suggested that to some degree this problem can be solved by development ("if my hometown was more developed and if people had better education, then this probably would not happen"). Third, my discussion appears to have implicitly and somewhat arrogantly lauded my own privilege and good fortune that I have access to a different lifestyle beyond compulsory familism, which I owe not only to my migration and mobility but also to China's growth that enabled such opportunities in the first place. Fourth, I seem to have argued for the West as an unproblematic place for queer migrants, where their socioeconomic achievement may save them from various disadvantages and visible and invisible discrimination facing them as both racial and sexual minorities. Fifth, I have suggested that there exist other and better ways to fulfill one's filial piety beyond marriage and reproduction, such as honoring the family and providing for the parents' material and cultural wellbeing with one's socioeconomic and sociocultural wealth, where compulsory development seems to have offered a partial solution to compulsory familism. However, at any rate, to what extent do these assumptions hold true? These questions should not have gone unchecked, and I would like to leave these to my readers who have been bearing with me the question of ineluctable development as well as the conditions and consequences of mobilities and immobilities from the start of the book.

Then, in light of these discussions, can we still talk about hope and remain hopeful for a queer future? Is that possible to locate a queer futurity not only within but beyond familism and development? There is no easy answer to these questions. One thing I am certain about is that we will not see a linear-progressive development of queer social acceptance and equal rights in China, although changes will come, for better or for worse, and however small and trivial. The society and the culture still mandate the filial responsibility of reproduction, which deprives the wider social acceptance of homosexuality and makes it difficult for grassroots activism to attract broad support across a large country with a complex demography. While the bottom-up activism is abysmal, a top-down reform is equally unlikely, due to the regime's refusal of the equal-rights agenda. The newly emerged queer meritocratic class is relatively small in number and lacks the incentive to call for wider social changes, while overall China lacks an effective civil society for informed discussions of gender and sexual diversity. We still have a long way to go for any substantive social progression to take place. Here, I hope *Queer Chinese Cultures and Mobilities* will open up new avenues for critical considerations of these issues—if this book can offer any value for us to reflect upon the past and think through the present, then tomorrow's paths may be better illuminated.

I still remember that, after each interview during my fieldwork, my interlocutors would ask me why I had chosen to conduct this research. After my explanation of the academic purposes, they often told me that it would be great if my research could benefit queer people instead of being circulated only within academic circles. They were mostly polite, but I could see in their eyes the suspicion that researchers may only focus on intellectual pursuits whose work offers little relevance to the people and the communities under scrutiny. Each time I returned from the field, what I thought was exactly how to make this research both intellectually rigorous and practically relevant to the lived experiences of queer people who have real stakes in this project. I hope my work has been able to fulfill these purposes and this book can speak to minds and hearts alike. Without being sentimental, I remain cautiously hopeful that there will be a queer future that we can build together.

One day this research will be forgotten. The ashes of time will dust my book, the pages unturned and the cover untouched. However, those recorded in this research will be remembered for their creations of such diverse and dynamic queer cultures and social practices against all the odds in the early twenty-first century. Nested in the many imperatives and contingencies of the entangled forces of mobilities and immobilities, future generations will carry on their great legacy and continue to write the never-ending stories of queer people's struggles and successes in kinship negotiation, geographical relocation, and social class migration. As a researcher, I am deeply grateful that I have had this opportunity to put their cultures and creations in front of the world—for me, for them, and for everyone who would like to see a better tomorrow and a brighter future. When the cold pages of this book feel the warmth of your fingers, I hope you can also feel the hearts of the people behind this project.

Notes

Introduction

1. See "Official Record of Proceedings of the Legislative Council (Hansard)" [*Lifaju huiyi guocheng zhengshi jilu*], 10 July 1991, 2058–69, Legislative Council of Hong Kong; and "Civil Appeal No. 317," 2005, Court of Appeal, High Court of the Hong Kong Special Administrative Region of China.
2. See Gao and Jia (2008, 462), Guo (2007a, 51–64), and Wang (2011, 83). Also consult Guo (2007b, 2008) and Zhou (2009) for relevant legal issues concerning same-sex relationships, and Chen (2008) for the development of homosexual studies in China.
3. These are outlined in Taiwan's *Gender Equity Education Act* (2004) and *Act of Gender Equality in Employment* (2007).
4. According to the IMF, China has overtaken the US since 2014 as the world's largest economy measured by gross domestic product (GDP) based on purchasing power parity (PPP). The data are available (with regular updates) on the IMF website: https://www.imf.org/en/Data. Key measures of economic performance are also published by the World Bank (https://databank.worldbank.org/data/home.aspx) and the United Nations (https://unstats.un.org/unsd/snaama/dnlList.asp).
5. These orders were released as "SARFT's Reaffirmation of the Standard for Film Censorship [*Guangdian zongju guanyu chongshen dianying shencha biaozhun de tongzhi*]," 7 March 2008; and "The Order of SARFT No. 65 [*Guojia guangbo dianying dianshi zongju ling di 65 hao*]," 12 November 2010, State Administration of Radio, Film, and Television of China.
6. In March 2013, SARFT merged with the General Administration of Press and Publication (GAPP) to become the State Administration of Press, Publication, Radio, Film and Television (SAPPRFT).
7. This was confirmed by Fan Popo during my interview with him in 2014.
8. The state tolerance still has its limits—mobile gay dating app ZANK, for instance, was terminated by the authority in 2017 together with other mobile social networking platforms for user-generated "obscene content." See Chapter 5.
9. In 2016, the Kuomintang once again lost the leadership to Taiwan's local Democratic Progressive Party.
10. Collectively, these might be termed post-2008 queer screen cultures—queer social practices and cultural productions on and off various forms of screen: silver screens

in movie theaters, digital projection screens in film clubs, computer and TV screens at home, and small smartphone screens in people's palms.

11. My approach to the cultural materials in question is more akin to Graeme Turner's "film as social practice" (2006) that departs from a predominately aesthetic focus in film studies and instead turns to the social meanings of films and relevant cultural practices.
12. The issue of mobilities is central to many social analyses and cultural critiques in the names of cultural flows (Appadurai 1996), speed and politics (Virilio [1977] 2006), the network society (Castells [1996] 2009), global complexity (Urry 2003, 2007), and liquid modernity (Bauman 2000). Also consider Cresswell (2006), Hannam, Sheller, and Urry (2006), Kaufmann (2002), and Urry (2000).
13. For further considerations of gender and sexuality through the lens of mobilities, see, for instance, Agustín (2007), Ahmadi (2003), Huang and Yeoh (2008), Pain (2001), Plummer (2008), and Walsh, Shen, and Willis (2008). For queer mobility studies that have emerged from various disciplinary areas, consult, for example, Bryson et al. (2006), Fortier (2001, 2003), Fu and Wu (2010), Gopinath (2005), Gorman-Murray (2007, 2009), Kunstman (2009), Luibhéid (2005, 2008), Luibhéid and Cantú Jr. (2005), Manalansan (2006), Oswin (2014), Puar (2002a, 2002b), Waitt and Gorman-Murray (2007, 2011a, 2011b), and Yue (2012b).
14. Further discussions on "emotional geographies" as a field of investigation can be found in Davidson, Bondi, and Smith (2005). For "queer geographies" and "geographies of sexualities," consider the works by humanistic geographers including Bell (1991), Brown (2000), Browne, Lim, and Browne (2007), Gorman-Murray (2012), Gorman-Murray, Waitt, and Johnston (2008), Johnston and Longhurst (2010), Knopp (2007), and Oswin (2008).
15. Another regional term that has become popular is *rayray*, a portmanteau replacing the first letter of "gay" with "r" as a more implicit nickname descriptor. It is mainly used among young gay men in Taiwan and less known in other Chinese societies.
16. I should note that Xiaomingxiong (a.k.a. Samshasha) believed that Hinsch's *Passions of the Cut Sleeve: The Male Homosexual Tradition in China* (1990) heavily borrowed from his Chinese-language book *The History of Homosexuality in China* (1st ed. 1984) without due acknowledgement. For more information about this alleged plagiarism, see an interview with Samshasha by McLelland (2000) and a discussion by Leung (2007).
17. More specifically, according to Tze-lan Sang (1999, 2003), *tongxing'ai* is a direct adoption of the Japanese word *doseiai*, a term described by James Valentine (1997, 100) as the most direct translation of the English word "homosexuality" in Japan's interpretation of Western sexology. Sang (2003) argues that *tongxing'ai* was less an identity than a modality of love when the term was first adopted from Japanese (118, 292–93, 297), while Frank Dikötter shows that then-Chinese sexologists already saw homosexuality as a mark of the pathological and uncivilized "other" (1995, 143–44). Howard Chiang (2010) believes that *tongxing'ai* in Republican China was equally trapped in the medical and scientific discourse, or what Michel Foucault (1978) calls *scientia sexualis*, to pathologize same-sex desire and same-sex attracted people (see also Chiang 2014a, 28–30). For more discussions on *doseiai*, see Gregory M. Pflugfelder (1999, 235–85). In Japanese, "homosexual" was also translated/transliterated as *homosekusharu* (McLelland 2005, 82).

18. For Wenqing Kang (2009, 2010), the spread of Western sexology into China in the first half of the twentieth century was contingent on the similarity between local and Western understandings of same-sex relationships. My concern, however, is whether such similarity was mere historical contingency or was born within the transformations of local sexual morality and sex-related values caused by China's increased interactions and tensions with the West. I consider this a process through which previous social stigmatization of same-sex bonding found its modern "scientific" ground from the imported Western sexology. China is not alone in this process. Julian Lee observes that contemporary state policies and regulations across many countries "commonly seek to prevent certain forms of sexuality from being expressed, even when, as is often the case, the country concerned has a rich history of diverse and socially legitimate sexual conduct" (2011, 2).
19. I should also note that this assumed paradigm shift from conduct-based to identity-based understandings of sexuality has been frequently questioned and challenged. In a Western context, Eve Sedgwick (1990, 44–48) criticizes that the historical search for the so-called "Great Paradigm Shift" (e.g., David M. Halperin's work in 1990) may have over-stretched Michel Foucault's (1978) periodization of sexuality and obscured the present conditions of sexual identities. In his later work, Halperin (2002, 13) himself notes that the assumption of a simple, epochal "shift" rather (1) lacks reflexivity on our current attitudes to the past; (2) takes for granted the connection between modern and premodern non-heterosexual formations; (3) appears inadequate in addressing homosexuality within its own history; and (4) implies "a Eurocentric progress narrative" potentially rendering non-Western and non-white sexualities as "backward." Following Halperin and writing on Sinophonicity, Howard Chiang (2014a, 24) criticizes this "paradigm shift" as a linear and reductionist view of "a broader rearrangement of earlier patterns of erotic organizations" in the late nineteenth century. This assumed linear progression (i.e., from "acts" to "identities" of erotic desire) is inadequate in recognizing the epistemological factors in this shift, such as the importation and translation of Western medical sciences and the rise of *scientia sexualis* in the late imperial and early Republican China (28).
20. This process, the loss of the same-sex tradition from the end of the imperial period to China's Cultural Revolution, is vividly captured in the film *Farewell My Concubine* (*Ba Wang Bie Ji*, Chen Kaige, 1993). See my previous work (Wei 2012) for a detailed analysis along with a discussion of the changing local same-sex social discourse in the twentieth century.
21. For example, the English version of *Global Times* (*Huanqiu Shibao*) published a report on 23 May 2013 about the problem of homophobic textbooks in China (see Yang 2013).
22. This comes from an old English idiom "work while you work, play while you play, that is the way, to be cheerful and gay." I owe this pun to late sci-fi writer Sir Arthur C. Clarke, who often told journalists that he was "merely mildly cheerful" when asked whether he was gay; while the journalists were curious about his sexuality, he took the pun of "gay" to avoid discussions about his homosexuality that was known to the public. See also Wong (2010) for an analysis of the emergence of the "gay" identity in China and Hong Kong.
23. Arjun Appadurai has a more nuanced description of such local and global, and homogenizing and heterogenizing, forces as "mutual effort of sameness and difference to cannibalize one another and thereby proclaim their successful hijacking of the

twin Enlightenment ideas of the triumphantly universal and the resiliently particular" (1996, 43).

24. While etymologists have debated over its historical usage and early association with sex and prostitution (Aman 1979, 257; Cawqua 1982, 224; Simes 2005, 8), it was not until the early twentieth century that "gay" started to emerge in popular culture as a slang word and eventually gained popularity. A well-documented (and much-debated) early use of "gay" in mass culture was in the film *Bringing Up Baby* (Howard Hawks, 1938), where Cary Grant's character, clad in a woman's gown, remarked that he "just went gay all of a sudden"—although the word "gay" in his line can still be interpreted in its original meaning as "happy and cheerful."
25. The minoritarian self-conception appears to predate the emergence of the gay identity in the West. For example, Eric Garber's documentation of the Harlem Renaissance as a significant moment in gay American history sees the feeling of kinship among lesbian and gay men as the beginning of homosexual "minority consciousness" (1989, 329). In addition, today's open and proud gay culture sharply contrasts with the "furtive and sad" homosexual lifestyle in the first half of the twentieth century, which has been described by some American intellectuals as "not worthy of being graced with the term *culture*" (see Newton 1993, 39, 311; see also 237–38 about how the Gay Liberation movement challenged and compromised the "old gay survival methods").
26. To that end, even the seemingly neutral term "same-sex" is also a socially constructed notion with its own genealogy. The view seeing men and women as two opposite sexes was an eighteenth-century construction, according to historian Thomas Laqueur (1990), vis-à-vis the previous anatomical understanding of men and women as two mirrored forms of "one sex." If we agree with Laqueur, then we can argue that the modern understandings of sexuality are based on the two-sex model rather than on the idea of a mirroring or neighboring sex. Here, it is noteworthy that "same-sex" itself is a constructed idea with its own socio-historical genealogy that may be easily overlooked.
27. The modern meaning of "lesbian" probably emerged in the mid-nineteenth century: when French poet Charles Baudelaire was in trial for his "obscene" *Les Fleurs du mal*, a volume of erotic verses initially considered by the poet to be titled *Les Lesbiennes* (*The Lesbians*), the word *lesbian* began to be known by the educated public, in France at least (Bonnet 1997, 157–58). Later in a 1904 French dictionary, the feminine form of homosexual ("*homosexuelle*") is found together with its masculine lexical form ("*homosexuel*"), implying a gender-distinctive understanding of homosexuality that had already come into being (Bonnet 160).
28. LGBTQQIAAP refers to Lesbian, Gay, Bisexual, Transgender, Queer, Questioning, Intersex, Asexual, Allies, and Pansexual. Corrêa, Petchensky, and Parker (2008, 7–8) describe this kind of naming as "throwing together a wide range of sexual and gender identity categories into one alphabet soup."
29. See Bao (2011a), Chou (2000), and Wong (2008) for more on these.
30. Along with *tongzhi*, there emerges a non-confrontational strategy that brings same-sex relationships into the register of the family—Chou Wah-shan's famous and much-debated "coming out as coming home" strategy (2000, 2001)—in comparison with the confrontational and unapologetic "coming out" strategy in the West. For discussions and critiques, see Bao (2011b), Liu and Ding (2005), and my previous work (Wei 2012). In this book, I point out that "coming out as coming home" has become

impossible and we need a new understanding of and a strategy for queer kinship negotiation. See Chapter 1 and the closing remarks.

31. The historical background and initial emergence of queer theory is discussed most notably by Annamarie Jagose in her book *Queer Theory* (1997). The development of the theory from a queer "niche" to a conceptual framework widely adopted by various academic disciplines has been well-documented by *The Year's Work in Critical and Cultural Theory*, an annual review journal published by Oxford University Press that has been documenting and commenting on queer theory (among other critical theories) since 1993.
32. I should note that all the interviews and data collection were carried out after I disclosed my researcher's identity.
33. Also, female participants were often scarce in the film clubs I visited, even in those co-organized by lesbian groups. Many films shown in these urban queer cultural spaces were selected from a male perspective by the organizers, and the events were often publicized through gay-male-dominated queer social media platforms with very limited numbers of lesbian women and "rotten girls" (*fu nü*, female fans of inter-male romance). On a relevant note, although numerous lesbian mobile dating apps have emerged in China, only gay dating apps and gay-male entrepreneurs seem to have attracted large venture capital investments and public media attention. In the wider society, anecdotal evidence also suggests a higher social visibility of gay-male cultures than of lesbian women. Moreover, during my fieldwork, gay men often saw me under a double light—first as their gay-male "comrade" and then as a researcher. For women, however, I was nothing but an ethnographer sniffing around and peeping into the female world that I did not (biologically and socially) belong to. Some of my informants believe that the gap and distance are in fact quite considerable between local gay and lesbian communities in today's China, and lesbian women will feel uncomfortable if a gay man intrudes into their own social and cultural spaces. Here, the researcher's identity can be used to advantage in approaching the field and building rapport, as much as it can be an obstacle to expanding the scope of the research.

Chapter 1 Stretched Kinship

1. For more on gay "coming-out migration" and identity negotiation, see Brown (2000), Cant (1997), Lewis (2012), Maddison (2002), Plummer (1995), and Weston (1995).
2. I owe this analysis to Rahul Rao's critique of family and homocapitalism in a different context (2015, 47).
3. Further research on China's internal migration can be found in Gaetano and Jacka (2004), Dong (2011), He, Li, and Chan (2015), Li and Roulleau-Berger (2013), Li, Chan, and He (2015), Nyíri (2010), Wallis (2013), Wong, Han, and Zhang (2015), and Zhang and Duncan (2014).
4. These urban queer spaces include gay bars and nightclubs, gay saunas and bathhouses, LGBT centers, gay-friendly coffee houses, *tongzhi* bookshops, book clubs, film clubs, gay sports groups, and LGBT counseling services, to name a few from my field research.
5. See BBC's report at http://www.bbc.co.uk/news/blogs-trending-31549731 (23 February 2015).

6. Along with stretched kinship, "closeted parents" is an emerging phenomenon in Chinese societies that deserves our attention. Although some people openly accept gay friends and co-workers, they often have trouble accepting a gay family member (Yeo and Chu 2018). This further indicates that the family is still a low-tolerant entity for sexual deviation, echoing anecdotal evidence that the young generation in Chinese societies tends to be more open to accept gays and lesbians in the wider society, as long as their own children are not queer.
7. For news reports, see, for example, http://www.tudou.com/programs/view/jg2N-RQbj-OA (23 July 2012).
8. Their complaint resembles that of the older gay men in post-Stonewall America who were unhappy about the exposure of the previously underground gay world to the public. See Newton (1993, 237–38) for a brief discussion.
9. The third season of *Rainbow Family* (2017) was only released in a paid online streaming service in China, not through YouTube or any mainstream Chinese video-sharing sites.
10. The founder aimed to create a regular communal event structured as a psychotherapy group through the medium of film, after a Concentric Circle book club had enjoyed success in Beijing's gay community since 2010 and subsequently extended to other cities in provincial China. After its establishment in May 2012, the film club started by showing feature-length movies followed by long discussions, which proved unpopular. The organizers soon switched to short films and videos and incorporated sketching as part of the post-screening discussion, after a cartoon-themed session was enthusiastically received.

Chapter 2 Home and Migration

1. These early queer cinematic masterpieces have gained an international reputation and have been intensively written about by film scholars. See Berry (1998, 2001), Chan (2008), Chiang (1998), C. Y. Chiang (2011), M. Chiang (2011), Chua (1999), Dai (2000), Dilley (2007), Eng (2010b), Grossman (2000), Lau (1995), Leung (2008), Leung (2010), Lim (2006), Metzger (2000), Tambling (2003), Wei (2012), Xu (1997), and Zhang (1999).
2. For critical analyses of individual films that fit into the queer youth genre, see, for example, Hu (2005) on *Formula 17* (*Shiqisui de Tiankong*, Chen Yin-jung, 2004), Shiau (2008) on *Eternal Summer* (*Shengxia Guangnian*, Leste Chen, 2006), and Yue (2007) on *Rice Rhapsody*. For recent discussions on lesbian films and cultures, see, for instance, Khoo (2014), Martin (2010), Shi (2015), and Wong (2012).
3. Cui Zi'en is one of the most renowned and prolific filmmakers in this underground digital film movement in China, with about twenty works under his belt including short film, feature-length drama, and documentary. He is the most frequently discussed DV (digital video) filmmaker in English-language academia, most recently by Liu (2015), Spencer (2012), Yue (2012a), and Zhou (2011, 2014), and is widely considered a queer auteur (Berry 2004). Cui often challenges heteronormative cultures through a consistent queer theme in his works and his distinctive queer visual and narrative styles that seldom follow the convention of mainstream cinema. However, other DV filmmakers who do not share Cui's high profile appear to spark much less curiosity for scholarly investigation, although their works are distributed through the same (underground) networks within small queer film circles such as queer film

festivals. These underground films seldom attract public attention and often remain in an uncandled darkness, barely known outside the independent film circuits, even in local queer communities. That said, these digital works nonetheless constitute a brook of non-mainstream queer undercurrents paralleling other cinematic waves that flow into the queer cultural reservoirs.

4. As Taiwanese filmmaker Pan Chih-yuan puts it, when the queer youth genre becomes popular, Taiwan's commercial film market seems to be left with two genres: homosexual film and non-homosexual film (Yuan 2007; see Shiau 2008 for a critical discussion). The focus on youth beauty echoes the Chinese male same-sex tradition that favors juvenile charm and delicate youth corporeality (Wei 2012) and intermingles with the boys' love fandom that is popular in East Asia (Wei 2014). The youth genre is also deeply rooted in Taiwan cinema's focus on and deep solicitude for youth issues, exemplified most notably by such Taiwan New Cinema masterpieces as *Dust in the Wind* (*Lian Lian Fengchen*, Hou Hsiao-Hsien, 1986) and *A Brighter Summer Day* (*Gulingjie Shaonian Sharen Shijian*, Edward Yang, 1991).
5. See an interview with Kit Hung (Zhao 2009) in *Gay Spot*, a self-published gay magazine based in Beijing: http://www.danlan.org/dispArticle_24890.htm (8 October 2009).
6. The year 2047 is also the fiftieth anniversary of Hong Kong's handover as well as the end of the "One Country, Two Systems" governance promised by China.

Chapter 3 Sinophone Mobilities

1. These forces are "mutual effort of sameness and difference to cannibalize one another" and thereby proclaim "the triumphantly universal and the resiliently particular." See Arjun Appadurai (1996, 43).
2. For further discussions on the conditions of mobilities and immobilities, consider Bauman (1998), Cass, Shove, and Urry (2005), Cohen and Gössling (2015), Gössling and Stavrinidi (2016), Urry (2005, 2011), and Urry and Larsen (2011).
3. Mobility scholars have also demonstrated that roads and routes themselves can be used as ethnographic sites for cultural-spatial critiques. See, for example, Dalakoglou and Harvey (2012).
4. See Baba (2001), Lee (2011), Williams (2009), and Yue (2012b) for further considerations of the impact of Malaysia's Islamization on gender and sexual non-conformity.
5. Department of Statistics, Malaysia (2011).
6. According to the 2010 census, Malays account for 60.3 percent of the total population with 22.9 percent Chinese and 7.1 percent Indians. At its peak, the Chinese used to make up 45 percent of the population in the late 1950s. While the Chinese ethnic population has multiplied in absolute numbers, the ratio they account for has dropped significantly during the second half of the twentieth century (see Mahari 2011).
7. For more in-depth discussions of the *bumiputera* privilege, consult Gabriel (2015), G. C. Khoo (2005, 2006), O. Khoo (2003), and Lee (2012).
8. See Kane (2006, 94–98) for more discussions in a lingua-historical context.
9. In Malaysia, Ti uploaded his films to YouTube and shared them on Facebook. Since both services are blocked in China, he switched to local video-sharing websites and queer social media. China's block of Western web services offers an opportunity for local businesses to develop similar products but inevitably creates a self-confined cyber island in the global and transnational flows of information. Here, China's

internet censorship is twofold: it not only controls and regulates content and access but also allows local companies to monopolize the domestic market by eliminating foreign competitors.

10. Chua (2012, 39, 158) also reminds us that Shih's coinage of "Sinophone" (2007, 2–8) owes to the multi-accented Mandarin dialogues in the film *Crouching Tiger, Hidden Dragon* (*Wohu Canglong*, Ang Lee, 2000).
11. More recently, Ti has been focusing on his role as a singer-songwriter and music video director popular on YouTube and Facebook. He has gained mainstream media attention through his songs such as *Malaysia Boy* (2017) that speaks to unprivileged single youth earnestly longing for girls' love and attention. Opening this song with a prescribed and proud "Malaysian" identity and waiving the national flag throughout the music video, Ti has continued with a conspicuously nationalist approach to include the iconic urban landmarks in Kuala Lumpur and Malaysia's cultural symbols from local foods and drinks to famous shopping districts in his visual and lyrical narrative. This has further shown the multilingual and multicultural Malaysian Sinophonicities that we have seen in Ti's early works. However, targeting the mainstream market, Ti's recent works focus mostly on straight people's singleness and loneliness to attract a larger audience, although this theme equally and perhaps more fundamentally concerns young queer people whose longing for racial and sexual equality in Sinophone Malaysia lacks state tolerance and family support. See the closing remarks for a discussion of the economy of loneliness in today's China and Sinophone Asia.
12. See Rosen and Wang (2011).
13. In China, a commercial coffee house is also more likely to survive under state regulation and censorship, compared to the politicized (in the eyes of the authorities at least) local LGBT NGOs. This echoes my observation in the introduction that queer cultures in today's China are often channeled through the process of capitalist development and urban consumerism, which the party-state has to some extent tolerated and incentivized.
14. Here, Yeh-tzu's remark itself offers a critical reflection on the issue of mobilities that strongly echoes my analysis in this chapter.
15. For further discussions on East Asian (Sinophone) migrations and cultural flows, see, for example, Chan, Haines, and Lee (2014), Fielding (2016), Martin (2015), and Rosen and Wang (2011).

Chapter 4 The Myth of Quality

1. Andrew Kipnis (2006, 296) has a parallel discussion based on Chinese dictionaries that traces the etymology of *suzhi* to early Chinese texts published more than 2,000 years ago.
2. The resolution was approved in the Sixth Plenary Session of the Twelfth Central Committee of the CCP. A summary/digest is available at http://dangshi.people.com.cn/GB/151935/176588/176597/10556334.html.
3. I should note that *suzhi* has also been generalized across a diverse range of contexts that may once again encompass natural qualities or shared common qualities. Delia Lin's book (2017) on the diverse glossary of *suzhi* has shed further light on the complexity of the issue.

4. In gender and sexuality studies, for example, this body of scholarship ranges from "queering the habitus" in lesbianism (Ross 2004) and "queer habitus" in bodily performance (Merabet 2014) to critiques of commercial LGBT media and market (Sender 2003, 2004; Henderson 2013) and a substantive feminist scholarship on gender and class (Adkins 2000, 2004; Christin 2012; Lizardo 2006; Lovell 2000; Skeggs 1997, 2000, 2004).
5. However, the softening of class boundaries in cultural taste appears to have occurred only from the top down and not from the bottom up: those down the social hierarchy have not shown a significant growth of interest in "high cultures" (Peterson 2005). In other words, the cultural capital of high-status social elites has diversified, but that of lower social classes remains at the same limited level. Also, as Warde, Wright, and Gayo-Cal (2007, 160) point out, "omnivore" is hardly a homogeneous category but encompasses a diverse range of cultural interests and various ways in pursuing different cultural tastes. On top of that, an increasing body of literature has constituted a "qualitative counter-attack against the statistics-based thesis that [cultural] tastes are increasingly 'omnivorous' in character," reconfirming Bourdieu's original argument and debunking the "cultural omnivore" thesis (Atkinson 2011, 169). For further discussions and debates on these issues, see Bennett et al. (2009), Bunting et al. (2008), Chan (2010), Chan and Goldthorpe (2007), Coulangeon and Roharik (2005), Goldberg (2011), López-Sintas and García-Álvarez (2002), Peterson (1992), Peterson and Kern (1996), Peterson and Simkus (1992), Roose, van Eijck, and Lievens (2012), van Eijck (2001), and van Eijck and Lievens (2008).
6. For more discussions on *suzhi* and China's emerging urban middle classes, see Goodman (2014), Hsu (2007), Kipnis (2007), Tang (2013), and Tomba (2008, 2009, 2010, 2014).
7. These photo albums include paintings (fine art), CD covers (music), film posters (cinema), manga and anime (comics), scenery pictures and urban landscapes (travel), fine dining and home cooking (culinary culture), book covers (literature or professional/academic publications), and much more. Here, the diverse interests shown through the user-created albums mark Feizan's signature cultural pursuits that Ling has envisioned since the very beginning.
8. See Henderson (2013, 48–49) for a parallel analysis in the West.
9. Consult Chen (2013), Chen and Qin (2014), Cheng (2010), Goodman (2013, 2014, 2016), and Tsang (2014) for further discussions on the state-led privatization and China's middle classes.

Chapter 5 Gated Communities

1. For writings on mobile LBS, consult Evans (2015), Farman (2012), Frith (2015), Gudelunas (2012), Hjorth and Arnold (2013), Katz and Lai (2014), and Wilken and Goggin (2014). For gay mobile social networking services, see Batiste (2013), Blackwell, Birnholtz, and Abbot (2015), Brubaker, Ananny, and Crawford (2016), Chiou (2012), and Licoppe, Rivière, and Morel (2016). For cultural critiques, consider Altman (2014), Fox (2014), Hartman (2013), Penney (2014), Quiroz (2013), and Race (2015a, 2015b). Researchers in HIV/AIDS prevention have also actively used locative mobile gay dating apps like Grindr to recruit research participants (Burrell et al. 2012, Gibbs and Rice 2016, Holloway et al. 2014, Landovitz et al. 2012, Martinez et al. 2014, Miller 2015, Rendina et al. 2014, Su et al., 2015, Sun et al. 2015, Winetrobe et al. 2014).

2. ZANK, for example, received angel investment in 2013 from Matrix Partners (China), a branch of the US-based private equity firm whose global investments focus on information and communication technologies (ICTs). This was followed by two more rounds of financing from Beijing-based Ce Yuan Investment in 2014 and Beijing Kunlun Tech Co. in 2016, totaling tens of millions of Chinese yuan (RMB) in capital injection. The latter investor, Beijing Kunlun, is a publicly traded online game company that also acquired 61.5 percent of Grindr in January 2016 for US $93 million and announced on 23 May 2017 that it would acquire 100 percent of Grindr for an additional US $152 million.
3. *Yuan* traditionally refers to a young lady, and the term *ming yuan* ("famous lady") often implicitly attributes a woman's fame to her own or her family's high socioeconomic stance. In today's cyber-slang, *ming yuan* applies to those who have attracted considerable attention on social media where the content they share indicates their social status and lifestyle. It is sometimes conflated with *wang hong*, another slang term designating self-made internet celebrities, although the latter mainly conveys popularity without the prestige of *ming yuan*. Nonetheless, both expressions may be used in a jocular manner to mock cyber celebrities whose fame may not come from or become productive of real-life social status. More important, today's social media users often portray themselves selectively, even when they cannot afford what they have shared online as part of a regular lifestyle. Hence, *ming yuan* may be used sarcastically to expose an overspread misrepresentation of a pretentious lifestyle above one's means. Among gay men, *ming yuan* can also imply effeminate demeanor and behaviors or allude to those passively patronized by other men. The use of *ming yuan* in the public dispute between Blue'd and Aloha implies the complex formulations and interventions of quality and capital in dating and relationship building, where users have been actively and selectively showing their privileged lifestyle or their desire for such privilege to "win" in the dating market.
4. Although the wage earners and the more privileged leisure class might be termed lower- and upper-middle classes, Miao's (2017) study shows that these classifications often fail to align with Chinese people's experiences and perceptions of class. "Lower/upper-middle class" is neither their term of choice nor their identification and conscious articulation of social distinctions.
5. Thinking retrospectively, even the name "Aloha" implies a mobility and a leisure pursuit—an exotic holiday in Hawai'i where "aloha" is a common local greeting meaning "love" and "affection." Since its early development, this Beijing-based mobile gay social network allows users to register with mobile phone numbers in eighteen countries, many of which have a large Chinese immigrant population. It looks like Aloha has been intentionally attracting those who have succeeded in migration and can afford cultural and leisure pursuits beyond the needs for survival.
6. See the report released by the Fourth Plenary Session of the Sixteenth Central Committee of the CCP: http://cpc.people.com.cn/GB/64162/66174/4527266.html.
7. In early 2016, Beijing LGBT Center initiated a new series of film screenings under the name *Guan Ying Si Xiang Hui* or "Private Sharing of Films."
8. It is interesting to note that the founder of the Concentric Circle book club and film club was initially a member of the Fellowship. Increasingly dissatisfied with the latter's obsession with cinematic art and lack of mental connections in the heavily film-orientated discussions, he left the Fellowship and established Concentric Circle with a psychotherapeutic focus.

9. On the other hand, the rise and fall of Feizan shows how an online queer space initially gated by cultural interests develops into a large and open-gate community, whose early cultural capital has been diluted and quality impaired. Those who have abandoned Feizan have made a choice similar to those who have fled a neighborhood when its demography starts to change and the quality of the community begins to decline. This further indicates how the mechanism of gating and walling functions to engender social inclusion and exclusion in today's queer communities along the lingering myth of quality.

References

English-Language References

Adkins, Lisa. 2000. "Objects of Innovation: Post-Occupational Reflexivity and Re-traditionalizations of Gender." In *Transformations: Thinking Through Feminism*, edited by Sarah Ahmed, Jane Kilby, Celia Lury, Maureen McNeil, and Beverley Skeggs, 259–72. London & New York: Routledge.

Adkins, Lisa. 2004. "Introduction: Feminism, Bourdieu and After." In *Feminism after Bourdieu*, edited by Lisa Adkins and Beverley Skeggs, 3–18. Oxford: Blackwell.

Agustín, Laura María. 2007. *Sex at the Margins: Migration, Labour Markets and the Rescue Industry*. London: Zed Books.

Ahmadi, Nader. 2003. "Migration Challenges Views on Sexuality." *Ethnic and Racial Studies* 26 (4): 684–706.

Ahmed, Sara, Claudia Castañeda, Anne-Marie Fortier, and Mimi Sheller, eds. 2003. *Uprootings/Regroundings: Questions of Home and Migration*. Oxford & New York: Berg.

Aksoy, Cevat Giray, Christopher S. Carpenter, Jeff Frank, and Matt L. Huffman. 2018. *Gay Glass Ceilings: Sexual Orientation and Workplace Authority in the UK*. Bonn: IZA Institute of Labor Economics.

Altman, Dennis. 1996. "Rupture or Continuity? The Internationalization of Gay Identities." *Social Text* 14 (3): 77–94.

Altman, Dennis. 1997. "Global Gaze/Global Gays." *GLQ: A Journal of Lesbian and Gay Studies* 3 (4): 417–36.

Altman, Dennis. 2001. *Global Sex*. Chicago, IL: University of Chicago Press.

Altman, Dennis. 2014. "In Defense of Grindr." *The Gay & Lesbian Review* 21 (6): 6.

Aman, Reinhold. 1979. "On the Etymology of Gay." *Maledicta: The International Journal of Verbal Aggression* 3: 257–58.

Anagnost, Ann. 2004. "The Corporeal Politics of Quality (*Suzhi*)." *Public Culture* 16 (2): 189–208.

Anagnost, Ann. 2008. "From 'Class' to 'Social Strata': Grasping the Social Totality in Reform-Era China." *Third World Quarterly* 29 (3): 497–519.

Anderson, Benedict. [1983] 2006. *Imagined Communities: Reflections on the Origin and Spread of Nationalism* (rev. ed). New York: Verso.

Ang, Ien. 2001. *On Not Speaking Chinese: Living Between Asia and the West*. London & New York: Routledge.

Appadurai, Arjun. 1996. *Modernity at Large: Cultural Dimensions of Globalization*. Minneapolis: University of Minnesota Press.

Atkinson, Will. 2011. "The Context and Genesis of Musical Tastes: Omnivorousness Debunked, Bourdieu Buttressed." *Poetics* 39 (3): 169–86.

Augé, Marc. 1995. *Non-Places: Introduction to an Anthropology of Supermodernity*. London: Verso.

Baba, Ismail. 2001. "Gay and Lesbian Couples in Malaysia." In *Gay and Lesbian Asia: Culture, Identity, Community*, edited by Gerard Sullivan and Peter A. Jackson, 143–63. London & New York: Routledge.

Bachner, Andrea. 2014. "Queer Affiliations: Mak Yan Yan's *Butterfly* as Sinophone Romance." In *Queer Sinophone Cultures*, edited by Howard Chiang and Ari Larissa Heinrich, 201–20. London & New York: Routledge.

Bakken, Børge. 2000. *The Exemplary Society: Human Improvement, Social Control, and the Dangers of Modernity in China*. Oxford: Oxford University Press.

Bao, Hongwei. 2011a. "'Queer Comrades': Transnational Popular Culture, Queer Sociality, and Socialist Legacy." *English Language Notes* 49 (1): 131–38.

Bao, Hongwei. 2011b. "People's Park: The Politics of Naming and the Right to the City." In *Queer Paradigm II: Interrogating Agendas*, edited by Matthew Ball and Burkhard Scherer, 115–32. Oxford: Peter Lang Publishers.

Bao, Hongwei. 2013. "A Queer 'Comrade' in Sydney." *Interventions: International Journal of Postcolonial Studies* 15 (1): 127–40.

Batiste, Dominique Pierre. 2013. "'0 Feet Away': The Queer Cartography of French Gay Men's Geo-social Media Use." *Anthropological Journal of European Cultures* 22 (2): 111–32.

Bauman, Zygmunt. 1998. *Globalization: The Human Consequences*. Cambridge: Polity.

Bauman, Zygmunt. 2000. *Liquid Modernity*. Cambridge: Polity.

Bell, David J. 1991. "Insignificant Others: Lesbian and Gay Geographies." *Area* 23 (4): 323–29.

Bell, David J., and Gill Valentine. 1995. Introduction to *Mapping Desire: Geographies of Sexualities*, by David J. Bell and Gill Valentine. London & New York: Routledge.

Bennett, Tony, Mike Savage, Elizabeth Bortolaia Silva, Alan Warde, Modesto Gayo-Cal, and David Wright. 2009. *Culture, Class, Distinction*. London & New York: Routledge.

Berghahn, Daniela. 2006. "No Place like Home? Or Impossible Homecomings in the Films of Fatih Akin." *New Cinema: Journal of Contemporary Film* 4 (3): 141–57.

Berry, Chris. 1998. "*East Palace, West Palace*: Staging Gay Life in China." *Jump Cut: A Review of Contemporary Media* 42: 84–89.

Berry, Chris. 2000. "Happy Alone? Sad Young Men in East Asian Gay Cinema." In *Queer Asian Cinema: Shadows in the Shade*, edited by Andrew Grossman, 187–200. New York, London, & Oxford: Harrington Park Press.

Berry, Chris. 2001. "Asian Values, Family Values: Film, Video, and Lesbian and Gay Identities." In *Gay and Lesbian Asia: Culture, Identity, Community*, edited by Gerard Sullivan and Peter A. Jackson, 211–31. New York: Harrington Park Press.

Berry, Chris. 2004. "The Sacred, the Profane, and the Domestic in Cui Zi'en's Cinema." *Positions: East Asia Cultures Critique* 12 (1): 195–201.

Bérubé, Allan. 1997. "Intellectual Desire." In *Queerly Classed: Gay Men and Lesbians Write About Class*, edited by Susan Raffo, 43–66. Cambridge: South End Press.

Binnie, Jon. 1997. "Coming out of Geography: Towards a Queer Epistemology?" *Environment and Planning D: Society and Space* 15 (2): 223–37.

Blackwell, Courtney, Jeremy Birnholtz, and Charles Abbott. 2015. "Seeing and Being Seen: Co-situation and Impression Formation Using Grindr, a Location-aware Gay Dating App." *New Media & Society* 17 (7): 1117–36.

Blackwood, Evelyn, and Mark Johnson. 2012. "Queer Asian Subjects: Transgressive Sexualities and Heteronormative Meanings." In "Queer Asian Subjects," edited by Evelyn Blackwood and Mark Johnson, special issue, *Asian Studies Review* 36 (4): 441–51.

Bockman, Johanna. 2013. "Neoliberalism." *Contexts* 12 (3): 14–15.

Bonnet, Marie-Jo. 1997. "Sappho, or the Importance of Culture in the Language of Love: Tribade, Lesbienne, Homosexuelle." In *Queerly Phrased: Language, Gender, and Sexuality*, edited by Anna Livia and Kira Hall, 147–66. New York & Oxford: Oxford University Press.

Bourdieu, Pierre. [1984] 2010. *Distinction: A Social Critique of the Judgement of Taste*. London & New York: Routledge.

Brah, Avtar. 1996. *Cartographies of Diaspora: Contesting Identities*. London & New York: Routledge.

Bray, David. 2005. *Social Space and Governance in Urban China: The* Danwei *System from Origins to Reform*. Stanford, CA: Stanford University Press.

Brooks, Siobhan. 2010. *Unequal Desires: Race and Erotic Capital in the Stripping Industry*. Albany: State University of New York Press.

Brown, Michael P. 2000. *Closet Space: Geographies of Metaphor from the Body to the Globe*. London & New York: Routledge.

Browne, Kath. 2006. "Challenging Queer Geographies." *Antipode: A Radical Journal of Geography* 38 (5): 885–93.

Browne, Kath, Jason Lim, and Gavin Brown, eds. 2007. *Geographies of Sexualities: Theory, Practices, and Politics*. Farnham & Burlington: Ashgate Publishing Group.

Brubaker, Jed R., Mike Ananny, and Kate Crawford. 2016. "Departing Glances: A Sociotechnical Account of 'Leaving' Grindr." *New Media & Society* 18 (3): 373–90.

Bryson, Mary, Lori MacIntosh, Sharalyn Jordan, and Hui-Ling Lin. 2006. "Virtually Queer? Homing Devices, Mobility, and Un/Belongings." *Canadian Journal of Communication* 31 (4): 791–814.

Bunting, Catherine, Tak Wing Chan, John Goldthorpe, Emily Keaney, and Anni Oskala. 2008. *From Indifference to Enthusiasm: Patterns of Arts Attendance in England*. London: Arts Council England.

Burrell, Earl R., Heather A. Pines, Edward Robbie, Leonardo Coleman, Ryan D. Murphy, Kristen L. Hess, Peter Anton, and Pamina M. Gorbach. 2012. "Use of the Location-Based Social Networking Application GRINDR as a Recruitment Tool in Rectal Microbicide Development Research." *AIDS and Behavior* 16 (7): 1816–20.

Cant, Bob, ed. 1997. *Invented Identities? Lesbians and Gays Talk About Migration*. London: Cassell.

Cass, Noel, Elizabeth Shove, and John Urry. 2005. "Social Exclusion, Mobility and Access." *The Sociological Review* 53 (3): 539–55.

Castells, Manuel. [1996] 2009. *The Rise of Network Society* (2nd ed. with a new preface ed.). Walden & Oxford: Wiley-Blackwell.

Cawqua, Urson. 1982. "Two Etymons and a Query. Gay—Fairies—Camping." *Maledicta: The International Journal of Verbal Aggression* 6: 224–30.

Chambers, Iain. 2001. *Culture after Humanism: History, Culture, Subjectivity*. London & New York: Routledge.

Chan, Felicia, and Andy Willis. 2012. "Articulating British Chinese Experiences On-Screen: *Soursweet* and *Ping Pong*." *Journal of Chinese Cinemas* 6 (4): 27–39.

Chan, Felicia, and Andy Willis. 2014. "British Chinese Short Films: Challenging the Limits of the Sinophone." In *Sinophone Cinemas*, edited by Audrey Yue and Olivia Khoo, 169–84. Basingstoke & New York: Palgrave Macmillan.

Chan, Kenneth. 2008. "Tactics of Tears: Excess/Erasure in the Gay Chinese Melodramas of *Fleeing by Night* and *Lan Yu*." *Camera Obscura: Feminism, Culture, and Media Studies* 23 (2): 141–66.

Chan, Tak Wing, ed. 2010. *Social Status and Cultural Consumption*. Cambridge: Cambridge University Press.

Chan, Tak Wing, and John H. Goldthorpe. 2007. "Class and Status: The Conceptual Distinction and Its Empirical Relevance." *American Sociological Review* 72 (4): 512–32.

Chan, Yuk-Wah, David Haines, and Jonathan H. X. Lee, eds. 2014. *The Age of Asian Migration: Continuity, Diversity, and Susceptibility*. Newcastle upon Tyne: Cambridge Scholars Publishing.

Chang, Kai-man. 2015. "Sleeping with Strangers: Queering Home and Identity in *I Don't Want to Sleep Alone*." In *Cinematic Homecoming: Exile and Return in Transnational Cinema*, edited by Matthew D. Johnson, Keith B. Wagner, Tianqui Yu, and Luke Vulpiani, 250–68. London: Bloomsbury Academic.

Chen, Chen, and Bo Qin. 2014. "The Emergence of China's Middle Class: Social Mobility in a Rapidly Urbanizing Economy." *Habitat International* 44: 528–35.

Chen, Jie. 2013. *A Middle Class without Democracy: Economic Growth and the Prospects for Democratization in China*. Oxford & New York: Oxford University Press.

Cheng, Li. 2010. *China's Emerging Middle Class: Beyond Economic Transformation*. Washington, DC: Brookings Institution Press.

Chia, Robert. 2003. "From Knowledge-Creation to the Perfecting of Action: Tao, Basho and Pure Experience as the Ultimate Ground of Knowing." *Human Relations* 56 (8): 953–81.

Chiang, Chih-Yun. 2011. "Representing Chineseness in Globalized Cultural Production: Chen Kaige's *Farewell My Concubine*." *China Media Research* 7 (1): 101–11.

Chiang, Howard. 2010. "Epistemic Modernity and the Emergence of Homosexuality in China." *Gender & History* 22 (3): 629–57.

Chiang, Howard. 2011. "Sinophone Production and Trans Postcoloniality: Sex Change from Major to Minor Transnational China." *English Language Notes* 49 (1): 109–16.

Chiang, Howard. 2014a. "(De)Provincializing China: Queer Historicism and Sinophone Postcolonial Critique." In *Queer Sinophone Cultures*, edited by Howard Chiang and Ari Larissa Heinrich, 19–51. London & New York: Routledge.

Chiang, Howard. 2014b. "Queering China: A New Synthesis." *GLQ: A Journal of Lesbian and Gay Studies* 20 (3): 353–78.

Chiang, Mark. 1998. "Coming Out into the Global System: Postmodern Patriarchies and Transnational Sexualities in *The Wedding Banquet*." In *Q&A: Queer in Asian America*, edited by David L. Eng and Alice Y. Hom, 374–95. Philadelphia, PA: Temple University Press.

Chiang, Mei-Hsuan. 2011. "Policing Sexuality: Confession, Power, and the Heterosexist Authority in *East Palace, West Palace*." *Asian Cinema* 22 (1): 240–55.

Chou, Wah-shan. 2000. *Tongzhi: Politics of Same-Sex Eroticism in Chinese Societies*. New York: Haworth Press.

Chou, Wah-shan. 2001. "Homosexuality and the Cultural Politics of *Tongzhi* in Chinese Societies." In *Gay and Lesbian Asia: Culture, Identity, Community*, edited by Gerard Sullivan and Peter A. Jackson, 27–46. New York: Harrington Park Press.

Christin, Angèle. 2012. "Gender and Highbrow Cultural Participation in the United States." *Poetics* 40 (5): 423–43.

Chua, Beng Huat. 2012. *Structure, Audience and Soft Power in East Asian Pop Culture*. Hong Kong: Hong Kong University Press.

Chua, Ling-Yen. 1999. "The Cinematic Representation of Asian Homosexuality in *The Wedding Banquet*." *Journal of Homosexuality* 36 (3–4): 99–112.

Cohen, Scott A., and Stefan Gössling. 2015. "A Darker Side of Hypermobility." *Environment and Planning A* 47 (8): 1661–79.

Collins, Samuel Gerald, and Matthew Slover Durington. 2015. *Networked Anthropology: A Primer for Ethnographers*. Abingdon & New York: Routledge

Corrêa, Sonia, Rosalind Petchesky, and Richard Parker. 2008. *Sexuality, Health and Human Rights*. London & New York: Routledge.

Costa, Cristina, and Mark Murphy. 2015. "Bourdieu and the Application of *Habitus* across the Social Sciences." In *Bourdieu, Habitus and Social Research*, edited by Cristina Costa and Mark Murphy, 3–17. Basingstoke & New York: Palgrave Macmillan.

Coulangeon, Philippe, and Ionela Roharik. 2005. "Testing the 'Omnivore/Univore' Hypothesis in a Cross-national Perspective: On the Social Meaning of Eclecticism in Musical Tastes in Eight European Countries." Paper presented at the Summer Meeting of the International Sociological Association Research Committee 28, Los Angeles, August 2005.

Cresswell, Tim. 2006. *On the Move: Mobility in the Modern Western World*. London & New York: Routledge.

Cresswell, Tim. 2010. "Towards a Politics of Mobility." *Environment and Planning D: Society and Space* 28 (1): 17–31.

Dalakoglou, Dimitris, and Penny Harvey. 2012. "Roads and Anthropology: Ethnographic Perspectives on Space, Time and (Im)Mobility." *Mobilities* 7 (4): 459–65.

D'Andrea, Anthony, Luigina Ciolfi, and Breda Gray. 2011. "Methodological Challenges and Innovations in Mobilities Research." *Mobilities* 6 (2): 149–60.

Davidson, Joyce, Liz Bondi, and Mick Smith, eds. 2005. *Emotional Geographies*. London & New York: Routledge.

D'Emilio, John. 1983. "Capitalism and Gay Identity." In *Powers of Desire: The Politics of Sexuality*, edited by Ann Snitow, Christine Stansell, and Sharon Thompson, 100–113. New York: Monthly Review Press.

Department of Statistics, Malaysia. 2011. "Population Distribution and Basic Demographic Characteristics." June 28, 2011. http://www.statistics.gov.my/portal/

download_Population/files/census2010/Taburan_Penduduk_dan_Ciri-ciri_Asas_Demografi.pdf

Dikötter, Frank. 1995. *Sex, Culture, and Modernity in China: Medical Science and the Construction of Sexual Identities in the Early Republican Period*. Honolulu: University of Hawai'i Press.

Dilley, Whitney Crothers. 2007. *The Cinema of Ang Lee: The Other Side of the Screen*. London & New York: Wallflower Press.

Ding, Yu, and Petula Sik Ying Ho. 2012. "Sex Work in China's Pearl River Delta: Accumulating Sexual Capital as a Life-Advancement Strategy." *Sexualities* 16 (1–2): 43–60.

Dong, Jie. 2011. *Discourse, Identity, and China's Internal Migration: The Long March to the City*. Bristol, Buffalo, & Toronto: Multilingual Matters.

dos Santos, Gonçalo Duro. 2006. "The Anthropology of Chinese Kinship: A Critical Overview." *European Journal of East Asian Studies* 5 (2): 275–333.

Duggan, Lisa. 2003. *The Twilight of Equality? Neoliberalism, Cultural Politics, and the Attack on Democracy*. Boston, MA: Beacon Press.

Dyer, Richard. 2002. *The Culture of Queers*. London & New York: Routledge.

Eng, David L. 2010a. *The Feeling of Kinship: Queer Liberalism and the Racialization of Intimacy*. Durham & London: Duke University Press.

Eng, David L. 2010b. "The Queer Space of China: Expressive Desire in Stanley Kwan's *Lan Yu*." *Positions: East Asia Cultures Critique* 18 (2): 459–87.

Engebretsen, Elisabeth L. 2014. *Queer Women in Urban China: An Ethnography*. Abingdon & New York: Routledge.

Evans, Leighton. 2015. *Locative Social Media: Place in the Digital Age*. Basingstoke & New York: Palgrave Macmillan.

Farman, Jason. 2012. *Mobile Interface Theory: Embodied Space and Locative Media*. London & New York: Routledge.

Farrer, James. 2010. "A Foreign Adventurer's Paradise? Interracial Sexuality and Alien Sexual Capital in Reform Era Shanghai." *Sexualities* 13 (1): 69–95.

Fielding, Tony. 2016. *Asian Migrations: Social and Geographical Mobilities in Southeast, East, and Northeast Asia*. Abingdon & New York: Routledge.

Fortier, Anne-Marie. 2000. *Migrant Belongings: Memory, Space, Identity*. Oxford & New York: Berg.

Fortier, Anne-Marie. 2001. "'Coming Home': Queer Migrations and Multiple Evocations of Home." *European Journal of Cultural Studies* 4 (4): 405–24.

Fortier, Anne-Marie. 2003. "Making Home: Queer Migrations and Motions of Attachment." In *Uprootings/Regroundings: Questions of Home and Migration*, edited by Sara Ahmed, Claudia Castañeda, Anne-Marie Fortie, and Mimi Sheller, 115–35. Oxford & New York: Berg.

Foucault, Michel. 1978. *The History of Sexuality, Vol. 1: An Introduction*. Translated by Robert Hurley. New York: Pantheon Books.

Foucault, Michel. 1986. "Of Other Spaces: Utopias and Heterotopias." Translated by Jay Miskoviec. *Diacritics* 16 (1): 22–27.

Fox, Max. 2014. "Grindr's Lonely Crowd." *The Gay & Lesbian Review* 21 (5): 19–21.

Fraser, Nancy. 1992. "Rethinking the Public Sphere: A Contribution to the Critique of Actually Existing Democracy." In *Habermas and the Public Sphere*, edited by Craig Calhoun, 109–42. Cambridge, MA: MIT Press.

Fraser, Nancy. 2013. *Fortunes of Feminism: From State-Managed Capitalism to Neoliberal Crisis*. London & New York: Verso.

Frith, Jordan. 2015. *Smartphones as Locative Media*. Cambridge: Polity.

Gabriel, Sharmani P. 2015. "The Meaning of Race in Malaysia: Colonial, Post-colonial and Possible New Conjunctures." *Ethnicities* 15 (6): 782–809.

Gaetano, Arianne M., and Tamara Jacka. 2004. *On the Move: Women and Rural-to-Urban Migration in Contemporary China*. New York: Columbia University Press.

Gao, Ge, and Stella Ting-Toomey. 1998. *Communicating Effectively with the Chinese*. London: Sage.

Garber, Eric. 1989. "A Spectacle in Color: The Lesbian and Gay Subculture of Jazz Age Harlem." In *Hidden from History: Reclaiming the Gay and Lesbian Past*, edited by Martin Bauml Duberman, Martha Vicinus, and George Chauncey, 318–31. New York: New American Library.

Gibbs, Jeremy J., and Eric Rice. 2016. "The Social Context of Depression Symptomology in Sexual Minority Male Youth: Determinants of Depression in a Sample of Grindr Users." *Journal of Homosexuality* 63 (2): 278–99.

Goodman, David S. G. 2013. "Middle Class China: Dreams and Aspirations." *Journal of Chinese Political Science* 19 (1): 49–67.

Goodman, David S. G. 2014. *Class in Contemporary China*. Cambridge: Polity.

Goodman, David S. G. 2016. "Locating China's Middle Classes: Social Intermediaries and the Party-State." *Journal of Contemporary China* 25 (97): 1–13.

Goldberg, Amir. 2011. "Mapping Shared Understandings Using Relational Class Analysis: The Case of the Cultural Omnivore Reexamined." *American Journal of Sociology* 116 (5): 1397–436.

Gonzales, Alicia M., and Gary Rolison. 2005. "Social Oppression and Attitudes toward Sexual Practices." *Journal of Black Studies* 35 (6): 715–29.

Gopinath, Gayatri. 2005. *Impossible Desires: Queer Diasporas and South Asian Public Cultures*. Durham & London: Duke University Press.

Gorman-Murray, Andrew. 2007. "Rethinking Queer Migration through the Body." *Social & Cultural Geography* 8 (1): 105–21.

Gorman-Murray, Andrew. 2009. "Intimate Mobilities: Emotional Embodiment and Queer Migration." *Social & Cultural Geography* 10 (4): 441–60.

Gorman-Murray, Andrew. 2012. "Revisiting Geographies of Sexuality and Gender Down Under." *New Zealand Geographer* 68 (2): 77–80.

Gorman-Murray, Andrew, Gordon Waitt, and Lynda Johnston. 2008. "Geographies of Sexuality and Gender 'Down Under'." *Australian Geographer* 39 (3): 235–46.

Gössling, Stefan, and Iliada Stavrinidi. 2016. "Social Networking, Mobilities, and the Rise of Liquid Identities." *Mobilities* 11 (5): 723–43.

Green, Adam Isaiah. 2008a. "Erotic Habitus: Toward a Sociology of Desire." *Theory and Society* 37 (6): 597–626.

Green, Adam Isaiah. 2008b. "The Social Organization of Desire: The Sexual Fields Approach." *Sociological Theory* 26 (1): 25–50.

Green, Adam Isaiah, ed. 2014. *Sexual Fields: Toward a Sociology of Collective Sexual Life*. Chicago, IL: University of Chicago Press.

Grossman, Andrew. 2000. "The Rise of Homosexuality and the Dawn of Communism in Hong Kong Film: 1993–1998." In *Queer Asian Cinema: Shadows in the Shade*, edited by Andrew Grossman, 149–86. New York, London, & Oxford: Harrington Park Press.

Gudelunas, David. 2012. "There's an App for That: The Uses and Gratifications of Online Social Networks for Gay Men." *Sexuality and Culture* 16 (4): 346–65.

Hakim, Catherine. 2010. "Erotic Capital." *European Sociological Review* 26 (5): 499–518.

Hakim, Catherine. 2011a. *Erotic Capital: The Power of Attraction in the Boardroom and the Bedroom*. New York: Basic Books.

Hakim, Catherine. 2011b. *Honey Money: The Power of Erotic Capital*. London: Allen Lane.

Halperin, David M. 1990. *One Hundred Years of Homosexuality, and Other Essays on Greek Love*. London & New York: Routledge.

Halperin, David M. 2002. *How to Do the History of Homosexuality*. Chicago & London: University of Chicago Press.

Hannam, Kevin, Mimi Sheller, and John Urry. 2006. "Editorial: Mobilities, Immobilities and Moorings." *Mobilities* 1 (1): 1–22.

Hartman, Stephen. 2013. "Bondless Love." *Studies in Gender and Sexuality* 14 (1): 35–50.

Harvey, David. 2007. *A Brief History of Neoliberalism*. Oxford: Oxford University Press.

He, Shenjing, Si-Ming Li, and Kam Wing Chan. 2015. "Migration, Mobility, and Segregation in Chinese Cities." *Eurasian Geography and Economics* 56 (3): 223–30.

Hee, Wai Siam, and Ari Larissa Heinrich. 2014. "Desire against the Grain: Transgender Consciousness and Sinophonicity in the Films of Yasmin Ahmad." In *Queer Sinophone Cultures*, edited by Howard Chiang and Ari Larissa Heinrich, 179–200. London & New York: Routledge.

Heinrich, Ari Larissa. 2014. "'A Volatile Alliance': Queer Sinophone Synergies across Literature, Film, and Culture." In *Queer Sinophone Cultures*, edited by Howard Chiang and Ari Larissa Heinrich, 3–16. London & New York: Routledge.

Henderson, Lisa. 2013. *Love and Money: Queers, Class, and Cultural Production*. New York: New York University Press.

Hine, Christine. 2008. "Virtual Ethnography: Modes, Varieties, Affordances." In *The SAGE Handbook of Online Research Methods*, edited by Nigel G. Fielding, Raymond M. Lee, and Grant Blank, 257–70. London: Sage.

Hine, Christine. 2015. *Ethnography for the Internet: Embedded, Embodied and Everyday*. London: Bloomsbury Academic.

Hinsch, Bret. 1990. *Passions of the Cut Sleeve: The Male Homosexual Tradition in China*. Berkeley: University of California Press.

Hjorth, Larissa, and Michael Arnold. 2013. *Online@AsiaPacific: Mobile, Social and Locative Media in the Asia-Pacific*. Abingdon & New York: Routledge.

Ho, Loretta Wing Wah. 2010. *Gay and Lesbian Subculture in Urban China*. London & New York: Routledge.

Holloway, Ian W., Eric Rice, Jeremy Gibbs, Hailey Winetrobe, Shannon Dunlap, and Harmony Rhoades. 2014. "Acceptability of Smartphone Application-Based HIV Prevention Among Young Men Who Have Sex with Men." *AIDS and Behavior* 18 (2): 285–96.

Horst, Heather A., and Daniel Miller. 2012. *Digital Anthropology*. Oxford & New York: Berg.

Hsu, Carolyn L. 2007. *Creating Market Socialism: How Ordinary People are Shaping Class and Status in China*. Durham & London: Duke University Press.

Hu, Brian. 2005. "Formula 17: Testing a Formula for Mainstream Cinema in Taiwan." *Senses of Cinema*, no. 34. http://sensesofcinema.com/2005/feature-articles/formula_17/.

Hu, Yang. 2016. "Sex Ideologies in China: Examining Interprovince Differences." *Journal of Sex Research* 53 (9): 1118–30.

Huang, Ana. 2017. "Precariousness and the Queer Politics of Imagination in China." *Culture, Theory and Critique* 58 (2): 226–42.

Huang, Shirlena, and Brenda S. A. Yeoh. 2008. "Heterosexualities and the Global(izing) City in Asia: Introduction." *Asian Studies Review* 32 (1): 1–6.

Hubbard, Phil. 2000. "Desire/Disgust: Mapping the Moral Contours of Heterosexuality." *Progress in Human Geography* 24 (2): 191–217.

Jagose, Annamarie. 1997. *Queer Theory: An Introduction*. New York: New York University Press.

Jamieson, Lynn, and Roona Simpson. 2013. *Living Alone: Globalization, Identity and Belonging*. Basingstoke & New York: Palgrave Macmillan.

Johnston, Lynda, and Robyn Longhurst. 2010. *Space, Place, and Sex: Geographies of Sexualities*. Lanham, Boulder, New York, Toronto, & Oxford: Rowman & Littlefield Publishers.

Kam, Lucetta Yip Lo. 2012. *Shanghai Lalas: Female Tongzhi Communities and Politics in Urban China*. Hong Kong: Hong Kong University Press.

Kane, Daniel. 2006. *The Chinese Language: Its History and Current Usage*. North Clarendon, VT: Tuttle Publishing.

Kang, Wenqing. 2009. *Obsession: Male Same-Sex Relations in China, 1900–1950*. Hong Kong: Hong Kong University Press.

Kang, Wenqing. 2010. "Male Same-Sex Relations in Modern China: Language, Media Representation, and Law, 1900–1949." *Positions: East Asia Cultures Critique* 18 (2): 489–510.

Kang, Wenqing. 2018. "Violence and Awakening: Male Same-Sex Relations during the Cultural Revolution." Paper presented at the Association for Asian Studies Annual Conference, Washington, DC, March 2018.

Katz, James E., and Chih-Hui Lai. 2014. "Mobile Locative Media: The Nexus of Mobile Phones and Social Media." In *The Routledge Companion to Mobile Media*, edited by Gerard Goggin and Larissa Hjorth, 53–62. London & New York: Routledge.

Kaufmann, Vincent. 2002. *Re-thinking Mobility*. Farnham & Burlington: Ashgate Publishing Group.

Khoo, Gaik Cheng. 2005. "Recuperating Malay Custom/Adat in Female Sexuality in Malaysian Films." In *Asian Media Studies: Politics of Subjectivities*, edited by John Nguyet Erni and Siew Keng Chua, 207–24. Hoboken, NJ: Wiley-Blackwell.

Khoo, Gaik Cheng. 2006. *Reclaiming Adat: Contemporary Malaysian Film and Literature*. Vancouver & Toronto: UBC Press.

Khoo, Olivia. 2003. "Sexing the City: Malaysia's New Cyberlaws and Cyberjaya's Queer Success." In *Mobile Cultures: New Media in Queer Asia*, edited by Chris Berry, Fran Martin, and Audrey Yue, 222–44. Durham & London: Duke University Press.

Khoo, Olivia. 2014, "The Minor Transnationalism of Queer Asian Cinema: Female Authorship and the Short Film Format." *Camera Obscura* 29 (1): 32–57.

Kipnis, Andrew. 2006. "*Suzhi*: A Keyword Approach." *The China Quarterly* 186: 295–313.

Kipnis, Andrew. 2007. "Neoliberalism Reified: *Suzhi* Discourse and Tropes of Neoliberalism in the People's Republic of China." *Journal of the Royal Anthropological Institute* 13 (2): 383–400.

Knoblauch, Hubert. 2005. "Focused Ethnography." *Forum: Qualitative Social Research* [*Forum Qualitative Sozialforschung*] 6 (3). https://doi.org/10.17169/fqs-6.3.20.

Knopp, Larry. 2007. "On the Relationship between Queer and Feminist Geographies." *The Professional Geographer* 59 (1): 47–55.

Kong, Travis. 2011a. *Chinese Male Homosexualities: Memba, Tongzhi and Golden Boy*. London & New York: Routledge.

Kong, Travis. 2011b. "Transnational Queer Labor: The 'Circuits of Desire' of Money Boys in China." *English Language Notes* 49 (1): 139–46.

Kong, Travis. 2012. "A Fading *Tongzhi* Heterotopia: Hong Kong Older Gay Men's Use of Spaces." *Sexualities* 15 (8): 896–916.

Koo, Fung Kuen, Eric P. F. Chow, Liangmin Gao, Xiaoxing Fu, Jun Jing, Liang Chen, and Lei Zhang. 2014. "Socio-cultural Influences on the Transmission of HIV among Gay Men in Rural China." *Culture, Health & Sexuality* 16 (3): 302–15.

Koshy, Susan. 2004. *Sexual Naturalization: Asian Americans and Miscegenation*. Stanford, CA: Stanford University Press.

Kühn, Jan-Michael. 2013. "Focused Ethnography as Research Method: A Case Study of Techno Music Producers in Home-Recording Studios." Translated by Luis-Manuel Garcia. *Dancecult: Journal of Electronic Dance Music Culture* 5 (1). https://doi.org/10.12801/1947-5403.2013.05.01.10.

Kunstman, Adi. 2009. "The Currency of Victimhood in Uncanny Homes: Queer Immigrants' Claim for Home and Belonging through Anti-Homophobic Organizing." *Journal of Ethnic and Migration Studies* 35 (1): 133–49.

Landovitz, Raphael J., Chi-Hong Tseng, Matthew Weissman, Michael Haymer, Brett Mendenhall, Kathryn Rogers, Rosemary Veniegas, Pamina M. Gorbach, Cathy J. Reback, and Steven Shoptaw. 2012. "Epidemiology, Sexual Risk Behavior, and HIV Prevention Practices of Men Who Have Sex with Men Using GRINDR in Los Angeles, California." *Journal of Urban Health: Bulletin of the New York Academy of Medicine* 90 (4): 729–39.

Laqueur, Thomas. 1990. *Making Sex: Body and Gender from the Greeks to Freud*. Cambridge, MA: Harvard University Press.

Lau, Jenny Kwok Wah. 1995. "*Farewell My Concubine*: History, Melodrama, and Ideology in Contemporary Pan-Chinese Cinema." *Film Quarterly* 49 (1): 16–27.

Lee, Julian C. H. 2011. *Policing Sexuality: Sex, Society, and the State*. London & New York: Zed Books.

Lee, Yuen-Beng. 2012. "The Malaysian Digital Indies: New Forms, Aesthetics, and Genres in Post-2000 Malaysian Cinema." PhD thesis, University of Melbourne.

Leung, Helen Hok-Sze. 2007. "Archiving Queer Feelings in Hong Kong." *Inter-Asia Cultural Studies* 8 (4): 559–71.

Leung, Helen Hok-Sze. 2010. *Farewell My Concubine: A Queer Film Classic*. Vancouver, BC: Arsenal Pulp Press.

Leung, William. 2008. "So Queer Yet So Straight: Ang Lee's *The Wedding Banquet* and *Brokeback Mountain*." *Journal of Film and Video* 60 (1): 23–42.

Lévi-Strauss, Claude. [1949] 1969. *The Elementary Structures of Kinship*. Translated by James Strachey, James Harle Bell, John Richard von Sturmer, and Rodney Needham. Boston, MA: Beacon Press.

Lewis, Nathaniel M. 2012. "Remapping Disclosure: Gay Men's Segmented Journeys of Moving Out and Coming Out." *Social & Cultural Geography* 13 (3): 211–31.

Li, Peilin, and Laurence Roulleau-Berger. 2013. *China's Internal and International Migration*. London & New York: Routledge.

Li, Si-Ming, Kam Wing Chan, and Shenjing He. 2015. "Migration, Mobility, and Community Change in Chinese Cities." *Eurasian Geography and Economics* 55 (4): 307–12.

Licoppe, Christian, Carole Anne Rivière, and Julien Morel. 2016. "Grindr Casual Hook-Ups as Interactional Achievements." *New Media & Society* 18 (11): 2540–58.

Lim, Song Hwee. 2006. *Celluloid Comrades: Representations of Male Homosexuality in Contemporary Chinese Cinemas*. Honolulu: University of Hawai'i Press.

Lim, Song Hwee. 2008a. "How to Be Queer in Taiwan: Translation, Appropriation, and the Construction of a Queer Identity in Taiwan." In *AsiaPacifiQueer: Rethinking Genders and Sexualities*, edited by Fran Martin, Peter A. Jackson, Mark McLelland, and Audrey Yue, 235–50. Chicago: University of Illinois Press.

Lim, Song Hwee. 2008b. "The Singapore Failure Story, 'Slanged Up'." In *Chinese Films in Focus II*, edited by Chris Berry, 9–16. Basingstoke: Palgrave Macmillan, & London: BFI Publishing.

Lim, Song Hwee. 2014. "The Voice of the Sinophone." In *Sinophone Cinemas*, edited by Audrey Yue and Olivia Khoo, 62–76. Basingstoke & New York: Palgrave Macmillan.

Lin, Delia. 2017. *Civilising Citizens in Post-Mao China: Understanding the Rhetoric of* Suzhi. London & New York: Routledge.

Liu, Jen-peng, and Naifei Ding. 2005. "Reticent Poetics, Queer Politics." *Inter-Asia Cultural Studies* 6 (1): 30–55.

Liu, Petrus. 2010. "Why Does Queer Theory Need China?" *Positions: East Asia Cultures Critique* 18 (2): 291–320.

Liu, Petrus. 2015. *Queer Marxism in Two Chinas*. Durham & London: Duke University Press.

Liu, Petrus, and Lisa Rofel. 2010. "Beyond the Strai(gh)ts: Transnationalism and Queer Chinese Politics." *Positions: East Asia Cultures Critique* 18 (2): 283–88.

Liu, Shuo. 2014. "Homemaking and Middle Class Formation in Urban China." In *Chinese Middle Classes: Taiwan, Hong Kong, Macao, and China*, edited by Hsin-Huang Michael Hsiao, 132–53. London & New York: Routledge.

Lizardo, Omar. 2006. "The Puzzle of Women's 'Highbrow' Culture Consumption: Integrating Gender and Work into Bourdieu's Class Theory of Taste." *Poetics* 34 (1): 1–23.

López-Sintas, Jordi, and Ercilia García-Álvarez. 2002. "Omnivores Show Up Again: The Segmentation of Cultural Consumers in Spanish Social Space." *European Sociological Review* 18 (3): 353–68.

Lovell, Terry. 2000. "Thinking Feminism with and against Bourdieu." *Feminist Theory* 1 (1): 11–32.

Lu, Sheldon H. 2007. "Dialect and Modernity in 21st-Century Sinophone Cinema." *Jump Cut: A Review of Contemporary Media*, no. 49. https://www.ejumpcut.org/archive/jc49.2007/Lu/index.html.

Lu, Sheldon H. 2008. "Review of *Visuality and Identity: Sinophone Articulations across the Pacific* (Berkeley: University of California Press, 2007) by Shu-mei Shih." Columbus, OH: MCLC Resource Center. https://u.osu.edu/mclc/book-reviews/visuality-and-identity/.

Lu, Sheldon H. 2012. "Notes on Four Major Paradigms in Chinese-language Film Studies." *Journal of Chinese Cinemas* 6 (4): 15–25. Reprinted as "Genealogies of Four Critical Paradigms in Chinese-Language Film Studies." In *Sinophone Cinemas*, edited by Audrey Yue and Olivia Khoo, 2014, 13–25. Basingstoke & New York: Palgrave Macmillan.

Lu, Sheldon H., and Emilie Yueh-Yu Yeh. 2005. Introduction to *Chinese-Language Film: Historiography, Poetics, Politics*, edited by Sheldon H. Lu and Emilie Yueh-yu Yeh, 1–24. Honolulu: University of Hawai'i Press.

Lü, Xiaobo, and Elizabeth J. Perry. 1997. Danwei*: The Changing Chinese Workplace in Historical and Comparative Perspectives*. Armonk, NY: M.E. Sharpe.

Luibhéid, Eithne. 2005. "Heteronormativity and Immigration Scholarship: A Call for Change." *GLQ: A Journal of Lesbian and Gay Studies* 10 (2): 227–35.

Luibhéid, Eithne. 2008. "Queer/Migration: An Unruly Body of Scholarship." *GLQ: A Journal of Lesbian and Gay Studies* 14 (2–3): 169–90.

Luibhéid, Eithne, and Lionel Cantú Jr., eds. 2005. *Queer Migrations: Sexuality, U.S. Citizenship, and Border Crossings*. Minneapolis: University of Minnesota Press.

Maddison, Stephen. 2002. "Small Towns, Boys, and Ivory Towers: A Naked Academic." In *Temporalities, Autobiography and Everyday Life*, edited by Jan Campbell and Janet Harbord, 152–68. Manchester & New York: Manchester University Press.

Mahari, Zarinah. 2011. "Demographic Transition in Malaysia." Paper presented at the 15th Conference of Commonwealth Statisticians, New Delhi, February 2011.

Mai, Nicola, and Russell King. 2009. "Love, Sexuality and Migration: Mapping the Issue(s)." *Mobilities* 4 (3): 295–307.

Manalansan, Martin F. 2006. "Queer Intersections: Sexuality and Gender in Migration Studies." *International Migration Review* 40 (1): 224–49.

Martin, Fran. 2003. *Situating Sexualities: Queer Representation in Taiwanese Fiction, Film and Public Culture*. Hong Kong: Hong Kong University Press.

Martin, Fran. 2010. *Backward Glances: Contemporary Chinese Cultures and the Female Homoerotic Imaginary*. Durham & London: Duke University Press.

Martin, Fran. 2015. "Transnational Queer Sinophone Cultures." In *Routledge Handbook of Sexuality Studies in East Asia*, edited by Mark McLelland and Vera Mackie, 35–48. London & New York: Routledge.

Martin, John Levi, and Matt George. 2006. "Theories of Sexual Stratification: Toward an Analytics of the Sexual Field and a Theory of Sexual Capital." *Sociological Theory* 24 (2): 107–32.

Martinez, Omar, Elwin Wu, Andrew Z Shultz, Jonathan Capote, Javier López Rios, Theo Sandfort, Justin Manusov, Hugo Ovejero, Alex Carballo-Dieguez, Silvia Chavez Baray, Eva Moya, Jonathan López Matos, Juan J DelaCruz, Robert H Remien, and Scott D Rhodes. 2014. "Still a Hard-to-Reach Population? Using Social Media to Recruit Latino Gay Couples for an HIV Intervention Adaptation Study." *Journal of Medical Internet Research* 16 (4): e113. https://doi.org/10.2196/jmir.3311.

Maton, Karl. 2014. "*Habitus*." In *Pierre Bourdieu: Key Concepts* (2nd ed.), edited by Michael Grenfell, 48–64. London & New York: Routledge.

McLelland, Mark. 2000. "Interview with Samshasha, Hong Kong's First Gay Rights Activist and Author." *Intersections: Gender, History and Culture in the Asian Context*, no. 4. http://intersections.anu.edu.au/issue4/interview_mclelland.html.

McLelland, Mark. 2005. *Queer Japan from the Pacific War to the Internet Age*. Lanham, Boulder, New York, Toronto, & Oxford: Rowman & Littlefield Publishers.

Menget, Patrick. 2008. "Kinship Theory after Lévi-Strauss' *Elementary Structures*." *Journal de la Société des Américanistes* 94 (2): 29–37. https://doi.org/10.4000/jsa.10549.

Merabet, Sofian. 2014. "Queer Habitus: Bodily Performance and Queer Ethnography in Lebanon." *Identities* 21 (5): 516–31.

Metzger, Sean. 2000. "Farewell My Fantasy." In *Queer Asian Cinema: Shadows in the Shade*, edited by Andrew Grossman, 213–32. New York, London, & Oxford: Harrington Park Press.

Miao, Ying. 2017. "Middle Class Identity in China: Subjectivity and Stratification." *Asian Studies Review* 41 (4): 629–46.

Michael, Robert T. 2004. "Sexual Capital: An Extension of Grossman's Concept of Health Capital." *Journal of Health Economics* 23 (4): 643–52.

Miller, Brandon. 2015. "'They're the Modern-Day Gay Bar': Exploring the Uses and Gratifications of Social Networks for Men Who Have Sex with Men." *Computers in Human Behavior* 51 (A): 476–82.

Mirowski, Philip. 2013. *Never Let a Serious Crisis Go to Waste: How Neoliberalism Survived the Financial Meltdown*. New York & London: Verso.

Muñoz, José Esteban. 2009. *Cruising Utopia: The Then and There of Queer Futurity*. New York: New York University Press.

Murray, Heather. 2012. *Not in This Family: Gays and the Meaning of Kinship in Postwar North America*. Philadelphia: University of Pennsylvania Press.

Muthalib, Hassan Abd. 2007. "The Little Cinema of Malaysia: Out with the Old, In with the New." *KINEMA: A Journal of Film and Audiovisual Media*. http://www.kinema.uwaterloo.ca/article.php?id=31.

Naficy, Hamid. 2001. *An Accented Cinema: Exilic and Diasporic Filmmaking*. Princeton & Oxford: Princeton University Press.

Nail, Thomas. 2015. *The Figure of the Migrant*. Stanford, CA: Stanford University Press.

Nail, Thomas. 2016. *Theory of the Border*. Oxford: Oxford University Press.

Nakajima, Seio. 2014. "Chinese Film Spaces: Social Locations and Media of Urban Independent Screen Consumption." In *Continuum: Journal of Media and Culture Studies* 28 (1): 52–64.

Newton, Esther. 1993. *Cherry Grove, Fire Island: Sixty Years in America's First Gay and Lesbian Town*. Boston, MA: Beacon Press.

Nonini, Donald M. 2008. "Is China Becoming Neoliberal?" *Critique of Anthropology* 28 (2): 145–76.

Nyíri, Pál. 2010. *Mobility and Cultural Authority in Contemporary China*. Seattle: University of Washington Press.

Offord, Baden. 2013. "Queer Activist Intersections in Southeast Asia: Human Rights and Cultural Studies." *Asian Studies Review* 37 (3): 335–49.

Ong, Aihwa. 2006. *Neoliberalism as Exception: Mutations in Citizenship and Sovereignty*. Durham & London: Duke University Press.

Ong, Aihwa. 2007. "Neoliberalism as a Mobile Technology." *Transactions of the Institute of British Geographers* 32 (1): 3–8.

Oswin, Natalie. 2008. "Critical Geographies and the Uses of Sexuality: Deconstructing Queer Space." *Progress in Human Geography* 32 (1): 89–103.

Oswin, Natalie. 2010. "Sexual Tensions in Modernizing Singapore: The Postcolonial and the Intimate." *Environment and Planning D: Society and Space* 28 (1): 121–41.

Oswin, Natalie. 2012. "The Queer Time of Creative Urbanism: Family, Futurity, and Global City Singapore." *Environment and Planning A* 44 (7): 1624–40.

Oswin, Natalie. 2014. "Queer Theory." In *The Routledge Handbook of Mobilities*, edited by Peter Merriman, Mimi Sheller, Kevin Hannam, Peter Adey, and David Bissell. London & New York: Routledge.

Pain, Rachel. 2001. "Geographies of Gender and Sexuality." In *Introducing Social Geographies*, edited by Rachel Pain, Jamie Gough, Graham Mowl, Michael Barke, Robert MacFarlene, and Duncan Fuller, 120–40. London: Arnold.

Pellegrino, Giuseppina, ed. 2011. *The Politics of Proximity: Mobility and Immobility in Practice*. Farnham & Burlington: Ashgate Publishing Group.

Penney, Tom. 2014. "Bodies under Glass: Gay Dating Apps and the Affect-Image." *Media International Australia* 153 (1): 107–17.

Peterson, Richard A. 1992. "Understanding Audience Segmentation: From Elite and Mass to Omnivore and Univore." *Poetics* 21 (4): 243–58.

Peterson, Richard A. 2005. "Problems in Comparative Research: The Example of Omnivorousness." *Poetics* 33 (5–6): 257–82.

Peterson, Richard A., and Roger M. Kern. 1996. "Changing Highbrow Taste: From Snob to Omnivore." *American Sociological Review* 61 (5): 900–907.

Peterson, Richard A., and Albert Simkus. 1992. "How Musical Tastes Mark Occupational Status Groups." In *Cultivating Differences: Symbolic Boundaries and the Making of Inequality*, edited by Michèle Lamont and Marcel Fournier, 152–86. Chicago, IL: University of Chicago Press.

Pflugfelder, Gregory M. 1999. *Cartographies of Desire: Male-Male Sexuality in Japanese Discourse, 1600–1950*. Los Angeles: University of California Press.

Plummer, Ken. 1995. *Telling Sexual Stories: Power, Change, and Social Worlds*. London & New York: Routledge.

Plummer, Ken. 2008. "Studying Sexualities for a Better World? Ten Years of *Sexualities*." *Sexualities* 11 (1–2): 7–23.

Pow, Choon-Piew. 2009. *Gated Communities in China: Class, Privilege and the Moral Politics of the Good Life*. London & New York: Routledge.

Puar, Jasbir. 2002a. "A Transnational Feminist Critique of Queer Tourism." *Antipode: A Radical Journal of Geography* 34 (5): 935–46.

Puar, Jasbir. 2002b. "Circuits of Queer Mobility: Tourism, Travel, and Globalization." *GLQ: A Journal of Lesbian and Gay Studies* 8 (1–2): 101–37.

Puar, Jasbir. 2006. "Mapping US Homonormativities." *Gender, Place & Culture: A Journal of Feminist Geography* 13 (1): 67–88.

Quiroz, Pamela Anne. 2013. "From Finding the Perfect Love Online to Satellite Dating and 'Loving-the-One-You're Near': A Look at Grindr, Skout, Plenty of Fish, Meet Moi, Zoosk and Assisted Serendipity." *Humanity & Society* 37 (2): 181–85.

Race, Kane. 2015a. "'Party and Play': Online Hook-Up Devices and the Emergence of PNP Practices among Gay Men." *Sexualities* 18 (3): 253–75.

Race, Kane. 2015b. "Speculative Pragmatism and Intimate Arrangements: Online Hook-Up Devices in Gay Life." *Culture, Health & Sexuality* 17 (4): 496–511.

Rainie, Lee, and Barry Wellman. 2012. *Networked: The New Social Operating System*. Cambridge, MA: MIT Press.

Raiti, Gerard C. 2007. "Mobile Intimacy: Theories on the Economics of Emotion with Examples from Asia." *M/C Journal: A Journal of Media and Culture* 10 (1). http://journal.media-culture.org.au/0703/02-raiti.php.

Rao, Rahul. 2015. "Global Homocapitalism." *Radical Philosophy* 194: 38–49.

Rao, Rahul. 2018. "The State of 'Queer IR'." *GLQ: A Journal of Lesbian and Gay Studies* 24 (1): 139–49.

Ren, Hai. 2010. *Neoliberalism and Culture in China and Hong Kong: The Countdown of Time*. London & New York: Routledge.

Rendina, H. Jonathon, Ruben H. Jimenez, Christian Grov, Ana Ventuneac, and Jeffrey T. Parsons. 2014. "Patterns of Lifetime and Recent HIV Testing Among Men Who Have Sex with Men in New York City Who Use Grindr." *AIDS and Behavior* 18 (1): 41–49.

Riesman, David, Nathan Glazer, and Reuel Denney. [1950] 2001. *The Lonely Crowd: A Study of the Changing American Character*. New Haven, CT: Yale University Press.

Rofel, Lisa. 1999. "Qualities of Desire: Imagining Gay Identities in China." *GLQ: A Journal of Lesbian and Gay Studies* 5 (4): 451–74.

Rofel, Lisa. 2007. *Desiring China: Experiments in Neoliberalism, Sexuality, and Public Culture*. Durham & London: Duke University Press.

Rofel, Lisa. 2010. "The Traffic in Money Boys." *Positions: East Asia Cultures Critique* 18 (2): 425–58.

Roose, Henk, Koen van Eijck, and John Lievens. 2012. "Culture of Distinction or Culture of Openness? Using a Social Space Approach to Analyze the Social Structuring of Lifestyles." *Poetics* 40 (6): 491–513.

Rosen, Daniel H., and Zhi Wang. 2011. *The Implications of China-Taiwan Economic Liberalization*. Washington, DC: Peterson Institute for International Economics.

Ross, Charlotte. 2004. "Queering the Habitus: Lesbian Identity in Stancanelli's *Benzina*." *Romance Studies* 22 (3): 237–50.

Sang, Tze-lan D. 1999. "Translating Homosexuality: The Discourse of *Tongxing'ai* in Republican China (1912–1949)." In *Tokens of Exchange: The Problem of Translation in Global Circulations*, edited by Lydia H. Liu, 276–304. Durham & London: Duke University Press.

Sang, Tze-lan D. 2003. *The Emerging Lesbian: Female Same-Sex Desire in Modern China*. Chicago, IL: University of Chicago Press.

Sang, Tze-lan D. 2014. "From Flowers to Boys: Queer Adaptation in Wu Jiwen's *The Fin-de-siècle Boy Love Reader*." In *Queer Sinophone Cultures*, edited by Howard Chiang and Ari Larissa Heinrich, 67–83. London & New York: Routledge.

Schneider, David. [1968] 1980. *American Kinship: A Cultural Account*. Chicago, IL: University of Chicago Press.

Schneider, David. 1984. *A Critique of the Study of Kinship*. Ann Arbor: University of Michigan Press.

Sedgwick, Eve Kosofsky. 1990. *Epistemology of the Closet*. Berkeley: University of California Press.

Sender, Katherine. 2003. "Sex Sells: Sex, Class, and Taste in Commercial Gay and Lesbian Media." *GLQ: A Journal of Lesbian and Gay Studies* 9 (3): 331–65.

Sender, Katherine. 2004. *Business, not Politics: The Making of the Gay Market*. New York: Columbia University Press.

Shah, Nayan. 2012. *Stranger Intimacy: Contesting Race, Sexuality and the Law in the North American West*. Berkeley, Los Angeles, & London: University of California Press.

Shapiro, Warren. 2010. "The Old Kinship Studies Confronts Gay Kinship: A Critique of Kath Weston." *Anthropological Forum* 20 (1): 1–18.

Shi, Liang. 2015. *Chinese Lesbian Cinema: Mirror Rubbing, Lala, and Les*. Lanham, MD: Lexington Books.

Shiau, Hong-Chi. 2008. "Marketing Boys' Love: Taiwan's Independent Film, *Eternal Summer*, and Its Audiences." *Asian Cinema* 19 (1): 157–71.

Shih, Shu-mei. 2004. "Global Literature and the Technologies of Recognition." *PMLA* 119 (1): 16–30.

Shih, Shu-mei. 2007. *Visuality and Identity: Sinophone Articulations across the Pacific*. Berkeley: University of California Press.

Shih, Shu-mei. 2010a. "Against Diaspora: The Sinophone as Places of Cultural Production." In *Global Chinese Literature: Critical Essays*, edited by Jing Tsu and David Der-wei Wang, 29–48. Leiden: Brill Press. Reprinted in *Sinophone Studies: A Critical Reader*, edited by Shu-mei Shih, Chien-hsin Tsai, and Brian Bernards, 2013, 25–42. New York: Columbia University Press.

Shih, Shu-mei. 2010b. "Theory, Asia and the Sinophone." *Postcolonial Studies* 13 (4): 465–84.

Shih, Shu-mei. 2011. "The Concept of the Sinophone." *PMLA* 126 (3): 709–18.

Shih, Shu-mei. 2014. "On the Conjunctive Method." In *Queer Sinophone Cultures*, edited by Howard Chiang and Ari Larissa Heinrich, 223–25. London & New York: Routledge.

Simes, Gary. 2005. "Gay Slang Lexicography: A Brief History and a Commentary on the First Two Gay Glossaries." *Dictionaries: Journal of the Dictionary Society of North America* 26: 1–159.

Sinnott, Megan. 2010. "Borders, Diaspora, and Regional Connections: Trends in Asian 'Queer' Studies." *The Journal of Asian Studies* 69 (1): 17–31.

Skeggs, Beverley. 1997. *Formations of Class and Gender: Becoming Respectable*. London: Sage.

Skeggs, Beverley. 2000. "The Appearance of Class: Challenges in Gay Space." In *Cultural Studies and the Working Class: Subject to Change*, edited by Sally Munt, 129–51. London: Continnuum-3PL.

Skeggs, Beverley. 2004. *Class, Self, Culture*. London & New York: Routledge.

So, Alvin Y. 2013. *Class and Class Conflict in Post-Socialist China*. Hackensack, NJ: World Scientific.

Spencer, Norman A. 2012. "Ten Years of Queer Cinema in China." *Positions: Asia Critique* 20 (1): 373–83.

Stewart, Matthew. 2018. "The 9.9 Percent Is the New American Aristocracy." *Atlantic*, June 2018.

Stewart, Simon. 2014. *A Sociology of Culture, Taste and Value*. Basingstoke & New York: Palgrave Macmillan.

Su, Jiunn-Yih, Jan Holt, Rebecca Payne, Kim Gates, Andrew Ewing, and Nathan Ryder. 2015. "Effectiveness of Using Grindr to Increase Syphilis Testing among Men Who Have Sex with Men in Darwin, Australia." *Australian and New Zealand Journal of Public Health* 39 (3): 293–94.

Sun, Christina J., Jason Stowers, Cindy Miller, Laura H. Bachmann, and Scott D. Rhodes. 2015. "Acceptability and Feasibility of Using Established Geosocial and Sexual Networking Mobile Applications to Promote HIV and STD Testing Among Men Who Have Sex with Men." *AIDS and Behavior* 19 (3): 543–52.

Tambling, Jeremy. 1990. *Confession: Sexuality, Sin, the Subject*. Manchester & New York: Manchester University Press.

Tambling, Jeremy. 2003. *Wong Kar-wai's Happy Together*. Hong Kong: Hong Kong University Press.

Tang, Beibei. 2013. "Urban Housing-Status-Groups: Consumption, Lifestyles and Identity." In *Middle-Class China: Identity and Behaviour*, edited by Minglu Chen and David S. G. Goodman, 54–74. Cheltenham: Edward Elgar.

Teh, Yik Koon. 2008. "Politics and Islam: Factors Determining Identity and the Status of Male-to-Female Transsexuals in Malaysia." In *AsiaPacifiQueer: Rethinking Genders and Sexualities*, edited by Fran Martin, Peter Jackson, Mark McLelland, and Audrey Yue, 85–98. Chicago: University of Illinois Press.

Tomba, Luigi. 2004. "Creating an Urban Middle Class: Social Engineering in Beijing." *The China Journal* 51: 1–26.

Tomba, Luigi. 2008. "Making Neighbourhoods: The Government of Social Change in China's Cities." *China Perspectives* 76 (4): 48–61.

Tomba, Luigi. 2009. "Of Quality, Harmony, and Community: Civilization and the Middle Class in Urban China." *Positions: East Asia Cultures Critique* 17 (3): 591–616.

Tomba, Luigi. 2010. "Gating Urban Spaces in China: Inclusion, Exclusion and Government." In *Gated Communities: Social Sustainability in Contemporary and Historical Gated Developments*, edited by Samer Bagaeen and Ola Uduku, 27–37. London: Earthscan.

Tomba, Luigi. 2014. *The Government Next Door: Neighborhood Politics in Urban China*. Ithaca, NY: Cornell University Press.

Tomlinson, John. 2000. "Proximity Politics." *Information, Communication & Society* 3 (3): 402–14.

Tsang, Eileen Yuk-Ha. 2014. *The New Middle Class in China: Consumption, Politics and the Market Economy*. Basingstoke & New York: Palgrave Macmillan.

Turkle, Sherry. 2011. *Alone Together: Why We Expect More from Technology and Less from Each Other*. New York: Basic Books.

Turner, Graeme. 2006. *Film as Social Practice* (4th ed.). London & New York: Routledge.

Underberg, Natalie M, and Elayne Zorn. 2013. *Digital Ethnography: Anthropology, Narrative, and New Media*. Austin: University of Texas Press.

Urry, John. 2000. *Sociology beyond Societies: Mobilities for the Twenty-First Century*. London & New York: Routledge.

Urry, John. 2003. *Global Complexity*. Cambridge: Polity.

Urry, John. 2005. "The Complexities of the Global." *Theory, Culture & Society* 22 (5): 235–54.

Urry, John. 2007. *Mobilities*. Cambridge: Polity.

Urry, John. 2011. "Social Networks, Mobile Lives and Social Inequalities." *Journal of Transport Geography* 21: 24–30.

Urry, John, and Jonas Larsen. 2011. *The Tourist Gaze 3.0*. London: Sage.

Valentine, Gill. 2002. "Queer Bodies and the Production of Space." In *Handbook of Lesbian and Gay Studies*, edited by Diane Richardson and Steven Seidman, 145–60. London: Sage.

Valentine, James. 1997. "Pots and Pans: Identification of Queer Japanese in Terms of Discrimination." In *Queerly Phrased: Language, Gender, and Sexuality*, edited by Anna Livia and Kira Hall, 95–114. Oxford & New York: Oxford University Press.

van Eijck, Koen. 2001. "Social Differentiation in Musical Taste Patterns." *Social Forces*, 79 (3): 1163–84.

van Eijck, Koen, and John Lievens. 2008. "Cultural Omnivorousness as a Combination of Highbrow, Pop, and Folk Elements: The Relation between Taste Patterns and Attitudes concerning Social Integration." *Poetics* 36 (2–3): 217–42.

Virilio, Paul. [1977] 2006. *Speed and Politics*. Los Angeles, CA: Semiotext(e).

Vitiello, Giovanni. 2011. *The Libertine's Friend: Homosexuality and Masculinity in Late Imperial China*. Chicago & London: University of Chicago Press.

Waitt, Gordon, and Gorman-Murray, Andrew. 2007. "Homemaking and Mature-Age Gay Men 'Down Under': Paradox, Intimacy, Subjectivities, Spatialities, and Scale." *Gender, Place and Culture* 14 (5): 569–84.

Waitt, Gordon, and Gorman-Murray, Andrew. 2011a. "'It's About Time You Came Out': Sexualities, Mobility and Home." *Antipode: A Radical Journal of Geography* 43 (4): 1380–403.

Waitt, Gordon, and Gorman-Murray, Andrew. 2011b. "Journeys and Returns: Home, Life Narratives and Remapping Sexuality in a Regional City." *International Journal of Urban and Regional Research* 35 (6): 1239–55.

Wall, Sarah. 2015. "Focused Ethnography: A Methodological Adaptation for Social Research in Emerging Contexts." *Forum: Qualitative Social Research* [*Forum Qualitative Sozialforschung*] 16 (1). https://dx.doi.org/10.17169/fqs-16.1.2182.

Wallis, Cara. 2013. *Technomobility in China: Young Migrant Women and Mobile Phones*. New York: New York University Press.

Walsh, Katie, Hsiu-hua Shen, and Katie Willis. 2008. "Heterosexuality and Migration in Asia." *Gender, Place and Culture* 15 (6): 575–79.

Walsh, Michael. 1996. "National Cinema, National Imaginary." *Film History*, 8 (1): 5–17.

Wang, Ling-chi. 2006. "The Structure of Dual Domination: Toward a Paradigm for the Study of the Chinese Diaspora in the United States." In *The Chinese Overseas*, edited by Hong Liu, 279–96. London & New York: Routledge.

Warde, Alan, David Wright, and Modesto Gayo-Cal. 2007. "Understanding Cultural Omnivorousness: Or, the Myth of the Cultural Omnivore." *Cultural Sociology* 1 (2): 143–64.

Warner, Michael. 2002. *Publics and Counterpublics*. New York: Zone Books.

Wei, John. 2012. "East Palace, West Closet: Representing the Chinese Same-Sex Tradition and Same-Sex Identities in Contemporary Chinese-Language Cinema." MA diss., University of Auckland.

Wei, John. 2014. "Queer Encounters between *Iron Man* and Chinese *Boys' Love* Fandom." *Transformative Works and Cultures*, no. 17. https://doi.org/10.3983/twc.2014.0561.

Wei, Wei. 2006. "Going Public: The Production and Transformation of Queer Spaces in Postsocialist Chengdu, China." PhD diss., Loyola University Chicago.

Wei, Wei. 2007a. "'Wandering Men' no longer Wander Around: The Production and Transformation of Local Homosexual Identities in Contemporary Chengdu, China." *Inter-Asia Cultural Studies* 8 (4): 572–88.

Wei, Wei. 2017. "Good Gay Buddies for Lifetime: Homosexually Themed Discourse and the Construction of Heteromasculinity among Chinese Urban Youth." *Journal of Homosexuality* 64 (12): 1667–83.

Welker, James, and Lucetta Kam. 2006. "Introduction of Queer Import(s): Sexualities, Genders and Rights in Asia." *Intersections: Gender, History and Culture in the Asian Context*, no. 14. http://intersections.anu.edu.au/issue14/introduction.htm.

Weston, Kath. [1991] 1997. *Families We Choose: Lesbians, Gays, Kinship*. New York: Columbia University Press.

Weston, Kath. 1995. "Get Thee to a Big City: Sexual Imaginary and the Great Gay Migration." *GLQ: A Journal of Lesbian and Gay Studies* 2 (3): 253–77.

Wilken, Rowan. 2010. "A Community of Strangers? Mobile Media, Art, Tactility, and Urban Encounters with the Other." *Mobilities* 5 (4): 449–68.

Wilken, Rowan, and Gerard Goggin, eds. 2014. *Locative Media*. Abingdon & New York: Routledge.

Williams, Walter. 2009. "Strategies for Challenging Homophobia in Islamic Malaysia and Secular China." *Nebula* 6 (1): 1–20.

Wilson, Ara. 2006. "Queering Asia." *Intersections: Gender, History and Culture in the Asian Context*, no. 14. http://intersections.anu.edu.au/issue14/wilson.html.

Winetrobe, Hailey, Eric Rice, José Bauermeister, Robin Petering, and Ian W. Holloway. 2014. "Associations of Unprotected Anal Intercourse with Grindr-Met Partners among Grindr-Using Young Men Who Have Sex with Men in Los Angeles." *AIDS Care* 26 (10): 1303–8.

Wolf, Sherry. 2004. "The Roots of Gay Oppression." *International Socialist Review*, no. 37. https://www.isreview.org/issues/37/gay_oppression.shtml.

Wong, Alvin Ka Hin. 2012. "From the Transnational to the Sinophone: Lesbian Representations in Chinese-Language Films." *Journal of Lesbian Studies* 16 (3): 307–22.

Wong, Andrew D. 2008. "On the Actuation of Semantic Change: The Case of *Tongzhi*." *Language Sciences* 30 (4): 423–49.

Wong, Day. 2010. "Hybridization and the Emergence of 'Gay' Identities in Hong Kong and in China." *Visual Anthropology* 24 (1–2): 152–70.

Wong, Tai-Chee, Sun Sheng Han, and Hongmei Zhang, eds. 2015. *Population Mobility, Urban Planning and Management in China*. New York & London: Springer.

Wright, Kai. 2008. *Drifting Toward Love: Black, Brown, Gay, and Coming of Age on the Streets of New York*. Boston, MA: Beacon Press.

Wu, Cuncun. 2004. *Homoerotic Sensibilities in Late Imperial China*. London & New York: Routledge.

Wu, Fulong. 2005. "Rediscovering the 'Gate' under Market Transition: From Work-Unit Compounds to Commodity Housing Enclaves." *Housing Studies* 20 (2): 235–54.

Xie, Ying, and Minggang Peng. 2018. "Attitudes Toward Homosexuality in China: Exploring the Effects of Religion, Modernizing Factors, and Traditional Culture." *Journal of Homosexuality* 65 (13): 1758–87.

Xu, Ben. 1997. "*Farewell My Concubine* and its Nativist Critics." *Quarterly Review of Film and Video* 16 (2): 155–70.

Yan, Hairong. 2008. *New Masters, New Servants: Migration, Development, and Women Workers in China*. Durham, NC: Duke University Press.

Yang, Jinghao. 2013. "Activists Battle to Eliminate Discrimination Taught in Schools." *Global Times*, May 23, 2013. http://www.globaltimes.cn/NEWS/tabid/99/ID/783903/Activists-battle-to-eliminate-discrimination-taught-in-schools.aspx.

Yeh, Emilie Yueh-yu. 2012. "*Wenyi* and the Branding of Early Chinese Film." *Journal of Chinese Cinemas* 6 (4): 65–94.

Yeo, Tien Ee Dominic, and Tsz Hang Chu. 2018. "Beyond Homonegativity: Understanding Hong Kong People's Attitudes about Social Acceptance of Gay/Lesbian People, Sexual Orientation Discrimination Protection, and Same-Sex Marriage." *Journal of Homosexuality* 65 (10): 1372–90.

Yue, Audrey. 2007. "Hawking in the Creative City: *Rice Rhapsody*, Sexuality and the Cultural Politics of New Asia in Singapore." *Feminist Media Studies* 7 (4): 365–80.

Yue, Audrey. 2008. "Same-Sex Migration in Australia: From Interdependency to Intimacy." *GLQ: A Journal of Lesbian and Gay Studies* 14 (2–3): 239–62.

Yue, Audrey. 2012a. "Mobile Intimacies in the Queer Sinophone Films of Cui Zi'en." *Journal of Chinese Cinemas* 6 (4): 95–108.

Yue, Audrey. 2012b. "Queer Asian Mobility and Homonational Modernity: Marriage Equality, Indian Students in Australia and Malaysian Transgender Refugees in the Media." *Global Media and Communication* 8 (3): 269–87.

Yue, Audrey. 2015. "Regulating Queer Domesticity in the Neoliberal Diaspora." In *Blackwell Companion to Hong Kong Cinema*, edited by Esther Cheung, Esther Yau, and Gina Marchetti, 284–302. Walden & Oxford: Wiley-Blackwell.

Yue, Audrey, and Olivia Khoo. 2012. "From Diasporic Cinemas to Sinophone Cinemas: An Introduction." *Journal of Chinese Cinemas* 6 (1): 9–13.

Zhang, Benzi. 1999. "Figures of Violence and Tropes of Homophobia: Reading *Farewell My Concubine* between East and West." *The Journal of Popular Culture* 33 (2):101–9.

Zhang, Jijiao, and Howard Duncan, eds. 2014. *Migration in China and Asia: Experience and Policy*. New York & London: Springer.

Zhang, Li. 2010. *In Search of Paradise. Middle Class Living in a Chinese Metropolis*. Ithaca, NY: Cornell University Press.

Zhou, Yuxing. 2011. "Riding the Digital Wave: Grassroots Filmmaking in China from the Late 1990s." PhD diss., University of Melbourne.

Zhou, Yuxing. 2014. "Chinese Queer Images on Screen: A Case Study of Cui Zi'en's Films." *Asian Studies Review* 38 (1): 124–40.

Zhu, Jingshu. 2018. "'Unqueer' Kinship? Critical Reflections on 'Marriage Fraud' in Mainland China." *Sexualities* 21 (7): 1075–91.

Chinese-Language References

Chen, Xiuyuan. 2008. "Chinese Homosexuality Studies: The Past and Future—A Literature Review of 178 Academic Journal Articles between 1986 and 2006" [*Zhongguo tongxinglian yanjiu: huigu yu zhanwang—dui 1986~2006 nian jian 178 pian xueshu lunwen de wenxian zongshu*]. *The Chinese Journal of Human Sexuality* [*Zhongguo xing kexue*], no. 11: 30–35.

Chiou, Wei-Chuen. 2012. "Enhancement of Hierarchy or Empowerment: Gender as Performance of Gay Community on LBS Apps?" [*Nantongzhi* app *jiaoyou de xingbie zhanyan celue: baquan haishi fuquan?*]. Paper presented at the Chinese Communication Society Annual Conference [*Zhonghua chuanbo xuehui nianhui*], Taichung, July 2012. http://ccs.nccu.edu.tw/paperdetail.asp?HP_ID=1467.

CQIF (China Queer Independent Film). 2013. "Independent Filmmaker Applies for the Disclosure of Information on the International Day against Homophobia" [*Guoji buzai kongtong ri, duli dianyingren shenqing xinxi gongkai*]. Sina Blog. May 17, 2013. http://blog.sina.com.cn/s/blog_6765a5a60101eg4t.html.

Dai, Jinhua. 2000. *Landscape in the Mist: Chinese Film Culture 1978–1998* (*Wuzhong fengjing: zhongguo dianying wenhua 1978–1998*). Beijing: Peking University Press.

Fu, Xiaoxing, and Zhen Wu. 2010. "The Urban Spatial Distribution and Cultural Production of Gay Groups: A Case Study of Shenyang" [*Nantongxinglian qunti de chengshi kongjian fenbu ji wenhua shengchan: yi Shenyang weili*]. *Journal of Engineering Studies: Cross-disciplinary Perspectives* [*Gongcheng yanjiu: kuaxueke shiye zhong de gongcheng*], no. 1: 38–52.

Gao, Shuyan, and Xiaoming Jia. 2008. "Domestic Research on Homosexuality during the Recent 15 Years" [*Jin 15 nian lai guonei tongxinglian de yanjiu gaikuang*]. *China Journal of Health Psychology* [*Zhongguo jiankang xinlixue zazhi*], no. 4: 461–63.

Guo, Xiao-fei. 2007a. "Did China Ever Decriminalize Homosexual?" [*Zhongguo youguo tongxinglian de feizuihua ma?*]. *Law and Social Development* [*Fazhi yu shehui fazhan*], no. 4: 51–65.

Guo, Xiao-fei. 2007b. *Homosexuality in the Spotlight of Chinese Jurisprudence* [*Zhongguo fa shiye xia de tongxinglian*]. Beijing: Intellectual Property Publishing House.

Guo, Xiao-fei. 2008. "The Legal Environment for Chinese *Tongzhi* Community—A Case Study" [*Zhongguo tongzhi renqun de falv huanjing—yi anli wei zhongxin*]. In *Ecological Report on the Chinese Homosexual Population (Part 1)*, edited by Ge Tong, Xiaopei He, Yini Guo, Zi'en Cui, Yanling Mao, and Xiao-fei Guo. Beijing: Beijing Gender Health Education Institute.

Li, Yinhe. 1998. *Subculture of Homosexuality* [*Tongxinglian yawenhua*]. Beijing: China Today Press.

Li, Yinhe, and Xiaobo Wang. 1993. *The World of Others: Perspectives on a Chinese Male Homosexual Community* [*Tamen de shijie: zhongguo nan tongxinglian qunluo toushi*]. Hong Kong: Cosmos Press.

Shen, Yimin. 1991. "The Status of Our Country's Population Control during the 'Seventh Five-Year Plan'" ['Qiwu' qijian woguo renkou kongzhi zhuangkuang]. *Sociological Studies* [*Shehuixue yanjiu*], no. 3: 16–19.

Tang, Ying, and Jing Qu. 2008. "The Origin of *Tongzhi* and the Reasons behind Its Discursive Evolution" [*Tongzhi chengwei de yuanliu ji qi yanbian yuanyin*]. *Social Science Front* [*Shehui kexue zhanxian*], no. 3: 270–72.

Ti, Bing-yen. 2013a. "Director's Notes on the Malaysian *Tongzhi* Micro-film *Exchange 2012*" [*Malaixiya tongzhi weidianying Tongchuang Yimeng daoyan shouji*]. Feizan. March 4, 2013. http://www.feizan.com/space-182513-do-blog-id-85422.html.

Ti, Bing-yen. 2013b. "Singing out My Inner Self: The Theme Song of *Exchange 2012—Way to Love*" [*Tongchuang Yimeng zhutiqu Xiangai Fangshi, changchu wo xinsheng*]. Feizan. March 8, 2013. http://www.feizan.com/space-182513-do-blog-id-86013.html.

Wang, Qingfeng. 2011. "The Status, the Evolution of Discourse, and a Different Voice: Homosexual Studies since the 1990s" [*Shengcun xianzhuang, huayu zhuanbian he yizhi de shengying: 90 niandai yilai de tongxinglian yanjiu*]. *Youth Studies* [*Qingnian yanjiu*], no. 5: 83–93.

Wei, Wei. 2007b. "'Piaopiao' in the City: The Emergence and Change of Homosexual Identities in Local Chengdu" [*Chenli de 'piaopiao': Chengdu bendi tongxinglian shenfen de goucheng he bianqian*]. *Society* [*Shehui*] 27 (1): 67–97.

Wei, Wei. 2010. "From the Symbolic Extinction to Censored Openness: The Representation of Homosexual in *If You Are the One*" [*Cong fuhaoxing miejue dao shenchaxing gongkai:* Fei Cheng Wu Rao *dui tongxinglian de zaixian*]. *Open Times* [*Kaifang shidai*], no. 2, 83–99.

Xiaomingxiong (Samshasha). [1984] 1997. *The History of Homosexuality in China* [*Zhongguo tongxingai shilu*]. Hong Kong: Rosa Winkel Press.

Yuan, Xiangyi. 2007. "An Interview with the Director of *Da-Yu: The Touch of Fate*: Too Many Youth-*Tongzhi* Films Will Be Boring" [*Zhuanfang* Zhijian de Zhongliang *daoyan: taiduo qingchun tongzhi pian hui ni*]. Mtime. June 23, 2007. http://group.mtime.com/huayu/discussion/79073/.

Zhao, Ke. 2009. "'I use Film to Express Myself': An Interview with Filmmaker Kit Hung" [*'Wo yong dianying biaoda ziji': zhuanfang daoyan Hong Rongjie*]. *Gay Spot* [*Dian*], no. 3. http://www.danlan.org/disparticle_24890_4_2.htm.

Zhou, Dan. 2009. *The Pleasure of Love and Discipline: Homosexual Desire, Jurisprudence and Chinese Modernity* [*Aiyue yu guixun: zhongguo xiandaixing zhong tongxing yuwang de fali xiangxiang*]. Guilin: Guangxi Normal University Press.

Index